# THE
# *Herb*
# BIBLE

# THE
# *Herb*
# BIBLE

Peter McHoy

Pamela Westland

A QUANTUM BOOK

Published in 2007 by
Baker & Taylor (UK) Ltd,
Bicester, Oxfordshire.

ISBN: 978-1-903938-78-2

QUMHBI

This book is produced by
Quantum Publishing Ltd.
6 Blundell Street
London N7 9BH

Printed in Singapore by
Star Standard Industries Pte Ltd

**Important Notice**
The HERB BIBLE is intended to be a general introduction to
the use of herbs. The information contained in this book is
neither comprehensive nor prescriptive, and the advice does
not address individual circumstances and conditions. Any
person may develop an allergic reaction at any time to a plant-
derived substance, whether taken internally, as a food or for
self-medication, or used topically. Some plants are toxic if
taken in large quantities or over a long period of time. Others
may have an unpleasant effect in specific circumstances. The
authors and publisher cannot be held responsible for adverse
reactions to plant substances used inappropriately. This book is
not a guide to self-diagnosis and treatment, and professional
advice should be sought before using any herb remedy except
for minor and self-limiting symptoms. Always consult a
physician or qualified herbal practitioner if you are already
receiving treatment for a medical conditions. Herbal remedies
are not innocuous and the effect of concomitant medication are
potentially dangerous. Professional advice should be sought for
any persistence conditions.

# CONTENTS

# INTRODUCTION

Most of us have a clear idea of what is meant by a herb, yet it is exceedingly difficult to define in precise terms. At its loosest, a herb can be any plant with a useful property, such as a source of dye, medicine or insect repellent. Such a definition obviously includes edible plants, leading to the inclusion in some herb books of fruits such as rhubarb, pomegranates and oranges; similarly chicory and Welsh onion are sometimes considered as herbs and at other times as vegetables.

Some experts debate the difference between a herb and a spice, the argument being that a herb is an annual, perennial or biennial that can be grown from seed and that has practical or

*Philipsburg Manor, in New York State, was built in the late seventeenth century. The adjoining herb garden is still arranged as it would have been at that date, with all the herbs which would have been in day-to-day use at the time.*

*The Elizabethan palace at Hatfield in Hertfordshire, showing the formal knot-garden made in the seventeeth century, much of which is given over to herbs.*

*Dandelion (left), one of the herbs recommended by John Gerard.*

*Selfheal (right) was gathered from the wild for use long before it was added to the cultivated herb garden.*

culinary uses – woody plants and those not grown from seed being spices. This seems a fruitless debate, as plants such as bay (*Laurus nobilis*) and sage would be classed as spices, while almost every cook regards them as herbs.

In this book a pragmatic approach has been taken. We have included the plants with a culinary, medicinal or practical use that you would expect to find in a traditional herb garden – along with some that you may prefer to gather from the wild rather than introduce into your garden, such as nettles and horsetail. A few are no longer used for their original purpose, or are impractical to harvest on a small scale (you will not extract a useful amount of oil from a couple of evening primrose plants, for example, nor harvest sufficient woad to yield enough dye to make the effort worthwhile). However, both plants are traditional inhabitants of the herb garden. Growing herbs that are of historical importance makes the herb garden that bit more interesting, and often more ornamental too.

THE HERB HERITAGE
Wild plants were used in food and medicines long before records were kept. Their culinary and medicinal uses must have been discovered largely by trial and error – no doubt with disastrous consequences for those who experimented with the poisonous ones! At first only native plants would have been used, and not

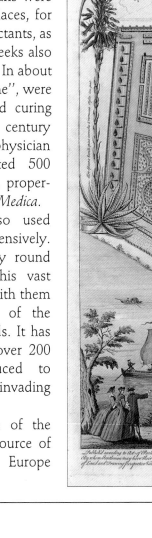

*Ancient Egyptian musicians (above) wear cones of scented grease, heavily perfumed with herbs.*

*An illustration from a fourteenth century Italian herbal (below).*

imported species cultivated in gardens. The widespread use of introduced plants began as trade routes became established, so enabling the dissemination of knowledge and plants among different cultures and lands.

We know that the Hebrews used herbs to flavour their food in biblical times, and most well-known culinary herbs, such as rosemary, thymes and marjorams, grew in the Middle East.

Early documented evidence of medicinal uses is sparse, but records from Babylon dated about 2000 B.C. give instructions for the preparation and administration of medicinal herbs. The ancient Egyptians were importing oils and spices from India amongst other places, for use as medicines, cosmetics, perfumes, dyes and disinfectants, as well as for the highly skilled art of embalming. The Greeks also possessed considerable knowledge of the uses of herbs. In about 400 B.C. students of Hippocrates, the "father of medicine", were learning about the use of herbs for easing pain and curing diseases. By the first century A.D., the Greek physician Dioscorides had listed 500 plants with medicinal properties in his *De Materia Medica*.

The Romans also used medicinal herbs extensively. Conquering their way round Europe, they took this vast knowledge of herbs with them together with many of the actual plants and seeds. It has been estimated that over 200 herbs were introduced to Britain by the invading Romans.

After the demise of the Roman Empire, the source of herbal knowledge in Europe

lay largely with the Christian monks, who often had a "physick" garden attached to their monasteries. Throughout the Middle Ages, herbal knowledge and folklore also proliferated in lay communities, largely passed on by word of mouth.

Herbals, early herbalists' manuals, contained the accumulated knowledge of centuries. John Gerard's *Herball* was published in England in 1579, and although based on a translation of an earlier Latin text, contained much original information. In 1640 this was followed by John Parkinson's massive *Theatrum Botanicum*, which covered about 3,800 plants.

Both authors combined received wisdom and fact, and were prone, at times, to flights of vivid imagination. Nicolas Culpeper was even more wide-ranging in his herbal *The English*

*Frontispiece to John Gerard's Herbal, dated 1597 (above).*

*Plan (left), of the Chelsea Physic Garden in London, dated 1751.*

Physician (also called *The Complete Herbal*), published about 1651. In it he propounded the theories of astrological botany and the Doctrine of Signatures – the idea that the shape and appearance of a plant indicates its medicinal uses. His books were the accepted orthodoxy of the day and were very successful.

So important are these volumes in the history and development of herb growing that hardly a book on herbs is published that does not make reference to them.

The "Age of Herbals" was succeeded by a more scientific approach to the study of herbs. By 1673, the Worshipful Society of Apothecaries had established a physic garden at Chelsea in London, with the objective of advancing the understanding of the botany of medical plants. This indicated the more rational and scientific approach, stemming from the development of the scientific method, that had begun to influence herbal medicine.

### THE NEW WORLD

Colonists of the New World took with them their books by Gerard, Parkinson and Culpeper, along with some of the herbs they used. Culinary and medicinal plants would have been particularly important to settlers who knew little or nothing of the qualities of the native flora. However, the settlers soon discovered that the indigenous peoples also had a vast herbal knowledge of their own. A cross-fertilization of knowledge between the two peoples

*Bee balm (above), which was used by the Oswego tribe to make a form of tea.*

*An early print of Native Americans transporting the fruits of a gathering trip (right). Incoming Europeans found the Native Americans had a rich store of herbal knowledge.*

*The Indian pepper harvest, from a fifteenth-century illumination.*

resulted in the development of a new body of herbal lore. This was, in the main, recorded by the naturalized Americans.

A Mexican Indian doctor named Juan Badianus gave us the first recorded written evidence of native American herb lore. In 1552 he wrote a manuscript, in Latin, recording medical practices of the time.

### DECLINE AND REVIVAL

Since the late 18th century, herbal medicine has come to be supplanted as the conventional practice by allopathic medicine, although the culinary uses of herbs have always been retained. However, in more recent times, people have become more aware of the practical value of fresh herbs, and nowadays few people would consider a garden complete without at least a small patch devoted to them. Even town gardeners often like to grow a small selection in windowboxes and tubs.

Most herbs these days are grown for culinary or decorative use, or for fragrant or cosmetic products. However, herbal medicine still has a vital role to play alongside conventional medicine: for instance, controlled trials by hospital doctors have shown that some herbs used in Chinese medicine achieved better results in the treatment of eczema than the strongest preparations available from the pharmaceutical industry.

The practice of herbal medicine is not for the amateur, however. Although the tisanes and mild preparations suggested in this book are unlikely to do you any harm, this is *not* a medical manual, and self-diagnosis of any medical condition is not advisable. Do not embark upon self-treatment of any serious illness without professional advice – from a medical practitioner or a qualified herbalist.

Though caution has to be observed when using herbs medicinally, culinary experiment-ation can be indulged in more enthusiastically.

*Chinese medicine makes extensive use of herbal remedies. Here, herbs are displayed in the window of a Chinese chemist.*

As we travel more freely and further afield, most of us are more ready to discover the delights of new herbs and spices, and to try new tastes.

Although the main uses of herbs are culinary and medicinal, they have many other potential uses, such as in perfumery, cosmetics and round the house. Many creative ideas for using herbs will be found within this book, and if you are prepared to experiment, you will discover a wide variety of interesting and useful arts and crafts that may with time become part of your way of life.

# DIRECTORY

# OF *H*ERBS

# HOW TO USE THE DIRECTORY

This directory includes all the useful herbs that you are likely to want to grow in a practical working garden, with hints and tips on how to get the best from them. You will find uses of all the herbs in the Directory summarized in the chart on pages 212–217. The plants are listed alphabetically by botanical – Latin – name. If this is not known, you can find it in the index under its common name.

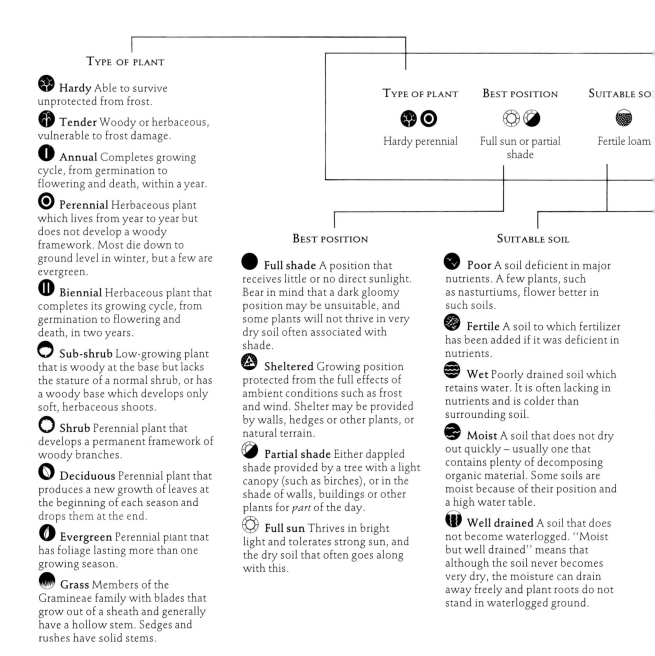

## TYPE OF PLANT

**Hardy** Able to survive unprotected from frost.

**Tender** Woody or herbaceous, vulnerable to frost damage.

**Annual** Completes growing cycle, from germination to flowering and death, within a year.

**Perennial** Herbaceous plant which lives from year to year but does not develop a woody framework. Most die down to ground level in winter, but a few are evergreen.

**Biennial** Herbaceous plant that completes its growing cycle, from germination to flowering and death, in two years.

**Sub-shrub** Low-growing plant that is woody at the base but lacks the stature of a normal shrub, or has a woody base which develops only soft, herbaceous shoots.

**Shrub** Perennial plant that develops a permanent framework of woody branches.

**Deciduous** Perennial plant that produces a new growth of leaves at the beginning of each season and drops them at the end.

**Evergreen** Perennial plant that has foliage lasting more than one growing season.

**Grass** Members of the Gramineae family with blades that grow out of a sheath and generally have a hollow stem. Sedges and rushes have solid stems.

### TYPE OF PLANT

Hardy perennial

### BEST POSITION

Full sun or partial shade

### SUITABLE SO...

Fertile loam

## BEST POSITION

**Full shade** A position that receives little or no direct sunlight. Bear in mind that a dark gloomy position may be unsuitable, and some plants will not thrive in very dry soil often associated with shade.

**Sheltered** Growing position protected from the full effects of ambient conditions such as frost and wind. Shelter may be provided by walls, hedges or other plants, or natural terrain.

**Partial shade** Either dappled shade provided by a tree with a light canopy (such as birches), or in the shade of walls, buildings or other plants for *part* of the day.

**Full sun** Thrives in bright light and tolerates strong sun, and the dry soil that often goes along with this.

## SUITABLE SOIL

**Poor** A soil deficient in major nutrients. A few plants, such as nasturtiums, flower better in such soils.

**Fertile** A soil to which fertilizer has been added if it was deficient in nutrients.

**Wet** Poorly drained soil which retains water. It is often lacking in nutrients and is colder than surrounding soil.

**Moist** A soil that does not dry out quickly – usually one that contains plenty of decomposing organic material. Some soils are moist because of their position and a high water table.

**Well drained** A soil that does not become waterlogged. "Moist but well drained" means that although the soil never becomes very dry, the moisture can drain away freely and plant roots do not stand in waterlogged ground.

If you are unable to find a particular herb in the Directory, it may be because the plant is potentially very hazardous for amateurs to use medicinally. For example, foxgloves (which yield the powerful heart drugs digitalin and digitoxin) and opium poppies are decorative herbs that you might want to grow ornamentally, but not to use herbally. Other herbs, such as horsetail and nettles, are not suitable for cultivating in the confines of a herb garden.

The Directory has been designed as a quick source of information on the main characteristics of a herb, how to grow it and where to plant it. The main uses are also outlined. Even if you already grow the plant in your garden, the cross-reference will open up many possibilities you may not have thought about.

To include as much information as possible the key facts for each herb are summarized at the end of the main entries as shown in the panel below. The following explanation of terms will help you get the best from the Directory.

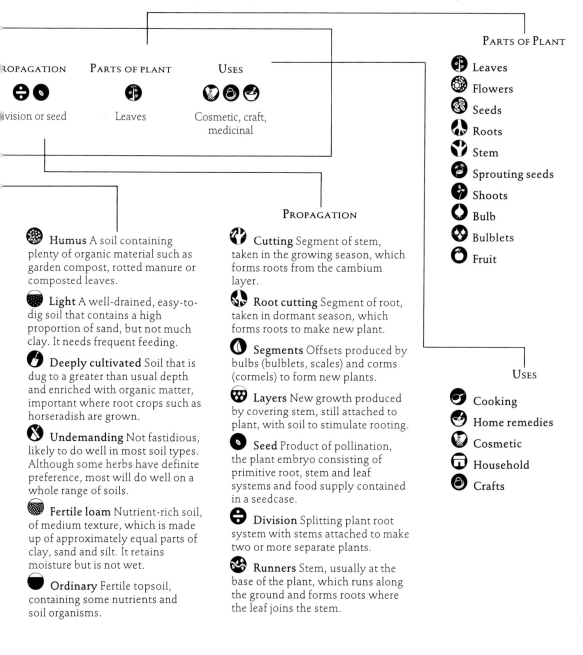

PROPAGATION

Division or seed

PARTS OF PLANT

Leaves

USES

Cosmetic, craft, medicinal

PARTS OF PLANT

- Leaves
- Flowers
- Seeds
- Roots
- Stem
- Sprouting seeds
- Shoots
- Bulb
- Bulblets
- Fruit

USES

- Cooking
- Home remedies
- Cosmetic
- Household
- Crafts

**Humus** A soil containing plenty of organic material such as garden compost, rotted manure or composted leaves.

**Light** A well-drained, easy-to-dig soil that contains a high proportion of sand, but not much clay. It needs frequent feeding.

**Deeply cultivated** Soil that is dug to a greater than usual depth and enriched with organic matter, important where root crops such as horseradish are grown.

**Undemanding** Not fastidious, likely to do well in most soil types. Although some herbs have definite preference, most will do well on a whole range of soils.

**Fertile loam** Nutrient-rich soil, of medium texture, which is made up of approximately equal parts of clay, sand and silt. It retains moisture but is not wet.

**Ordinary** Fertile topsoil, containing some nutrients and soil organisms.

PROPAGATION

**Cutting** Segment of stem, taken in the growing season, which forms roots from the cambium layer.

**Root cutting** Segment of root, taken in dormant season, which forms roots to make new plant.

**Segments** Offsets produced by bulbs (bulblets, scales) and corms (cormels) to form new plants.

**Layers** New growth produced by covering stem, still attached to plant, with soil to stimulate rooting.

**Seed** Product of pollination, the plant embryo consisting of primitive root, stem and leaf systems and food supply contained in a seedcase.

**Division** Splitting plant root system with stems attached to make two or more separate plants.

**Runners** Stem, usually at the base of the plant, which runs along the ground and forms roots where the leaf joins the stem.

## *Achillea millefolium*

# YARROW

THE NAME YARROW is applied to several achilleas, but this is the one most often used as a herb. A common roadside plant in many parts of Europe and America, it is tough with creeping roots that enable it to spread rapidly. It will thrive in almost any soil and position other than shade, and may be a weed in lawns. In a mown lawn it is no more than 5 cm (2 in)

*Wild yarrow is usually white, but it's best to grow a coloured variety such as 'Cerise Queen'.*

tall, but elsewhere grows to about 60 cm (24 in).

The foliage is feathery with a pleasant smell when crushed. The species has small white flowers carried in flat heads from early summer to late autumn. Less invasive are coloured varieties such as 'Cerise Queen', which is cherry red, and others less common in shades of pink and yellow. These achilleas look well in borders, but must be kept in check.

Although the species can be raised from seed, named varieties are propagated by cuttings or division. If you choose to grow the species in a herb garden you may be able to transplant "weed" plants growing elsewhere in the garden.

| TYPE OF PLANT | BEST POSITION | SUITABLE SOIL | PROPAGATION | PARTS OF PLANT | USES |
|---|---|---|---|---|---|
|  |  |  |  |  |  |
| Hardy perennial | Full sun or partial shade | Undemanding. Tolerates poor and dry soil | Cuttings, division, seed | Leaves and flowers | Cosmetic, craft, culinary, household, medicinal |

# *Agrimonia eupatoria*
# AGRIMONY

THIS MODEST PLANT with slender spikes of flowers blooms all summer. All parts of the plant – flowers, downy leaves, even the root – are slightly aromatic with a smell reminiscent of apricots, fainter than the similar but less common *A. odorata* (syn. *A. repens*).

Agrimony is very undemanding. It will even tolerate partial shade and dry soil. The fact that it grows commonly on hedge banks and edges of fields in Britain and many parts of southern Europe gives a clue to its undemanding nature.

A creeping rootstock means that it can spread, but

*Agrimony is a rather weedy-looking plant, at its best in a wild part of the garden.*

it often develops just a single upright stem with a few weak branches. Its appearance does not warrant a prime site, so plant it where its unpredictable habit will not spoil a neat and formal herb garden.

Although perennial it tends to be short-lived, so it is worth growing spare plants. Plants can be bought from nurseries and garden centres, but the herb is easy to grow from seed.

| TYPE OF PLANT | BEST POSITION | SUITABLE SOIL | PROPAGATION | PARTS OF PLANT | USES |
|---|---|---|---|---|---|
| Hardy perennial | Full sun or partial shade | Undemanding, but well drained | Cuttings or seed | Leaves | Household, cosmetic, medicinal |

## *Alchemilla vulgaris*
# LADY'S MANTLE

THIS SPECIES RESEMBLES the widely grown *A. mollis*, so popular with gardeners and flower arrangers. The small yellowish green flowers are carried in fuzzy heads above folded and pleated leaves that collect dew, or raindrops after a shower. The first flush is in early summer but flowering can continue into early autumn. Lady's mantle is one of the prettiest herbs to grow and can form a foamy edging to a formal herb garden or border. Alternatively try planting it with catmint or lavender for a happy colour combination. This trouble-free plant grows to about 23–30 cm (9–12 in), but where conditions suit it can reach 45 cm (18 in).

Although this lady's mantle is listed in catalogues under *A. vulgaris*, some botanists refer to it as *A. xanthochlora*. It is the species traditionally grown for herbal use, but some herb growers treat *A. mollis* in the same way. If you already have the latter in the garden, and simply want to include it in the herb garden for its decorative effect, you are almost sure to find self-sown seedlings in the herbaceous border or between paving to transplant.

| TYPE OF PLANT | BEST POSITION | SUITABLE SOIL | PROPAGATION | PARTS OF PLANT | USES |
|---|---|---|---|---|---|
| Hardy perennial | Full sun or partial shade | Fertile loam | Division or seed | Leaves | Cosmetic, craft, medicinal |

*Allium cepa proliferum*

# EGYPTIAN TREE ONION

THIS PLANT, ALSO KNOWN as the Egyptian top onion, has bulbs on the stem tops as well as at the base. The 90 cm (36 in) flowering stems produce inconspicuous white flowers which are followed by clusters of small bulbs which sprout leaves. Both types of bulbs are used like onions to season soups, sandwiches and salads. If you need only a small quantity for seasoning, use the stem bulblets so the ground bulbs form a large clump – especially if the plant is growing in a border. The bulbs are small in comparison with an onion, so regard them as a variation rather than a substitute for onions.

This culinary herb is very hardy and simple to propagate – most easily from the bulblets that form on the tall, hollow stems. When harvesting, save a few bulbs to replant as for shallots.

*Tree onions are neat, well-behaved plants, sure to fascinate when the stem bulbs appear.*

| TYPE OF PLANT | BEST POSITION | SUITABLE SOIL | PROPAGATION | PARTS OF PLANT | USES |
|---|---|---|---|---|---|
| Hardy perennial | Full sun | Fertile loam | Bulbs, bulblets | Leaves, bulbs, bulblets | Culinary |

## *Allium fistulosum*

# WELSH ONION

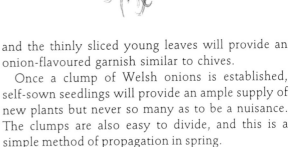

THE WELSH ONION or Japanese bunching onion is a compact, well-behaved, clump-forming plant that does not become invasive. Drumstick white flowerheads form on hollow stems about 45–75 cm (18–30 in) tall, then new leaves sprout around the base of the plant. Although the flowers are less attractive than chives, they are bold enough for a place in the border and their ability to form clumps makes them suitable for a tall permanent edging to a vegetable plot.

The bulbs, although small, can be used like onions

*Welsh onions form neat clumps that make quite an attractive edging in the kitchen or herb garden.*

and the thinly sliced young leaves will provide an onion-flavoured garnish similar to chives.

Once a clump of Welsh onions is established, self-sown seedlings will provide an ample supply of new plants but never so many as to be a nuisance. The clumps are also easy to divide, and this is a simple method of propagation in spring.

| TYPE OF PLANT | BEST POSITION | SUITABLE SOIL | PROPAGATION | PARTS OF PLANT | USES |
|---|---|---|---|---|---|
|  |  |  |  |  |  |
| Hardy annual | Full sun or partial shade | Fertile loam, preferably moist | Division or seed | Leaves, bulbs | Culinary |

# *Allium sativum*

# GARLIC

T HE TASTE AND SMELL of garlic is familiar to practically everyone and in many countries it is one of the most widely used culinary herbs. Garlic has flat grey-green leaves about 2.5 cm (1 in) wide and 30 cm (12 in) long. The willowy flower stalks produce clusters of mauvish-white flowers which can reach 60 cm (24 in) or more.

If you like garlic, this is a herb you will certainly want to grow. The "cloves" are tightly clustered bulblets, each sheathed in a papery skin, and "tissue-wrapped" to hold them together.

Plant individual bulblets in early spring, 2.5 cm (1 in) deep and 15–20 cm (6–8 in) apart. If spring planting gives disappointing results, producing "solid" bulbs that have not split into cloves, try planting in late autumn. Alternatively plant in spring but put the bulbs in the fridge (not the freezing compartment) a week before to give them a cold spell before planting. Where summers are cold, dull and damp, results can be disappointing, but early planting in the autumn usually improves results. Garlic responds well to feeding, so apply a general garden fertilizer if growth seems poor.

| TYPE OF PLANT | BEST POSITION | SUITABLE SOIL | PROPAGATION | PARTS OF PLANT | USES |
|---|---|---|---|---|---|
| Hardy perennial | Full sun | Fertile loam | Segments of bulb "cloves" | Bulb | Cosmetic, culinary, medicinal |

# *Allium schoenoprasum*
# CHIVE

THE COMMON, OR ONION, CHIVE is such a versatile plant that you can use it all around the garden. It makes compact clumps of grass-like foliage about 30 cm (12 in) tall, covered with pink or purple flowers in early summer. A clump of chives is just as pretty as thrift (*Armeria maritima*), which it resembles from a distance, and makes an excellent edging for a flower bed or border. Use it as well in herb pots and windowboxes. You can even grow it indoors by a light window.

If you want chives primarily for culinary use, remove the flowers to prevent the plants becoming exhausted. Harvest the young leaves by pinching them off at the base to avoid the stubs dying back and leaving unsightly brown edges. By using

*Chives make a very pretty edging, bright enough for a flower garden.*

cloches for protection in spring and autumn, the harvesting period can be extended to about nine months.

As even young leaves can be harvested for an onion-flavoured garnish, try raising some plants from seed by a light window, perhaps in a glass kitchen jar for a more interesting effect. Otherwise grow them in seed trays and prick them out into flowerpots.

| TYPE OF PLANT | BEST POSITION | SUITABLE SOIL | PROPAGATION | PARTS OF PLANT | USES |
|---|---|---|---|---|---|
| Hardy perennial | Full sun or partial shade | Fertile, moist but well-drained | Division or seed | Leaves | Cosmetic, culinary |

# *Allium tuberosum*
# GARLIC CHIVE

The garlic chive or Chinese chive is a vigorous plant forming upright clumps about 60 cm (24 in) tall. The snowy white flowerheads which appear in summer are surprisingly sweetly scented despite the strong garlic smell of the leaves and bulbs. With its height and attractive flowers it has a place in borders as well as herb gardens, and it forms clumps which are easy to divide.

The flavour is not as strong and pungent as true garlic, so this is a useful herb for those who prefer a milder flavour.

*If you find garlic difficult to grow, or the flavour too strong, try garlic chives instead.*

| TYPE OF PLANT | BEST POSITION | SUITABLE SOIL | PROPAGATION | PARTS OF PLANT | USES |
|---|---|---|---|---|---|
| Hardy perennial | Full sun or partial shade | Fertile, moist but well-drained | Division or seed | Leaves | Cosmetic, culinary |

*Aloysia triphylla*

# LEMON VERBENA

LEMON VERBENA IS ONE of those plants that has suffered from renaming and it may also be sold as *Lippia citriodora*. But whatever its name, this is an excellent herb to grow. The pale purple flowers, clustered along the stems in late summer, are not very showy, but the plant's main attraction is the foliage which gives off a strong citrus scent when crushed. Lemon verbena is at its most aromatic in the early evening.

Grow lemon verbena in a warm, protected position as it is not frost-hardy and needs protection during winter except in the mildest areas. It is a wise precaution to take cuttings unless you choose to grow the herb in a container and overwinter it in a conservatory or greenhouse. Where it is mild enough to survive out of doors, lemon verbena will grow into a bushy shrub 1.5 m (5 ft) high and as much across. However it will be smaller when grown in a container.

Prune in mid spring to remove dead wood and cut the main stems to about 30 cm (12 in) from the ground to keep the shrub compact.

Although it can be raised from seed, it is easier to take softwood cuttings in late summer to overwinter under glass.

| TYPE OF PLANT | BEST POSITION | SUITABLE SOIL | PROPAGATION | PARTS OF PLANT | USES |
|---|---|---|---|---|---|
|  |  | | | | |
| Tender deciduous shrub | Full sun or partial shade | Fertile loam | Cuttings or seed | Leaves | Cosmetic, culinary, medicinal, household |

## *Althaea officinalis*
# MARSHMALLOW

THE CONFECTION OF MARSHMALLOW was formerly made from the mucilage present in the stems, leaves and especially the roots, but substitutes are now used commercially. The herb has other uses, however, and it is such a pretty perennial that little justification is needed to include it in the garden. The pale pink, or occasionally white, saucer-shaped flowers in late summer have a cottage-garden appeal, and where conditions suit it will make a bushy plant about 1.2 m (4 ft) tall.

Marshmallow can grow rather tall and straggly for a formal herb garden, and is more at home in a moist area of a cottage-style garden where it looks best planted with border plants or in front of shrubs.

*You are unlikely to grow enough marshmallow to make the confection, but it's a pretty plant to enjoy as an ornamental herb.*

As its common name implies, this is a plant that grows wild in marshes, mainly near the sea. It is often disappointing in the hot, dry soils that most herbs prefer and needs watering freely in dry weather unless the ground is naturally moist.

It is easy to increase by pulling pieces from the crown of large plants in the autumn. It can also be raised from seeds sown in spring.

| TYPE OF PLANT | BEST POSITION | SUITABLE SOIL | PROPAGATION | PARTS OF PLANT | USES |
|---|---|---|---|---|---|
| Hardy perennial | Sun or partial shade | Moist | Division or seed | Leaves, roots, stems | Cosmetic, culinary, medicinal |

## *Anethum graveolens*

# DILL

Dill is a very aromatic annual herb and one that is quick and easy to grow. With its feathery dark blue-green leaves and starry clusters of yellowish green flowers in mid summer, it looks rather like a small version of fennel (with which it will hybridize if planted too close).

Its fine-cut foliage looks attractive in a border, but avoid an exposed position as strong winds can flatten the plants. Because the seeds are allowed to ripen on the plant they multiply freely and self-sown seedlings may be a problem. So a corner on its own in the herb garden may be a more practical planting position than a border.

*Dill is attractive enough to grow in a border, but self-sown seedlings can be a problem.*

Seed is usually sown in spring, but in mild areas, autumn sowing produces earlier plants. For a succession of young leaves, make a regular sowing every two or three weeks throughout early and mid summer. The seedlings do not transplant well and respond by flowering prematurely, so sow where they are to grow.

| TYPE OF PLANT | BEST POSITION | SUITABLE SOIL | PROPAGATION | PARTS OF PLANT | USES |
|---|---|---|---|---|---|
|  | | |  | |  |
| Hardy annual | Full sun, sheltered | Light, well-drained | Seed | Leaves, seeds | Craft, culinary, medicinal |

# *Angelica archangelica*
# ANGELICA

Use angelica as a bold focal-point in the herb garden proper or as a group at the back of a border. In its second year this biennial will make a huge plant with 60 cm (24 in) bright green leaves topped in mid or late summer by its spectacular clusters of yellowish green flowerheads on stems about 1.8 m (6 ft) tall. All parts of this distinctive herb are fragrant to the touch.

Its large size will mean that unless you have lots of space, only two or three plants can be accommodated in a herb garden. The noble stature of angelica makes it an eye-catching feature, even in a wild part of the garden.

Although technically a biennial, if you prevent it flowering by cutting off stems that show signs of blooming you may keep it growing for a third year.

Sow a few seeds each year to ensure new plants are always available to replace those that die. The seed soon loses its viability, however, and to be sure of good germination try to save your own seed and sow within a couple of weeks if possible. If you have trouble germinating the seed, buy small plants in the spring. Once angelica is established, self-sown seedlings should ensure a continuing supply of plants without much effort on your part.

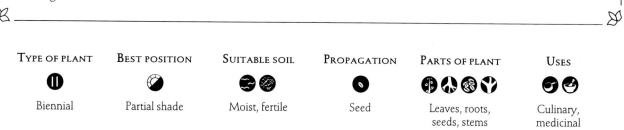

| TYPE OF PLANT | BEST POSITION | SUITABLE SOIL | PROPAGATION | PARTS OF PLANT | USES |
|---|---|---|---|---|---|
| Biennial | Partial shade | Moist, fertile | Seed | Leaves, roots, seeds, stems | Culinary, medicinal |

## *Anthemis nobilis*
# CHAMOMILE

THE CORRECT BOTANICAL NAME for chamomile is *Chamaemelum nobile* but it is usually sold by herb nurseries as an anthemis. Various related plants are sometimes called chamomile, so check descriptions and names before you buy. The plant illustrated is the type most often grown, and is sometimes described as English or perennial chamomile.

The dainty white daisy flowers with yellow centres are carried among feathery leaves. The plant has a spreading habit and seldom exceeds 30 cm (12 in) in height. It can be used for paths within a herb garden as it is a popular grass-substitute. The variety usually selected for this use is the non-flowering 'Treneague'. This variety is suitable for a lawn but not as a herb, for it is the flowers that have the useful properties.

Chamomile looks best planted in a bold drift as ground cover, as individual plants can look weedy. It will, in any case, self-sow freely.

*Chamomile is sometimes used as a grass substitute. In the herb garden it will make an attractive green carpet.*

| TYPE OF PLANT | BEST POSITION | SUITABLE SOIL | PROPAGATION | PARTS OF PLANT | USES |
|---|---|---|---|---|---|
|  |  | | | | |
| Hardy perennial | Full sun or partial shade | Undemanding, does well on poor soil | Division or seed | Flowers | Craft, cosmetic, household, medicinal |

# *Anthriscus cerefolium*
# CHERVIL

*Chervil is a pleasant, leafy herb that readily self-seeds.*

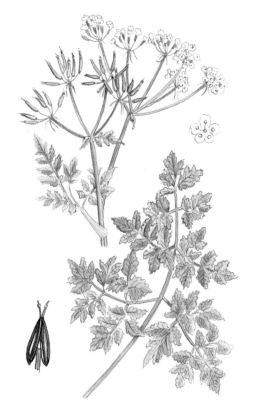

CHERVIL RESEMBLES ITALIAN PARSLEY, with bright green, divided leaves and growing to about 30 cm (12 in). The flavour is very different, however, with a hint of aniseed. It is one of the ingredients of *fines herbes*, so widely used in French cookery. Grow plenty because it can be used generously.

Chervil is an ideal herb to grow in tubs, troughs, large pots or even windowboxes, but keep it well watered or plants will run to seed prematurely. This is because this delicate-looking plant prefers a position in moist shade. It quickly deteriorates and runs to seed in extremes of heat or cold.

Sow a short row every two or three weeks in spring and summer for a succession of young leaves. In mild areas or when plants are under cloche protection, try sowing some seed in the autumn.

Always sow where the plants are to grow as the seedlings are too fragile to transplant, and thin to about 10 cm (4 in) apart when they are large enough to handle.

To avoid the need for resowing every year, allow a few plants in each row to produce their dainty white flowers and set seed. Self-sown seedlings should maintain a supply of plants in the bed.

| TYPE OF PLANT | BEST POSITION | SUITABLE SOIL | PROPAGATION | PARTS OF PLANT | USES |
|---|---|---|---|---|---|
| Hardy annual | Partial shade | Fertile, moist | Seed | Leaves | Cosmetic, culinary, medicinal |

## *Artemisia abrotanum*
# LAD'S LOVE/SOUTHERNWOOD

*Try planting lad's love where you will brush against the aromatic foliage.*

exposed to chilling winds. (The bedraggled appearance in winter may have given rise to another of its colloquial names, that of "old man".) Leave this old growth on as protection, but cut it back to 45 cm (18 in) in late spring to stimulate fresh shoots and to keep the plant compact.

Propagate by softwood cuttings from new growth in early summer, or hardwood cuttings with a heel in autumn.

THIS IS A HERB with many common names besides the ones given here. They all indicate its value as a traditional herb. In some the link is obvious, such as the French *garde-robe*, a reference to its use as a moth deterrent. Others, like "maiden's ruin", are less obvious (it was used as a love charm).

The soft green aromatic foliage is silky to touch, so grow it where you can brush it with your hand as you walk past to release its aroma of camphor. It is a compact shrub that grows to about 90 cm (36 in) with a spread of 60 cm (24 in). With its feathery foliage, sometimes topped with small yellow flowers in late summer, it looks perfectly at home in an herbaceous border. Try it as a tub plant too.

Although hardy in most areas except the very cold, it will become tatty in winter, especially if

| TYPE OF PLANT | BEST POSITION | SUITABLE SOIL | PROPAGATION | PARTS OF PLANT | USES |
|---|---|---|---|---|---|
|  |  |  | |  | |
| Shrub (hardy except cold areas) | Full sun, sheltered | Ordinary but well drained | Cuttings, layers | Leaves | Cosmetic, culinary, medicinal, household |

## *Artemisia absinthium*
# WORMWOOD

Like most artemisias, wormwood is an attractive and extremely aromatic foliage plant, useful in shrub and mixed borders as well as the herb garden. A sub-shrub, it makes a rounded bush about 1–1.2 m (3–4 ft) tall covered with dainty, finely cut foliage. The leaf colour is silvery when young but ages to pale green. However 'Lambrook Silver' retains its attractive silvery colour well. Yellowish green flowers are produced in mid summer but these are insignificant compared with the foliage.

Although it is hardy in many areas, wormwood is vulnerable in cold regions. Where winters are very cold, it ought to be grown in a tub that can be taken into the greenhouse or conservatory for protection.

*Wormwood needs annual pruning for the best foliage effect.*

Even in favourable areas it is worth protecting the plant in a harsh winter.

Plants become leggy unless trimmed back in spring. Be drastic and prune them back to about 15 cm (6 in) above the ground – new growth will soon have them looking good again.

Wormwood can be raised from seed, but it is easier to propagate from cuttings or division. Dividing the plant also encourages vigorous new growth.

| TYPE OF PLANT | BEST POSITION | SUITABLE SOIL | PROPAGATION | PARTS OF PLANT | USES |
|---|---|---|---|---|---|
| Sub-shrub | Full sun | Ordinary, well drained | Cuttings, division, seed | Leaves | Medicinal |

## *Artemisia dracunculus*

# FRENCH TARRAGON

*Tarragon is a valuable culinary herb but lacks ornamental value.*

Tarragon is one of the most sought-after culinary herbs, but beware what you buy. French tarragon has excellent flavour, but Russian tarragon (*A. dracunculoides*) is very inferior. Superficially they look similar, but the leaves of French tarragon are long, narrow and willowy while those of the Russian form are larger, coarser and more indented at the margins. The taste test will confirm the genuine French tarragon. Before buying a plant chew a leaf: French tarragon has a distinctive, slightly aniseed flavour, but Russian tarragon is bitter and less pleasant.

French tarragon makes a thick, bushy plant 60–90 cm (24–36 in) tall, with a spread of about 45 cm (18 in). It rarely flowers successfully, which is why it needs to be grown from cuttings or by division (Russian tarragon is often grown from seed.) Pinch out any flowering shoots that appear to encourage leaf growth.

Cold, damp winters pose a problem as tarragon does best in a warm, sunny position where the climate is mild throughout the year. To help it through the winter, cut back the top growth in early autumn, and cover the plant with dry bracken, straw, conifer shoots or a sheet of plastic. Otherwise pot up some small pieces of the plant, or take cuttings and overwinter these in a light, frost-free greenhouse or conservatory.

Try moving a plant to a cold frame for the winter: you may be able to enjoy fresh tarragon for a few more months.

| Type of plant | Best position | Suitable soil | Propagation | Parts of plant | Uses |
|---|---|---|---|---|---|
| Hardy perennial | Full sun or partial shade | Ordinary, well drained | Cuttings, division | Leaves | Culinary |

## *Artemisia vulgaris*

# MUGWORT

DESPITE ITS LACK OF visual appeal, this is a useful herb for flavouring that is easy to grow. It is a herbaceous perennial with 1–1.5 m (3–5 ft) purplish stems. The coarsely divided leaves are often slightly rolled at the edges and white felted beneath. The yellowish brown flowers which scarcely protrude from their scaly protection appear between mid summer and early autumn.

The plant is easy to raise in a seedbed outdoors in spring or summer. Seed is available from wild flower specialists. However, if you have trouble buying seeds, you may be able to collect them from the wild; mugwort is a common weed over most of the northern hemisphere including North America and Central Asia. Improved varieties are available as plants from specialist herb nurseries, including a variegated form.

*Mugwort can look rather weedy, but provides a useful filler in a herbaceous or mixed border.*

| TYPE OF PLANT | BEST POSITION | SUITABLE SOIL | PROPAGATION | PARTS OF PLANT | USES |
|---|---|---|---|---|---|
| Hardy perennial | Full sun | Undemanding | Division, seed | Leaves | Medicinal |

## *Borago officinalis*
# BORAGE

root means it does not transplant easily nor does it do well in containers. Bees and wasps are attracted by borage, so do not plant it too close to a path.

For summer use sow in mid or late spring where the plants are to grow, and again in early and mid summer for succession. In mild areas or if seedlings are under cloche protection, sow in the autumn to flower in late spring and early summer. Borage is an annual so plants will die at the end of the season, but self-sown seedlings germinate freely and you should always have replacement plants coming up.

For winter use only, a few seeds can be sown in a large pot and thinned to one if more germinate. Keep the pot near a very light window, or better still in a conservatory or greenhouse.

DECORATIVE BORAGE HAS BRIGHT blue star-like flowers, each with a cone of prominent black anthers, often described as a "beauty spot". Occasionally a plant may have pink, or more rarely white, flowers. The stems, leaves and flower buds are all covered with silvery hairs which catch the light and give the whole plant a rough feel.

Grow borage in a border among ornamental herbaceous plants if there is no space in a more formal herb garden. However, its long, fleshy tap

*Borage is loved by bees and gardeners alike. It's very decorative and thrives in a sunny position.*

| TYPE OF PLANT | BEST POSITION | SUITABLE SOIL | PROPAGATION | PARTS OF PLANT | USES |
|---|---|---|---|---|---|
|  |  |  |  |  |  |
| Hardy annual | Full sun or partial shade | Undemanding | Seed only | Flowers, leaves | Cosmetic, culinary, medicinal |

## *Calendula officinalis*

# POT MARIGOLD

THE POT MARIGOLD IS essential for any herb garden. Apart from bringing colour to salads and other dishes, its bright orange or yellow flowers introduce a cheerful note to a herb garden that may otherwise be dominated by greys and greens.

You can buy single calendulas of the traditional cottage-garden type, but most seed companies sell

*Pot marigolds are so decorative that many people grow them purely as ornamentals.*

the larger and more decorative double varieties. Both can be used herbally, so choose whichever fits in with your style of garden. If you allow them to self-sow, they will, in any case, deteriorate over the years and become dominated by small single flowers. Dwarf varieties grow to about 30 cm (12 in), while the traditional varieties, more suited to a herb garden, reach about 45 cm (18 in).

In spring sow seed where the plants are to grow. Thin out the seedlings when large enough to handle leaving about 23 cm (9 in) between plants. For a succession sow every two or three weeks throughout. In mild areas an autumn sowing will produce flowers by mid or late spring.

| TYPE OF PLANT | BEST POSITION | SUITABLE SOIL | PROPAGATION | PARTS OF PLANT | USES |
|---|---|---|---|---|---|
| Hardy annual | Full sun | Undemanding | Seed | Flowers, leaves | Cosmetic, craft, culinary, household, medicinal |

## *Carum carvi*
# CARAWAY

This is an invaluable herb to include in the garden despite its somewhat weedy appearance. The thread-like bright green leaves that resemble carrot tops have a mild flavour somewhere between dill and parsley. Stems 45–75 cm (18–30 in) high are topped by clusters of small white flowers which eventually produce the ribbed seeds used to flavour confectionery, cookies, cakes and breads. Even the finger-thick, parsnip-like roots can be eaten.

Caraway looks best in a large clump or bold drift, so plants can grow into each other and provide mutual support, rather than in rows. If you intend to use their roots, however, it is probably more convenient to grow them in rows.

A biennial, caraway can be sown in both spring and autumn for a succession of young foliage. In either case the plants will flower the following summer. Caraway does not transplant well, so always sow the seeds where the plants are to grow. Thin the seedlings to about 15 cm (6 in) apart when they are about 8 cm (3 in) high.

Harvest the seed before it drops, but allow a few plants to shed their seeds to provide a supply of self-sown seedlings if space permits.

*Caraway is an easy-to-grow biennial, best sown in bold drifts if you want to harvest its seeds.*

| TYPE OF PLANT | BEST POSITION | SUITABLE SOIL | PROPAGATION | PARTS OF PLANT | USES |
|---|---|---|---|---|---|
|  | | | | | |
| Hardy biennial | Full sun, sheltered | Undemanding, well drained | Seed | Leaves, roots, seeds | Craft, culinary, medicinal |

*Chenopodium bonus-henricus*

# GOOD KING HENRY

*Good King Henry does not look particularly attractive, but it has many culinary uses, and you can crop it over a long period.*

IN COMMON WITH MOST herbs this has several other colloquial names, including goosefoot. Described and sold as either a herb or a vegetable, good King Henry can certainly be prepared in a number of ways. The young leaves are harvested and cooked like spinach or eaten raw in salads, or the young emerging shoots can be blanched and used like asparagus. It is a good standby to have in the garden as it needs the minimum of attention.

The plants, also known as goosefoot, form clumps of dark green spear-shaped leaves about 45–60 cm (18–24 in) tall. Small spikes of insignificant flowers develop in spring, but pinch these out to encourage more leaf growth.

To stimulate young, succulent growth, mulch the area with garden compost or rotted manure after the top growth has died down. Apply a balanced garden fertilizer in spring. You should be able to crop good King Henry for several years, but after three or four it is worth starting again with new plants.

Sow in early or mid spring and thin the plants to about 30 cm (12 in) apart when large enough to handle. Small plants may be obtainable through specialist herb nurseries.

| TYPE OF PLANT | BEST POSITION | SUITABLE SOIL | PROPAGATION | PARTS OF PLANT | USES |
|---|---|---|---|---|---|
| Hardy perennial | Full sun | Fertile | Seed | Leaves, shoots | Culinary |

# *Chrysanthemum balsamita*
# COSTMARY

COSTMARY IS ALSO SOLD under its botanical name of *Balsamita major*. Also known as alecost, it is a leafy herb that forms an upright clump 60–90 cm (24–36 in) tall and looks best mixed in with more attractive border plants. Alternatively, grow it where the foliage can be brushed in passing to release its scent. The name "bible leaf" is sometimes applied to the plant in America and alludes to the fact that early settlers sometimes used the dried leaves as aromatic page markers.

Both leaves and pale yellow flowers are mint-scented. The young leaves are used mainly for culinary purposes, and as a mint substitute, but the herb can be used to make herb pillows.

It is best not to let flowers develop otherwise the plant will soon become leggy. Even with flowers removed the centre of the clump may die out after a few years, so propagate new plants regularly.

There are several ways to propagate costmary. If you can obtain seeds, sow them in spring. However, if you already have an established plant, the best way to propagate it is from root cuttings, as described on page 135, or simply sever and replant a creeping rooted portion in spring.

| TYPE OF PLANT | BEST POSITION | SUITABLE SOIL | PROPAGATION | PARTS OF PLANT | USES |
|---|---|---|---|---|---|
|  |  |  |  |  |  |
| Hardy perennial | Full sun or partial shade | Fertile | Division, root cuttings, seed | Leaves | Cosmetic, culinary, household, medicinal |

## *Chrysanthemum parthenium*

# FEVERFEW

THIS HAS ALWAYS BEEN an important herb and, today, is again regarded as having considerable medicinal potential. It is also a pretty plant, with soft, light green serrated leaves that form mounds 23–60 cm (9–24 in) high, generously sprinkled with white or yellow, single or double flowers for most of summer and into autumn. The aromatic leaves are also retained through the winter. In addition it is undemanding to grow, and does well in any well-drained soil. It will even self-sow into crevices in walls and between paving stones. Feverfew really is a plant of many virtues.

You will find feverfew sold under other names, among them the botanical name *Tanacetum parthenium*. In seed catalogues it may be listed as *Matricaria eximia*. The varieties with double and yellow flowers or golden foliage can be used in the same way. Many of the compact double varieties look attractive in containers. 'Aureum' has golden foliage that remains bright even in partial shade and into winter.

Feverfew is a short-lived perennial, so maintain a supply of new plants. Seed sown in spring or cuttings taken in summer are easy and reliable methods of propagation; division and leaf cuttings are possible but difficult.

*Feverfew is a pretty plant with white daisy flowers, but the golden form is especially attractive.*

| TYPE OF PLANT | BEST POSITION | SUITABLE SOIL | PROPAGATION | PARTS OF PLANT | USES |
|---|---|---|---|---|---|
|  |  |  |  |  | |
| Hardy evergreen perennial (often grown as a half-hardy annual) | Full sun, partial shade | Undemanding | Cuttings, division, seed | Leaves | Cosmetic, household, medicinal |

## *Cichorium intybus*
# CHICORY

CHICORY IS AN EXTREMELY useful plant to grow. The leaves are eaten as a vegetable, the roots can be ground to make a flavouring for coffee, and the very pretty blue flowers, once used to produce soothing eye drops, can simply be enjoyed.

Sow the seeds in rows in late spring or early summer and thin the plants to about 30 cm (12 in) apart. Some varieties produce heads rather like a cos lettuce that can be cut and eaten in late autumn or early winter; others need to be lifted and forced as a winter vegetable.

To produce tight heads of blanched leaves (chicons), lift the parsnip-like roots in late autumn or early winter. Plant them up in deep pots or boxes after trimming off the leaves and bottom of the root. Then keep them in a dark place at a temperature of at least 13°C (55°F). After three or four weeks a head of new leaves should have grown that can be harvested when about 15 cm (6 in). Consult seed catalogues to identify the particular varieties which are recommended for the different uses.

If you want chicory to flower, do not cut or lift the plants at the end of the first year but leave them to bloom in their second season.

| TYPE OF PLANT | BEST POSITION | SUITABLE SOIL | PROPAGATION | PARTS OF PLANT | USES |
|---|---|---|---|---|---|
|  | ✳ | 🌿 | ● | 🌿☮ | ☞ |
| Hardy perennial (usually treated as a hardy annual) | Full sun | Fertile | Seed | Leaves, roots | Culinary |

*Cochlearia armoracia*

# HORSERADISH

*Horseradish is not normally a pretty plant, but the variegated form can become a real focal point.*

Horseradish is a coarse-looking plant with dock-like leaves about 60 cm (24 in) long. There is a variegated variety with leaves splashed with white that makes a more decorative plant. Horseradish is also listed in some catalogues under its botanical name of *Armoracia rusticana*.

The useful part of the plant is the pungent thick fleshy root rather than the leaves. So despite the fact that it can be invasive in the garden, prepare the ground well before planting. Cultivate the soil to about 45 cm (18 in), working in plenty of garden compost or rotted manure. Plant about 30 cm (12 in) apart, and keep well watered to prevent the roots becoming coarse. Plant dormant roots of horseradish, known as thongs, with the top of the root about 5 cm (2 in) below the soil surface. Spikes of tiny white flowers may appear in late spring or early summer, but remove these to concentrate the plant's energy on leaf and root production.

The easiest way to propagate horseradish is to break off and replant small pieces of root in spring. These should soon grow new shoots.

Being soft and fleshy, the leaves are prone to attack by a whole range of leaf-eating insects, and snails can be a particular problem.

| Type of plant | Best position | Suitable soil | Propagation | Parts of plant | Uses |
|---|---|---|---|---|---|
| Hardy perennial | Full sun or partial shade | Ordinary but deeply cultivated | Root cuttings, seed | Roots | Cosmetic, culinary, medicinal |

## *Coriandrum sativum*

# CORIANDER

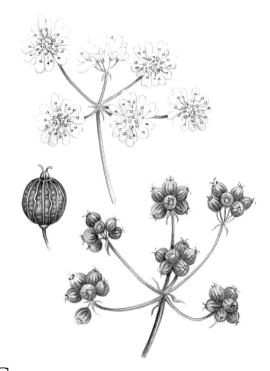

leaves are often called Chinese parsley, a reference to their inclusion in many Chinese dishes. The seeds that follow the mauve-tinted white flowers are also strongly but more pleasantly aromatic. The seeds are an important spice and have been used for centuries.

Sow this easy-to-grow annual in mid spring, where it is to grow. Choose a position sheltered from strong winds because the stems are weak and the plant tends to loll about, a problem that twiggy stakes should overcome. Water regularly in dry weather, especially if you want a long-lasting supply of fresh leaves.

*Coriander is an easy annual, best sown in a bold drift. Individual plants can look weedy.*

CORIANDER HAS LACY, feathery foliage and a frothy profusion of tiny white flowers in early and mid summer. It grows to about 60 cm (24 in) and tends to look best as single plants surrounded by colourful herbs like pot marigolds or in bold drifts in a wilder part of the garden. It can also be grown in tubs or large pots, provided you sow *in situ*. It also looks good in a herb border supported by other plants and so allowing its feathery foliage to fill in any gaps.

The leaves have a pungent smell that has been described as a cross between lemon peel and sage; it is one that many people find unpleasant. The fresh

| TYPE OF PLANT | BEST POSITION | SUITABLE SOIL | PROPAGATION | PARTS OF PLANT | USES |
|---|---|---|---|---|---|
| Hardy annual | Full sun | Undemanding, well drained | Seed | Leaves, seeds | Culinary, household, medicinal |

## *Cuminum cyminum*
# CUMIN

Sow seed in spring, where the plants are to grow, and thin them out to a few centimetres (inches) apart if too many germinate. The crop of seeds should be ready to harvest about three or four months later; the hotter and drier the summer, the better the crop should be.

*Cumin is an unimposing plant, so sow it in bold drifts. Provide a sunny spot for successful results.*

T HIS USEFUL SPICE WAS out of favour as a plant for the herb garden, until interest increased in Indian and Middle Eastern cookery, not to mention spicy Mexican dishes. Now there is every reason to grow it.

Cumin is a small and unimposing plant grown solely for its seeds. It does not reach much more than 30 cm (12 in), and has grass-like leaves on branching stems that are topped with small heads of tiny lilac or white flowers.

A sunny spot is essential to ensure that a good crop of seed matures and ripens, so grow cumin massed in a bed where it can be allowed to set seed.

| TYPE OF PLANT | BEST POSITION | SUITABLE SOIL | PROPAGATION | PARTS OF PLANT | USES |
|---|---|---|---|---|---|
|  | ☼ | ✖ | ● | ❀ |  |
| Hardy annual | Full sun | Undemanding | Seed | Seeds | Culinary, medicinal |

*Cymbopogon citratus*

# LEMON GRASS

ALTHOUGH COMMERCIALLY CULTIVATED in Florida, this lemon-scented tender perennial is not widely grown outside tropical climates. The grass rarely flowers, and it is grown for its long, slender, bright green strap-shaped leaves, which are used to impart a lemon flavour to candies and is also used for a refreshing tea.

A few specialist nurseries do sell plants. In areas where the winters are mild and frost-free it will survive outdoors over winter. Where conditions suit, the plant will make an upright clump up to 1.8 m (6 ft) tall. Elsewhere grow it in a container placed in partial shade, but where the aromatic

*Lemon grass is only suitable for growing outdoors in warm areas, but can be grown in a container and overwintered in a conservatory or in a greenhouse.*

leaves can be touched to release their fragrance as you pass. The leaves will only reach 90 cm (36 in), and the plant can overwinter indoors, preferably in a frost-free greenhouse or conservatory.

In mid or late spring cut the leaves back to just above the soil to stimulate new growth. An established clump should be divided in spring once it becomes too large for the container.

| TYPE OF PLANT | BEST POSITION | SUITABLE SOIL | PROPAGATION | PARTS OF PLANT | USES |
|---|---|---|---|---|---|
|  |  | | | |  |
| Tender perennial grass | Partial shade | Fertile | Division | Leaves | Culinary, household |

# *Filipendula ulmaria*
# MEADOWSWEET

Meadowsweet is a medicinal herb, attractive enough to be grown as an ornamental plant. It develops basal rosettes of leaves from creeping roots in spring, followed in early and mid summer by leafy stems topped with many-branched heads of small white flowers. Massed flowerheads create a foam-like effect to a height of 1–1.5 m (3–5 ft). Both leaves and flowers are aromatic; the leaves smell rather like wintergreen, yet the flowers have a sweet

*The golden variety 'Aurea' is a much more attractive garden plant than the green meadowsweet.*

almond-and-honey fragrance in the evening air.

In the wild, meadowsweet grows mainly by water, a clue to the need this plant has for ample moisture in the soil. It performs poorly in the hot, dry conditions that suit most herbs.

The variegated and golden varieties are ornamental. 'Variegata' has dark green leaves marked with deep yellow, but the yellow leaves of 'Aurea' are especially striking. The latter needs a shady or partially shaded spot as in strong sunlight the leaves scorch and turn brown. Like many golden-foliaged plants, the yellow tends to green as the season advances.

The easiest way to propagate is to divide clumps in autumn. Alternatively the species can be raised from seed sown in autumn.

| TYPE OF PLANT | BEST POSITION | SUITABLE SOIL | PROPAGATION | PARTS OF PLANT | USES |
|---|---|---|---|---|---|
|  | |  | | |  |
| Hardy perennial | Full sun or partial shade | Moist | Division | Flowers | Craft, medicinal |

## *Foeniculum vulgare*
# SWEET FENNEL

THERE ARE TWO WIDELY available forms of common, sweet or Roman fennel, one with green and the other with bronze foliage, *F. vulgare purpureum*. Both types are much used as a herb and as an ornamental garden plant – the green as a background to show off the bronze. Both are attractive from the moment the feathery new shoots appear in spring until the 1.8 m (6 ft) stems with distinctive seedheads need cutting down in the autumn.

The thread-like leaves smell strongly of anise and develop into great plumes. The stems, however, are strong and rigid, and by late summer bear flat heads of minute yellow flowers.

Fennel should be grown at the back of a herb border, or ornamentally in a herbaceous border. It will also make a striking focal point in a more open position, such as in a gravel garden, where the many insects that the flowers attract can be studied.

For best results sow in spring where the plants are to grow. Once you have a plant you will never be short of self-sown seedlings unless the flowerheads are cut off before the seeds ripen and fall – a wise precaution to prevent seedlings becoming a nuisance. Plants can be increased by division, but the deep tap root is difficult to lift.

*Fennel is one of the most decorative herbs, pretty enough to grow in a flower border.*

| TYPE OF PLANT | BEST POSITION | SUITABLE SOIL | PROPAGATION | PARTS OF PLANT | USES |
|---|---|---|---|---|---|
| Hardy perennial | Full sun | Undemanding, but well drained | Seed | Leaves, seeds | Cosmetic, craft, culinary, medicinal |

## *Foeniculum vulgare dulce*
# FLORENCE FENNEL

THE SEEDS AND LEAVES of the Florence fennel or finocchio can be used like sweet fennel, though they have a slightly milder flavour. However, Florence fennel is grown as a vegetable, primarily for its bulb-like stems which have a taste somewhere between anise and celery.

It is a compact plant, growing to about 60–90 cm (24–36 in), but pretty enough to be grown in groups in the flower border.

Florence fennel needs a long growing season with plenty of moisture. Sow about 12 mm (½ in) deep in late spring, and thin seedlings to 20 cm (8 in) apart. Earth up to blanch the "bulbs" once they have reached the size of golf balls. Flowerheads should be removed unless wanted for the seeds. The bulbs should be ready to harvest by late summer.

*Florence fennel is commonly grown as a vegetable, but makes a pretty foliage plant too.*

| TYPE OF PLANT | BEST POSITION | SUITABLE SOIL | PROPAGATION | PARTS OF PLANT | USES |
|---|---|---|---|---|---|
| Hardy annual | Full sun | Fertile | Seed | Leaves, seeds, stem | Culinary |

*Galium odoratum*

# SWEET WOODRUFF

THIS GROUND-HUGGING CARPETER was once scattered on floors to improve the smell of musty rooms, but nowadays it is grown as an outdoor carpet for a shady area.

Clusters of tiny white, delicately scented flowers appear in spring, set off by whorls of pointed leaves on square stems. The low growing plants will reach about 15–30 cm (6–12 in). As this is a woodland plant, it will not do well in the hot, sunny conditions that most herbs prefer. Use it instead as a dainty edging to the shady side of a herb garden and work in plenty of moisture-holding garden compost, rotted manure or rotted leaves before you plant.

When the leaves wilt in the autumn they fill the air with the sweet smell of hay as they dry. This

distinctive smell is scarcely present during the spring and summer, and it only develops when the herb is dried.

Divide plants in spring. Otherwise, raise them from seed in spring also, but be prepared for slow germination. Sweet woodruff may still be sold under its old name of *Asperula odorata*.

*Grow sweet woodruff in a bold drift or as a carpet. It's useful for a shady area.*

| TYPE OF PLANT | BEST POSITION | SUITABLE SOIL | PROPAGATION | PARTS OF PLANT | USES |
|---|---|---|---|---|---|
|  Hardy perennial |  Shade or partial shade |  Moist, rich in humus |  Division, seed | Leaves | Culinary, household |

## *Glycyrrhiza glabra*

# LICORICE

Licorice, also spelt liquorice, has been culti-vated in Europe and the New World for centuries. Old people will still remember the true licorice sticks: roots stripped of their bitter bark that are held like a lollipop and chewed as a sweet. These are still sold in some health-food shops.

Despite the well known uses of licorice, surpris-ingly few people recognize the plant. It has graceful ash-like foliage and in summer the spikes of pale violet-blue pea-like flowers are a bonus.

You need plenty of space for licorice. Despite being a herbaceous perennial it can reach 1.8 m (6 ft) once it has become established for a few years and the roots spread. However a more usual height is 1–1.2 m (3–4 ft). Cut down the foliage in the autumn as it begins to die back, and at the same time remove creeping stems close to the roots if you need to control the spread. The roots are ready to be har-vested the third year after planting.

To propagate, plant pieces of root, each with a bud, about 15 cm (6 in) apart in the autumn or at any time during the dormant season.

*You need plenty of space for the bushy and leafy licorice, but it's a useful back-of-border plant.*

| Type of plant | Best position | Suitable soil | Propagation | Parts of plant | Uses |
|---|---|---|---|---|---|
|  | | | | | |
| Hardy perennial | Full sun | Light | Division, root cuttings | Roots | Culinary, medicinal |

## *Hyssopus officinalis*
# HYSSOP

Hyssop is well worth growing for its decorative contribution to the herb garden and pleasant aroma. It resembles lavender in appearance and the blue, sometimes white or pink, flower spikes open from mid summer into autumn. Both flowers and foliage have a strong, slightly musky smell.

The plant makes a neat dwarf shrub about 60 cm (24 in) tall, with a spread about half that. This compact shape makes it suitable for growing in a container or as a low informal hedge within the herb garden, but bear in mind that it will attract bees and wasps. Plant rooted cuttings for a hedge in spring, 30 cm (12 in) apart, and once established clip regularly to maintain a neat profile.

Cut back plants in beds or borders to just above soil level in early spring to stimulate bushy new growth; shoots may, in any case, be damaged by a severe winter. The plant will deteriorate with time and is best replaced after four or five years. Self-sown seedlings will probably have established themselves in the garden to replace old plants. Otherwise new plants can be raised from cuttings taken in autumn.

*Try hyssop as an edging or low "hedge". It also makes a pretty plant in a container.*

| Type of plant | Best position | Suitable soil | Propagation | Parts of plant | Uses |
|---|---|---|---|---|---|
|  |  |  | | |  |
| Hardy evergreen sub-shrub | Full sun | Fertile, well drained | Cuttings, division, seed | Flowers, leaves | Culinary, household, medicinal |

# *Iris germanica* 'Florentina'
# ORRIS ROOT

ORRIS ROOT LOOKS LIKE a pale bearded iris, with the familiar fan of stiff sword-shaped leaves arising from thick rhizomes that lie at soil level. The white flowers with a hint of blue appear in early summer and last for a couple of weeks. The plant usually makes a clump about 60 cm (24 in) tall, but in warm areas can be larger.

The flowers have a faint but pleasant fragrance, but the true orris aroma – like vanilla or violets – is only released after the rhizomes have been dried. (Before drying they have an earthy smell.)

Do not expect to harvest rhizomes until the third year after planting, and if possible establish an area where a colony can be left to grow undisturbed for a few years. If you do not have enough space in the herb garden, plant it in the herbaceous border or in front of shrubs.

The easiest method of propagation is by lifting and dividing the rhizomes in mid summer after flowering, making sure there is a fan of leaves on each piece that you replant. Keep the rhizome horizontal to the surface and do not plant too far below the surface.

Orris root may be sold as *Iris florentina* or as *I.* 'Florentina' .

| TYPE OF PLANT | BEST POSITION | SUITABLE SOIL | PROPAGATION | PARTS OF PLANT | USES |
|---|---|---|---|---|---|
| Hardy perennial | Full sun | Undemanding, well drained | Division | Roots | Cosmetic, household |

## *Isatis tinctoria*
# WOAD

Woad is also known as dyer's weed in some countries. It was the traditional blue dye used in Europe for colouring cloth and decorating the body. The dye is slow to prepare and the smell disgusting as the crushed leaves ferment, so only the most enthusiastic traditionalist would want to use woad for this purpose nowadays. However it is an interesting plant to have in any herb collection because of its fascinating history.

The plant is a biennial that grows to about 60–90 cm (24–36 in). It looks rather leggy and

uninteresting during its first year of growth, but when it flowers in early summer the following year a group of them will make a bold splash of yellow that is difficult to ignore. The flowers resemble those of the yellow mustard and rape plants now widely grown for the oil their seeds yield. If woad is grown for its dye, however, the leaves are regularly cropped before the plant flowers.

You can buy plants from specialist herb nurseries, but it is easy to grow from seed sown in early or mid summer.

*Woad is quite pretty in flower, but you may need to stake it as the growth can be rather leggy.*

| TYPE OF PLANT | BEST POSITION | SUITABLE SOIL | PROPAGATION | PARTS OF PLANT | USES |
|---|---|---|---|---|---|
| Hardy biennial | Full sun | Fertile | Seed | Leaves | Household |

## *Laurus nobilis*

# SWEET BAY

No HERB GARDEN IS complete without a bay, and if trained and clipped into a formal shape, such as a pyramid or "lollipop", it makes an excellent centrepiece for a formal design. Clipped bays also make smart patio plants, and a pair in tubs on either side of the front or back door are always impressive. The small creamy flowers that appear in late spring are insignificant.

Where conditions suit, bay can make a very large bush or small tree, but it is possible to keep it to about 1.8 m (6 ft) by regular clipping and pruning. Use secateurs to clip sweet bay, not shears. This avoids slashing the large dark green, glossy leaves which would then turn brown at the cut edges.

*Sweet bay is an excellent, easily shaped, shrub for a container.*

Although bay will survive frost and quite cold winters, some of the leaves may be damaged. Freezing weather and strong winds make the worst combination, so erect a wind shelter for the necessary protection. Where winters are very cold, it should be grown in a tub and taken into a greenhouse bay or light porch for the winter.

When growing plants in tubs or large pots use a loam-based potting compost and remember to feed occasionally during summer. Repot in spring as necessary.

Cuttings are the preferred method of propagating sweet bay. It can also be raised from seed but germination is often slow and erratic.

| TYPE OF PLANT | BEST POSITION | SUITABLE SOIL | PROPAGATION | PARTS OF PLANT | USES |
|---|---|---|---|---|---|
|  |  |  |  |  | |
| Tender shrub | Full sun or partial shade | Well drained | Cuttings, seed | Leaves | Craft, culinary, household, medicinal |

# *Lavandula*
# LAVENDER

No HERB GARDEN IS complete without lavender. Whether grown in a border or bed, in a tub or large pot, or as a hedge, it is one of the most attractive and fragrant of all herbs. Lavender is also a traditional cottage-garden plant. It has grey-green aromatic foliage and fragrant spikes of blue or mauve flowers from mid summer to early autumn.

There are many species and varieties from which to choose, so it is worth considering growing a collection. Some of the best to start with are: *L. angustifolia* (syn. *L. spica*) 'Hidcote' (violet-blue); *L. angustifolia* 'Munstead' (lavender-blue, green leaves); *L. × intermedia* 'Twickel Purple' (lavender-blue); and French lavender, *L. stoechas* (dark purple flowers in congested terminal heads rather than long spikes). There are also white- and pink-flowered varieties, though these lack the impact of the more traditional colours. All grow to about 60–90 cm (24–36 in).

Clip over the plants lightly with shears in autumn or the following spring to keep them tidy and compact. Even clipped plants deteriorate in time, so raise some replacements every few years.

Lavenders can be grown from seed, but the preferred method of propagation is taking cuttings which will root readily in spring or late summer. Cuttings also ensure that named varieties will be the same as their parent.

*Lavandula
angustifolia
'Hidcote'*

| TYPE OF PLANT | BEST POSITION | SUITABLE SOIL | PROPAGATION | PARTS OF PLANT | USES |
|---|---|---|---|---|---|
| Hardy shrub | Full sun | Undemanding, well drained | Cuttings, seed | Flowers, leaves | Craft, cosmetic, culinary, medicinal, household |

*Use lavenders liberally . . . not only in the herb garden but in borders and among shrubs. They are excellent companions for roses.*

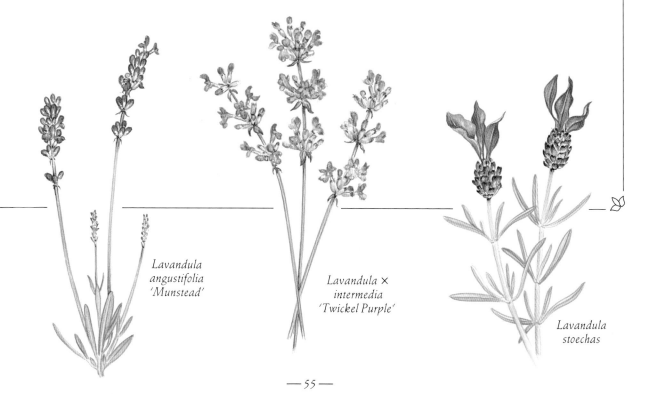

*Lavandula angustifolia 'Munstead'*

*Lavandula × intermedia 'Twickel Purple'*

*Lavandula stoechas*

# *Levisticum officinale*
# LOVAGE

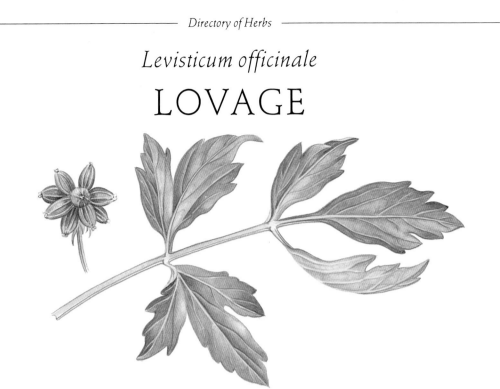

Lovage is a tall, leafy perennial herb that grows to about 1.5–1.8 m (5–6 ft). Umbrella-like clusters of small yellow flowers are produced in mid or late summer, but the leaves are the main feature of the plant, resembling those of celery but much larger. The flavour and smell is also celery-like.

As lovage is so tall, it is best grown at the back of a border, where its size will not be a problem. It is difficult to place in a formal herb garden with small beds. However it is useful for corners that are too shady for sun-loving herbs to thrive, as it grows happily in full sun or partial shade. Do not allow young plants to dry out, and always keep lovage well watered in dry weather. A balanced fertilizer applied in early summer will keep plants vigorous and lush.

The seed should be sown in spring. Sprinkle a few seeds where you want the plant to grow, and thin the seedlings to one in each position if more germinate. Otherwise start them off in pots or trays indoors and plant out the seedlings. Established plants do not divide successfully, but you can take root cuttings from established plants.

*Lovage demands plenty of space, but you can use it as a leafy border filler as well as in the herb garden.*

| Type of plant | Best position | Suitable soil | Propagation | Parts of plant | Uses |
|---|---|---|---|---|---|
|  |  |  |  |  |  |
| Hardy perennial | Full sun or partial shade | Fertile, moist | Root cuttings, seed | Leaves, stems, roots, seeds | Cosmetic, culinary, medicinal |

## *Marrubium vulgare*

# WHITE HOREHOUND

maintain a compact bushy appearance, old plants should be clipped over with shears each spring. White horehound is a versatile plant for although it prefers full sun, it also performs satisfactorily in partial shade.

Horehound is almost always grown from seed sown in mid spring, indoors or in a seedbed outdoors. Transplant the seedlings to where they are to grow, spacing them about 25 cm (10 in) apart, or take cuttings during the summer.

Horehound is seldom grown nowadays, but it is worth finding space for a clump as this perennial tolerates poor, impoverished soil and can look after itself. It makes a bushy plant about 60 cm (24 in) high, with small wrinkled leaves with crinkled edges that turn down. The small white flowers clustered along the stems in summer are much loved by bees.

Grow a couple of plants in a herb border or formal herb garden or use it as an ornamental edging. It can also be used in a container with other herbs. To

*The white horehound is unspectacular but useful and easy to grow.*

| TYPE OF PLANT | BEST POSITION | SUITABLE SOIL | PROPAGATION | PARTS OF PLANT | USES |
|---|---|---|---|---|---|
| Hardy perennial | Full sun or partial shade | Undemanding | Cuttings, seed | Leaves | Medicinal |

# *Melissa officinalis*
# LEMON BALM

*Melissa officinalis*

Lemon balm is a cottage-garden plant grown for its lemon-scented leaves as much as its herbal use. No garden should be without this plant which is as decorative as it is useful. It should be placed next to a path or in a low raised bed, where the strong lemon scent of the foliage will be released as the leaves are brushed against in passing.

The small white flowers clustered up the stem during the summer are insignificant visually, but very attractive to bees, as the name 'melissa' suggests. The plant makes a rounded mound 60–90 cm (24–36 in) high, with leaves that resemble those of mint. In warm climates it can grow up to 1.2 m (4 ft). Although it will grow in dry soils, the scent is stronger and more agreeable if the ground is moist and fertile.

*Plant lemon balm where you can brush against its aromatic foliage.*

| Type of Plant | Best Position | Suitable Soil | Propagation | Parts of Plant | Uses |
|---|---|---|---|---|---|
|  |  | |  |  |  |
| Hardy perennial | Full sun or partial shade | Fertile, moist | Cuttings, division, seed | Leaves | Cosmetic, culinary, medicinal, household |

*'Variegata' (syn. 'Aurea' )*

This is a herbaceous perennial that can easily be propagated by division, cuttings or seed. Seed tends to be slow to germinate but some self-sown seedlings can usually be found around an existing plant. The easiest way to multiply lemon balm is by dividing the clump in spring. If you need more than a few plants, take cuttings in late spring.

It is worth replacing plants every two or three years. This is because old plants are often over-large and have lost the neat form of youth.

### Variegated Varieties

The golden and variegated varieties look good towards the front of a herbaceous border or in front of shrubs, if the position is not too dark. The variety **'All Gold'** will bring a splash of yellow to a shady or partially shaded border. In full sun the leaves tend to scorch and turn brown.

**'Variegata'** (also called 'Aurea') will tolerate full sun. Its leaves are boldly splashed and speckled with yellow, and the foliage looks especially striking in early summer.

*The variety 'Variegata' is perhaps the brightest lemon balm, and the best choice for a border position.*

*The variety 'All Gold' is a bright choice for a shaded position.*

*'All Gold'*

# *Mentha*
# MINT

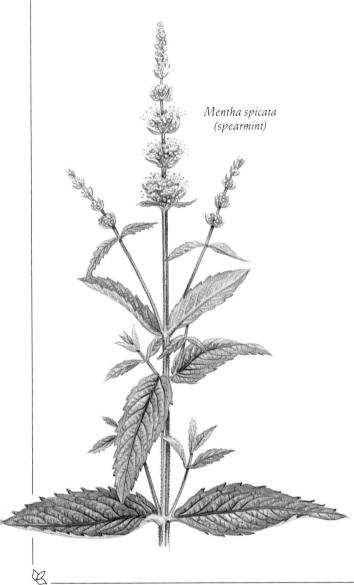

*Mentha spicata*
*(spearmint)*

No HERB GARDEN IS complete without a couple of different mints. All those described on the following pages are upright-growing to about 30–60 cm (12–24 in) and a spread that constantly increases as the plant expands its territory by underground stems unless restrained by some means (see pages 61, 62 and 63). (*Mentha pulegium*, pennyroyal, is a creeping plant described on page 64.)

There are a dozen or more mints widely available from garden centres and herb specialists, and a collection of six or so will add interest to the garden as well as your meals.

The mint most commonly grown is spearmint (*M. spicata*), the flavour and scent of which is readily associated with chewing gum. This and all the mints described have the same cultural requirements. They also have similar spikes of small, bluish mauve or purple flowers in late summer. As these are not very attractive, you may prefer to cut them off with shears to make more of a feature of the foliage.

Despite the ability of mints to cling to life tenaciously, and challenge their neighbours for space, they respond well to care and attention. They do least well in hot, dry positions, when diseases such as mildew and rust can be a problem. To encourage lush growth with succulent leaves, grow them in moist soil and partial shade. Once the shoots begin to age and the leaves look old, try cutting some of the shoots back to just above ground level to stimulate a fresh flush of growth.

Work plenty of garden compost or rotted manure

| TYPE OF PLANT | BEST POSITION | SUITABLE SOIL | PROPAGATION | PARTS OF PLANT | USES |
|---|---|---|---|---|---|
|  |  |  |  |  | |
| Hardy perennial | Full sun or partial shade | Moist, fertile | Division, runners | Leaves | Cosmetic, craft, culinary, household, medicinal |

*Mentha spicata, spearmint, is perhaps the best for culinary use.*

into the ground before planting. Set plants about 23–30 cm (9–12 in) apart. To propagate mint either divide an established clump in winter or spring or separate pieces of runners (underground stems) and bury 5 cm (2 in), ideally in late winter or early spring.

To help combat disease, cut off the shoots at ground level in autumn, using shears. Burn or otherwise dispose of the material so that disease spores cannot re-infect the garden.

If mint is cropped heavily, top dress plants with a layer of well-rotted manure during the winter, and if possible start a new bed every third year.

Extend the harvesting period by potting up a few plants in late summer. Cut the top growth down to about 15 cm (6 in) and take the pot into a greenhouse or place by a light window indoors. Lift some runners in late winter and plant them about 5 cm (2 in) in deep pots or trays. Keep in a warm greenhouse or a cold frame and you will have young fresh mint to enjoy a month or so before that growing in the garden is ready.

### Selected Species

The illustrations and main identification features given should help you to recognize most of the common mints, but they can be confusing and even the experts make mistakes in identification.

**Apple mint** (*M. × rotundifolia*) Also known as **round-leaved mint**, this has very hairy stems and

*Variegated apple mint looks good tumbling over a path.*

*Mentha suaveolens (variegated apple mint)*

rounded, rather woolly wrinkled leaves. It is sometimes called *M. suaveolens*, and you might find it sold under either name.

'**Variegata**', the variegated apple mint, is sometimes called **pineapple mint**. Its leaves are blotched and splashed with creamy white and some may be almost all white. The allusion to a pineapple scent is rather fanciful, but perhaps created to distinguish it from the plain-leaved apple mint.

Apple mint, especially the variegated form, is a compact plant that grows to about 30 cm (12 in), making it a good choice for the front of a border or in a container.

**Bowles' mint** (*M.* × *villosa* var. *alopecuroides*) Considered by some to be a hybrid of *M. spicata* and *M. rotundifolia*, the large woolly stalkless leaves are almost round. It is a rampant grower that tolerates dry soils better than most mints. Although not popular commercially because it wilts quickly when picked, it nevertheless makes excellent mint sauce.

**Curly mint** This mint is difficult to ascribe to a particular species. The name is given to several different mints, many of them hybrids, with waved,

*If you crush the leaves of the eau de Cologne mint, you will know why it has been given this name.*

*Mentha × piperita citrata (eau de Cologne mint)*

*Like the other mints, variegated apple mint will soon spread, but a bed of it can be really eyecatching.*

*Mentha × villosa alopecuroides (Bowles' mint)*

*Mentha × gentilis 'Variegata'*
*(variegated ginger mint)*

*Use the variegated ginger mint to provide a bold splash of foliage colour in the herb garden.*

twisted or curled leaves. Curly leaves add nothing to culinary merit, but contribute variety and interest to a mint collection.

**Eau de Cologne mint** (*M. × piperita* var. *citrata*) A hairless mint with thin smooth leaves and purple runners, it has purplish flowers. In full sun it develops a strong eau-de-Cologne scent and the whole plant is tinged purple. In shade the colour is more coppery. Use it as an aromatic herb in pot pourri or to make a honey-sweetened drink. The flavour is not so good for mint sauce.

**Ginger mint** (*M. × gentilis*) This strongly scented mint smells like spearmint. The short-stalked leaves are pointed at both ends, but the variegated form is the one usually grown and this is very distinctive with contrasting stripes of yellow along the midrib and main veins.

**Horse mint** (*M. longifolia*) The greyish and very hairy leaves are much longer than broad, and have a rather musty smell. It is not a good choice for culinary use.

**Peppermint** (*M. × piperita*) This has thin, hairy, stalked leaves. Two forms are widely available: black peppermint has deep purple stems and leaf blades up to about 6 cm (2½ in) long, white peppermint is a lighter green and has leaf blades up to about 7.5 cm (3 in) long. Its distinctive smell means it cannot be mistaken for any other mint. Peppermint is used to make a refreshing mint tea.

**Pineapple mint** see apple mint.

**Round-leaved mint** see apple mint.

**Spearmint** (*M. spicata*) The one that is usually used to make mint sauce, and the most generally cultivated of the culinary mints. The leaves are almost or completely stalkless, lance-shaped, bright green and hairless.

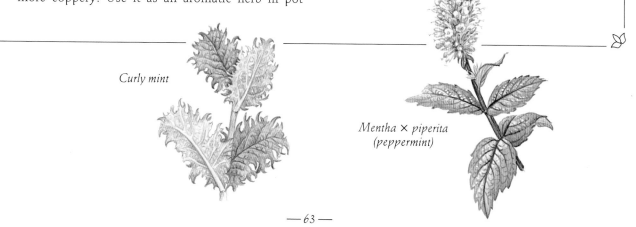

*Curly mint*

*Mentha × piperita*
*(peppermint)*

# *Mentha pulegium*
# PENNYROYAL

Pennyroyal makes a good ground-cover plant, with small oval leaves spaced evenly along slender 25–30 cm (10–12 in) tall stems that grow from creeping roots. Some forms of the plant are more compact, however, and grow only 10–15 cm (4–6 in) tall. The foliage has a peppermint smell but the leaves have a strong, rather bitter taste. The clusters of small lilac-pink flowers in mid summer are an attractive bonus.

Apart from its use as a ground cover (it can even be used as a grass substitute for lawns), it will grow in crevices and tumble over paving, but regular watering in very dry weather is essential. It is also worth planting in a windowbox or other container.

This is an undemanding plant that is not fussy about soil, and will grow in sun or shade. It is generally much lusher and healthier in moist shady conditions, however, and even where conditions suit it may require renewing after about four years. In very cold climates, pennyroyal benefits from protection in winter.

It is easy to grow from seed sown in spring, but propagation is easiest by division.

WARNING  Pennyroyal should not be consumed at any time during pregnancy. It can also be toxic to anyone if used to excess.

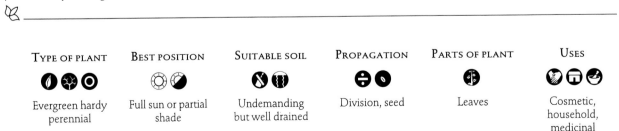

| TYPE OF PLANT | BEST POSITION | SUITABLE SOIL | PROPAGATION | PARTS OF PLANT | USES |
|---|---|---|---|---|---|
| Evergreen hardy perennial | Full sun or partial shade | Undemanding but well drained | Division, seed | Leaves | Cosmetic, household, medicinal |

# *Monarda citriodora*
# LEMON BEE BALM

ALTHOUGH LESS COMMONLY GROWN than *Monarda didyma*, lemon bee balm makes a pretty border plant 1–1.5 m (3–5 ft) tall topped with crowns of pale pink flowers. It makes a bushy clump that expands with age. The oval, pointed leaves smell strongly of lemon when bruised, and can be used in a similar way to those of the scarlet bee balm.

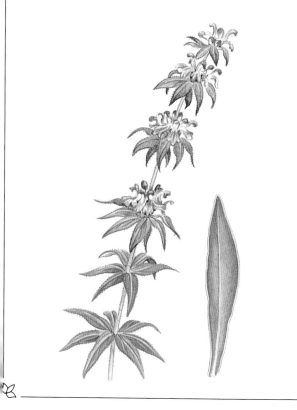

*Monarda citriodora is highly ornamental, and is also very attractive to butterflies and bees.*

The plant makes a bold splash of colour when it flowers in mid summer, and you can be sure it will attract plenty of bees and butterflies. It is thus a good plant for the herbaceous border, but try to find space for it in the herb garden too, where it will add both height and colour. It is also a good choice for a cottage garden.

Lemon bee balm should be obtainable from herb growers or nurseries specializing in more unusual plants. To propagate a large number of plants, take cuttings in spring. Otherwise just divide a large clump into several pieces; it benefits from division every third year, anyway.

| TYPE OF PLANT | BEST POSITION | SUITABLE SOIL | PROPAGATION | PARTS OF PLANT | USES |
|---|---|---|---|---|---|
| Hardy perennial | Full sun or partial shade | Fertile, moist | Cuttings, division | Leaves | Culinary |

# *Monarda didyma*
# BEE BALM

This useful herb, also known as bergamot or oswego tea, is a popular border plant grown for its decorative flowers as much as for its aromatic foliage. The tubular flowers, held like a crown at the top of the 1–1.2 m (3–4ft) stems in mid and late summer are normally bright scarlet. There are also varieties with pink, salmon, crimson, mauve, purple or white flowers, so you can create a really colourful show. As the common name implies, bee balm attracts bees which are appreciative of nectar-rich flowers. Hummingbirds are also attracted to the plant in countries where these tiny birds live.

Although flowers are the main attraction for many people, it is the dark green, resinous-scented leaves that are its justification in the herb garden. They are a prime ingredient of Earl Grey tea, and have other culinary uses. There is even a pleasant fragrance when the top growth has died down. The roots are also sweetly aromatic.

Work plenty of garden compost or rotted manure into the ground before planting, and apply a mulch of organic material each spring.

For a plentiful supply of plants raise them from seed or by taking cuttings. Otherwise just divide an established clump in autumn. The plants benefit from division every second year or else they become bare in the centre. Named varieties must always be propagated from cuttings or by division.

| Type of Plant | Best Position | Suitable Soil | Propagation | Parts of Plant | Uses |
|---|---|---|---|---|---|
|  |  |  |  |  |  |
| Hardy perennial | Full sun or partial shade | Fertile, moist | Cuttings, division, seed | Leaves | Cosmetic, craft, culinary, household, medicinal |

## *Myrrhis odorata*
# SWEET CICELY/MYRRH

*The flowers are dull, but sweet Cicely is a pleasant foliage plant.*

THIS TALL PERENNIAL HERB, also called garden myrrh, grows about 1.2–1.5 m (4–5 ft). It has pretty ferny foliage and small creamy white flowers arranged in umbrella-like heads in late spring and early summer. In spring, it is one of the first plants to produce new growth. Despite this it usually retains its foliage until mid winter.

The claw-like clusters of long brownish black seeds are quite attractive, but if you grow sweet Cicely primarily for its leaves, cut off the flower-heads to prevent seeding. Both the leaves and seeds give off a strong aroma that leaves a hint of licorice and aniseed.

This herb prefers a partially shaded spot with cool soil for the carrot-like tap roots (these can be eaten as a vegetable) to penetrate. It does not like the hot dry positions that suit most herbs. If you cannot find an appropriate space in the herb garden, grow it at the back of a herbaceous or mixed border. Its fresh green foliage is a good foil for more colourful plants and they in turn offer support, as sweet Cicely has a tendency to sprawl.

Seed can sometimes be slow to germinate, but there are nearly always some self-sown seedlings that can be transplanted while still young. Small pieces of root will usually grow if planted in spring, provided they have a bud, or eye, but the parent plant will object to being lifted.

| TYPE OF PLANT | BEST POSITION | SUITABLE SOIL | PROPAGATION | PARTS OF PLANT | USES |
|---|---|---|---|---|---|
|  |  |  |  |  | |
| Hardy perennial | Partial shade | Fertile | Division, seed | Leaves, roots, seeds | Craft, culinary, household |

# *Myrtus communis*
# MYRTLE

Myrtle is a charming evergreen shrub with small aromatic, dark green leathery leaves, and fragrant white flowers about 2.5 cm (1 in) across from early late summer. These are sometimes followed by purple-black oval berries. For decorative impact, 'Variegata' with its creamy white and green leaves is a better plant.

Where conditions suit, the green-leaved species will make a shrub 3 m (10 ft) or more high, but 'Variegata' is less vigorous. Both types can be kept to about 90 cm (36 in) if grown in a tub or large pot. Keep well watered in dry weather; this is especially important if growing in a container.

If space is at a premium, grow the dwarf species *M. Tarentina* (sometimes sold as 'Jenny Reitenback'). There is also a variegated dwarf variety available.

The reason why myrtle is not more widely grown is probably because it is not completely frost hardy. It will tolerate a light frost which will only cause superficial damage, but the shrub does best when kept above 5°C (41°F). This can be achieved by growing plants in large containers that can be moved indoors into a greenhouse or conservatory for winter. Outdoors it needs to be planted by a warm wall in a sheltered position. Prune out any frost-damaged shoots in spring.

Propagate by cuttings in late summer.

*Myrtle is a charming evergreen, but it is one that does best in a warm area.*

| TYPE OF PLANT | BEST POSITION | SUITABLE SOIL | PROPAGATION | PARTS OF PLANT | USES |
|---|---|---|---|---|---|
| Tender evergreen shrub | Full sun, sheltered | Light, well drained | Cuttings | Leaves, fruit | Culinary |

*Nasturtium officinale*

# WATERCRESS

THIS LEAFY PLANT GROWS from 5–60 cm (2–24 in) depending on conditions. It remains low and compact in cool running water, but grows tall and runs to seed in hot weather or in dry conditions. It spreads by the thread-like roots which may arise from each leaf joint. The tiny white flowers are uninteresting and their development is a sign that the plant is past its best.

The natural habitat for watercress is in a flowing stream, but it may be grown without natural running water. To do this a special bed must be made and kept wet by constant watering. Dig a trench about 30 cm (12 in) deep in a partially shaded position, and place 15 cm (6 in) of well-rotted manure or garden compost in the bottom. Cover it with a layer of about 8 cm (3 in) of soil to which has been added as much moisture-retaining material as possible.

If starting from seed, sow directly into the finished trench in mid spring, water thoroughly and ensure that the trench never dries out. For this reason it is sensible to dig the trench close to a water supply or outside tap.

Alternatively grow your watercress in a shallow trough half filled with soil. Plant the seedlings into the soil which must be kept moist. Gradually increase the level of the water in the trough as the cress grows. About once a week, drain off the water and refill with fresh.

| TYPE OF PLANT | BEST POSITION | SUITABLE SOIL | PROPAGATION | PARTS OF PLANT | USES |
|---|---|---|---|---|---|
| Hardy perennial | Full sun or partial shade | Moist, preferably wet but not stagnant | Cuttings, division, seed | Leaves | Culinary, medicinal |

# *Nepeta cataria*

# CATNIP/CATMINT

likely to be squashed flat by cats lying on it, so it is worth protecting with a low fence of wire netting.

Like other catmints, this makes an attractive edging for a shrub or mixed border, or to divide the herb garden into sections. But avoid using it where it will cascade over the edge of a path as it attracts bees and wasps.

Catnip is easy to propagate from seed, but unless you need a large number divide established clumps in early or mid spring; this will give you larger plants more quickly. Cuttings of basal shoots can also be taken in mid spring.

*Nepeta cataria is not as bright as the more popular catmints, but your cats will love it!*

SEVERAL SPECIES of nepeta have been given the name of catmint, but *N. cataria* is the one that cats really love to sniff and rub against. The herb is sometimes used to fill "toys" for cats. The grey-green leaves feel soft and crushing them releases the characteristic minty aroma. The shaded mauve to white flowers, on shoots up to 60–90 cm (24–36 in) high, are borne in clusters where the leaves join the stem.

Although not as showy as *N.* × *faassenii* and *N. mussinii* (syn. *N. racemosa*) which are more popular for the garden, try planting *N. cataria* as an ornamental in the herbaceous border if you are short of room in the herb garden. Bear in mind that it is

| TYPE OF PLANT | BEST POSITION | SUITABLE SOIL | PROPAGATION | PARTS OF PLANT | USES |
|---|---|---|---|---|---|
| Hardy perennial | Full sun | Undemanding | Cuttings, division, seed | Leaves | Cosmetic, medicinal |

*Ocimum basilicum*

# SWEET BASIL

The pungent foliage of basil is usually green, but try a coloured one such as 'Dark Opal' for a change.

Sweet basil is grown for its foliage which has a pungent smell. It can be grown indoors in pots or outside in the garden during summer. The kind most often seen has soft, dark green leaves, though the shape and size can vary, and some are ruffled. In poor light the plants soon become leggy, so keep pinching out the growing tips to encourage branching and a bushy shape. (This is worth doing even with plants in the garden.) The white flowers are not a feature of basil, so do not hesitate to pinch out flowering spikes.

For contrast grow green-leaved basil in combination with one of the purple-leaved varieties such as 'Dark Opal', *O. basilicum* 'Purpurascens', or 'Purple Ruffles'. These purple-leaved basils can look dull on their own, but are a good foil to their green counterpart. They also make attractive companions as patio plants in a container.

Unless you buy plants, propagate each year from seed sown indoors in spring. You then have the choice of growing them in pots by a light window, or planting them in the herb garden when there is no risk of frost and they have been acclimatized (this is very important as a sudden chill or very cold winds may kill basil even without a frost). If growing them outside, space plants about 30 cm (12 in) apart.

Bush basil (*O. basilicum* 'Minimum', sometimes listed as *O. minimum*) has much smaller leaves and grows to about 30 cm (12 in) rather than the 60 cm (24 in) or more of sweet basil.

| TYPE OF PLANT | BEST POSITION | SUITABLE SOIL | PROPAGATION | PARTS OF PLANT | USES |
|---|---|---|---|---|---|
|  | | |  |  |  |
| Tender annual | Full sun | Ordinary, well drained | Seed | Leaves | Craft, culinary, household, medicinal |

## *Oenothera biennis*
# EVENING PRIMROSE

THE EVENING PRIMROSE, also called night willow herb in North America, has the sort of wild-flower charm that looks good in a cottage garden. In the herb garden it makes a bold splash of yellow to contrast with the predominant greens. It is a biennial which in its first year forms a flat rosette of pale green leaves, then in the second produces upright stems about 1–1.2 m (3–4 ft) tall. These stems carry large fragrant yellow flowers from early summer and into autumn. Where conditions suit, flowers may even be produced late in the first year. The flowers are short lived, and are at their best in the evening, when the scent increases in intensity.

Evening primroses are now grown commercially on a large scale for the essential oil which is regarded as having important medicinal properties. On a garden scale the yield will not make harvesting a practical proposition. It is, however, such an attractive plant that it needs no excuse for a place in any herb garden.

Sow the seeds where the plants are to grow in late spring or early summer and thin the seedlings out when large enough to handle. Seeds are available from specialist seedsmen or those dealing in wild flower seeds, otherwise buy seedlings from a herb nursery. Once plants are established, self-sown seedlings should provide a supply of plants for subsequent years.

| TYPE OF PLANT | BEST POSITION | SUITABLE SOIL | PROPAGATION | PARTS OF PLANT | USES |
|---|---|---|---|---|---|
| Hardy biennial | Full sun | Undemanding | Seed | Leaves, stems, seeds | Medicinal |

# *Origanum majorana*
# SWEET MARJORAM

This desirable culinary herb needs to be treated as a half-hardy annual in most areas, although it is in fact a tender perennial that will overwinter outside where frosts are not a problem. The plant grows to about 25 cm (10 in), with tough trailing stems, covered in summer with clusters of small but dainty flowers, usually mauvish pink but sometimes white or purple. The plant's flowers are produced from pea-like buds that resemble knots which is why it became commonly known as knotted marjoram. The small oval leaves are pungently aromatic.

Sweet marjoram makes an attractive container plant and, by taking it indoors and placing it where it

*Sweet marjoram makes a pretty edging, but remember that it's not frost-hardy.*

gets natural light, you should be able to keep it through the winter.

Sow seeds indoors or, if possible, in a greenhouse and prick out into trays or pots. Plant out in early summer after hardening off. Sow seed outdoors in late spring where the plants are to flower, but cover them with a cloche to aid germination.

Overwintered plants can be propagated by cuttings or division, but it is usually easier to raise new plants from seed each year.

| Type of plant | Best position | Suitable soil | Propagation | Parts of plant | Uses |
|---|---|---|---|---|---|
|  |  |  |  |  | |
| Tender perennial | Full sun | Fertile | Cuttings, division, seed | Leaves | Cosmetic, craft, culinary, household, medicinal |

## *Origanum vulgare*
# OREGANO/WILD MARJORAM

Oregano is an invaluable culinary herb. It is easy to grow and a highly decorative garden plant. Unlike sweet marjoram it is hardy and will overwinter without problems. It dies down for the winter, but when growth starts in spring it will soon make a bushy plant about 30–45 cm (12–18 in) tall. An established plant will have a spread of about 45 cm (18 in), making an attractive mound of aromatic foliage studded with masses of small pink flowers from mid to late summer.

The flowers are very attractive to many kinds of insects, including butterflies, bees and wasps. Therefore, although it is useful as an edging plant in summer, do not plant it where it will overhang a path if insects bother you.

The golden-leaved variety makes an ideal edging plant as it is smaller and more compact than the

green-leaved species. The flowers can be trimmed off with shears to keep it as a neat foliage plant. Oregano tends to become woody and less attractive after about four years, so consider dividing and replanting, or raising new plants from cuttings, after the third year.

*Origanum vulgare is pretty in flower, and 'Aureum' makes an attractive foliage plant.*

| TYPE OF PLANT | BEST POSITION | SUITABLE SOIL | PROPAGATION | PARTS OF PLANT | USES |
|---|---|---|---|---|---|
| Hardy perennial | Full sun | Ordinary, well drained | Cuttings, division, seed | Leaves | Culinary |

# *Panax quinquefolius*
# GINSENG

HEALTH FOOD AND HERB enthusiasts rank ginseng as a medicinal herb of major importance. Chinese ginseng is a different species, but the two look similar and are used in the same way. The five-fingered leaves are held hand-like on 30–45 cm (12–18 in) stems that arise from the base of the plant. Smallish green flowers appear on mature plants in early summer – usually three or four years after sowing. Like the plant itself, the fleshy roots develop only slowly.

The plant is of no great ornamental value, but it can be used as a foliage ground cover in the right conditions. It is worth trying to grow as a curiosity, even if it struggles to thrive. In the wild it grows in moist woodland, so prepare a special small bed in partial shade, enriching it with plenty of humus-forming material such as garden compost, rotted manure or decomposed leaves.

It can be grown from seed but this may not be easy to obtain. Some herb nurseries also sell ginseng plants, but you are unlikely to find this herb in garden centres.

| TYPE OF PLANT | BEST POSITION | SUITABLE SOIL | PROPAGATION | PARTS OF PLANT | USES |
|---|---|---|---|---|---|
| Hardy perennial | Partial shade | Moist, fertile | Division, seed | Roots | Medicinal |

## *Pelargonium*

# SCENTED-LEAVED PELARGONIUMS

THE SCENTED-LEAVED PELARGONIUMS are species and hybrid species belonging to the same genus as the popular border plants known as geranium. In some species the scent released by the crushed leaves is unmistakable, but in others the aroma is more elusive and difficult to define. What one person describes as orange, another may consider smells of lemons, or even roses!

Most scented-leaved pelargoniums grow 30–

*Pelargonium graveolens has been described as smelling of lemons, oranges, and roses!*

60 cm (12–24 in) tall, but the shape and size of leaf vary considerably, and some are attractively variegated. The flowers are relatively unspectacular when compared to the showy display given by bedding pelargoniums (summer bedding geraniums).

All scented-leaved pelargoniums make good pot-plants for home or greenhouse, but outdoors they lack the impact of their more floriferous cousins. Once there is no risk of frost, however, they

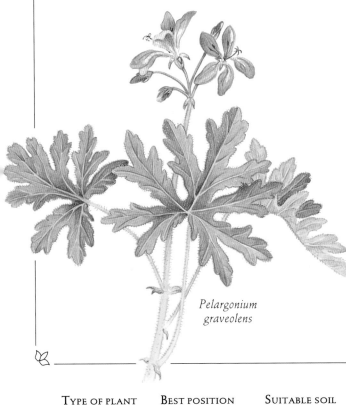

*Pelargonium graveolens*

| TYPE OF PLANT | BEST POSITION | SUITABLE SOIL | PROPAGATION | PARTS OF PLANT | USES |
|---|---|---|---|---|---|
| Tender perennial | Full sun or good light | Well drained, light (fill pots with loam-based compost) | Cuttings | Flowers, leaves | Cosmetic, culinary, household |

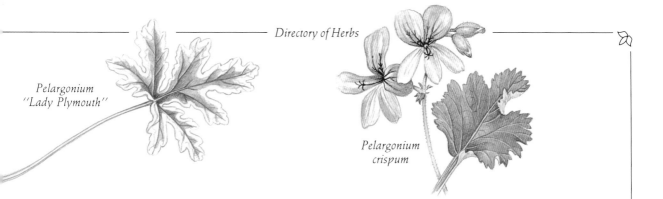

*Pelargonium "Lady Plymouth"*

*Pelargonium crispum*

can be planted in the herb garden for the summer. Alternatively a collection of them can be grown in a raised bed, perhaps on the patio where visitors will enjoy doing a "sniff test"!

Lift plants in the autumn and cut them back by about two-thirds before overwintering in a frost-free place. Keep on the dry side during the winter. You may find it more convenient to keep them in large pots throughout the year and plunge them, complete with pot, into the soil for the summer.

If the plants become straggly, pinch back the growing tips to keep them compact and induce branching. Feed during the summer, whether in pots or the garden. Cuttings taken in autumn and spring root easily.

### SELECTED SPECIES

Most herb growers sell scented-leaved pelargoniums, but to extend your collection you may have to obtain plants from a specialist nursery. There are many other species and varieties besides the ones listed here, some with different scents.

*P.* × *asperum* Pine scent (which some people find unpleasant); lilac flowers; rough grey-green leaves.

*P. capitatum* Rose scent; rose-purple flowers; hairy leaves; sometimes sold as 'Attar of Roses'; variegated variety available.

*P.* × *citrosum* Orange scent; mauve flowers.

*P. crispum* Lemon scent; mauve flowers; small crinkled leaves; variegated varieties available. Sometimes sold as the finger-bowl pelargonium (geranium) because it was used to scent finger bowls.

*P.* × *fragrans* Nutmeg/spice scent; white flowers; small grey-green leaves; a variegated variety with mauve flowers is also available.

*P. graveolens* Scent difficult to define, variously described as lemon, orange or rose; pink and purple flowers; grey-green leaves; **'Lady Plymouth'** is a variegated variety.

*P. grossularioides* Coconut scented; purple flowers; small leaves; creeping habit.

*P.* **'Mabel Grey'** Lemon scent; mauve flowers; other hybrids having a weaker lemon scent include **'Lemon Fancy'** and **'Little Gem'**.

*P.* × *nervosum* Lime scent; lavender flowers; small crinkled leaves.

*P. odoratissimum* Apple scent; small white flowers; sprawling habit.

*P. tomentosum* Peppermint scent; small white flowers; pale green leaves.

*Pelargonium tomentosum*

*Pelargonium quercifolium, oakleaf geranium*

*Petroselinum crispum*

# PARSLEY

*Curled parsley*

year. But by the time it flowers the plant is past its best and should be discarded.

Parsley seed has a reputation for being slow or difficult to germinate, but it will usually succeed if the ground is warm and moist. If you have problems try soaking the seeds in lukewarm water for a couple of hours before sowing in drills or furrows that have been well watered beforehand. Make sure the soil never dries out before the seeds germinate.

By sowing at various times, you should be able to pick fresh parsley at any time of the year. The earliest sowing can be under glass in late winter or early spring, followed by regular sowings outdoors in spring and summer. In autumn sow seed in a cold

*Curled varieties of parsley are the most attractive. Grow them in blocks, rows, or as an edging.*

Parsley needs little introduction. It is probably one of the most universal of culinary herbs, and a familiar sight in kitchen gardens with its tightly curled leaves.

Although a hardy biennial and easily overwintered, it is most often grown as an annual. The almost moss-like foliage will form a plant 23–30 cm (9–12 in) tall which will eventually produce tiny clusters of greenish yellow flowers in the second

| Type of plant | Best position | Suitable soil | Propagation | Parts of plant | Uses |
|---|---|---|---|---|---|
|  |  |  |  |  |  |
| Hardy biennial | Full sun or partial shade | Fertile, humus-rich | Seed | Leaves, roots | Cosmetic, culinary, household, medicinal |

*Plain-leaved parsley*

frame or under cloches for a winter crop. You can also try growing parsley in pots in a greenhouse or by a very light window indoors.

### SELECTED SPECIES

**Italian parsley** (*P. crispum* var. *neopolitanum*) This is also known as flat-leaved parsley according to where you live. It does not make such an attractive edging plant as the more familiar curled parsley (sometimes called French parsley in America), but it has a stronger flavour that some cooks prefer. The leaves are flat and resemble those of coriander (cilantro). Cultivation is the same as for curled parsley.

**Hamburg parsley** (*P. crispum* var. *tuberosum*) Also known as turnip-rooted parsley, the leaves of this distinctive type look like Italian or plain-leaved parsley, and they can be used in the same way. But this is a dual-purpose plant and the parsnip-like roots can be eaten as a vegetable. Cook the roots in the same way as parsnips, although the taste is closer to that of celeriac.

Sow Hamburg parsley in early or mid spring, where the plants are to grow, and lift the roots in autumn or winter.

*Hamburg parsley*

*Hamburg parsley has leaves that can be used like ordinary parsley, and roots that can be eaten as a vegetable.*

## *Pimpinella anisum*

# ANISE

Aɴɪꜱᴇ ɪꜱ ɢʀᴏᴡɴ ᴘʀɪᴍᴀʀɪʟʏ for its seeds which have the distinctive aniseed flavour. However, a piquancy can be given to soups and salads by adding a few of the leaves. The mature leaves of this hardy annual are feathery and resemble a coarse carrot, but those produced while the plant is still young are more rounded and less divided. Umbrella-like flower heads of tiny white blooms resembling those of dill are produced in mid or late summer.

The plant grows to about 45–60 cm (18–24 in) and is best used as a filler in a herb bed or border. The young plants are rather fragile, so put them in a sheltered position protected from strong winds. Be

*This rather flimsy annual does best in a sheltered position. Use it as a filler in a herb bed or border.*

sure to sow where you want the plants to grow as seedlings do not transplant well.

The main sowing time is spring, but in mild areas an autumn sowing will produce an earlier crop of seeds the following year. Once the plant is established you are assured of more in future years, although the self-sown seedlings are unlikely to become a major problem. Because it is grown for its seeds, these must be allowed to form after flowering and mature to harvest. Just keep a small quantity on one side to sow the next spring in case insufficient self-sown seedlings appear.

| TYPE OF PLANT | BEST POSITION | SUITABLE SOIL | PROPAGATION | PARTS OF PLANT | USES |
|---|---|---|---|---|---|
| 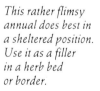 | ⊛ | 🍓🎲 | ◉ | 🌿🌀 | 🗝🏠🥄 |
| Hardy annual | Full sun | Light, well drained | Seed | Leaves, seeds | Culinary, household, medicinal |

## *Poterium sanguisorba*
# SALAD BURNET

Once popular in english cottage gardens and taken to North America by early settlers, salad burnet has become a rather neglected culinary herb. Its leaves have a flavour reminiscent of cucumber, and they are well worth including in summer salads.

The long cascading stems splay out from the centre of the plant, making a mound about 30 cm (12 in) tall. The small, toothed, blue-green leaves grow in opposite pairs along the stems, and in early summer these are topped by small reddish flower-heads. Although not evergreen, the plant is in leaf for most of the year as the new leaves appear very early and are retained well into winter.

Salad burnet is undemanding and will take care of itself once established. In the wild it grows especially well on chalk, but it will grow satis-

factorily in most gardens, given a sunny position.

The plant can be divided, but once established, self-sown seedlings will almost certainly be available. In fact, it is advisable to cut off flowerheads to prevent seedlings becoming a problem.

*Try growing salad burnet in a container if you can't find space in the herb garden.*

| Type of plant | Best position | Suitable soil | Propagation | Parts of plant | Uses |
|---|---|---|---|---|---|
| Hardy perennial | Full sun | Undemanding | Division, seed | Leaves | Culinary, medicinal |

# *Prunella vulgaris*
# SELFHEAL

Selfheal varies in height according to conditions; although normally a ground-hugger just a few centimetres (inches) high, it will grow to more than 45 cm (18 in) in poor light and moist soil. Mauve, purple, pink or white flowers appear in dense heads in mid and late summer.

It can be used as a ground cover or as an edging plant for beds and borders. However use it with care as it can become a persistent weed. For instance, it is not advisable to plant selfheal at the front of a border adjoining a lawn as it will easily spread into the grassed area and become a problem. Grow it instead in an area of the herb garden contained by paving to restrict its spread. Alternatively plant it in a large container, perhaps placed at the base of a tree or group of shrubs.

Selfheal can be bought as a plant, but it is easy to raise from seed. However, you may have to order from a seedsman specializing in herbs or wild flowers. Sow at any time between spring and autumn. Division is the easiest method of propagating established plants. The prostrate stems root freely, so there are plenty of young plants that can be separated from their parents.

| Type of plant | Best position | Suitable soil | Propagation | Parts of plant | Uses |
|---|---|---|---|---|---|
|  |  |  | | |  |
| Hardy perennial | Full sun or partial shade | Undemanding, well drained | Leaves | Leaves | Medicinal |

*Pulmonaria officinalis*

# LUNGWORT

Lungwort is a popular garden plant, grown mainly for its pretty spring flowers that are pink or red when they first open, then turn violet and blue, creating a multi-coloured effect. There are also white cultivars. The first flowers, on 23–30 cm (9–12 in) stems, appear in early spring, and the plant continues to bloom through to late spring. The variegated leaves, blotched silvery-white, remain attractive for many months.

The spots on the foliage were thought to resemble diseased lungs in early times, and made the plant popular in folk medicine as a treatment for lung

Pulmonaria officinalis
*'Sissinghurst white'*

diseases such as tuberculosis. It contains mucilage, tannin, saponins and silicic acid, and some of these can have a beneficial effect on the respiratory system. An infusion of the dried leaves is sometimes used for chesty coughs and sore throats. Some herbalists prescribe lungwort to control diarrhoea.

Lungwort makes effective ground cover for a shaded area; it also looks good in bold clumps at the front of herbaceous or mixed borders, as well as in the herb garden. The plant is undemanding provided there is sufficient moisture. Water freely in dry weather if the soil appears dry.

Division, preferably at the end of the season, is the easiest method of propagation.

| Type of plant | Best position | Suitable soil | Propagation | Parts of plant | Uses |
|---|---|---|---|---|---|
|  |  |  |  | | |
| Hardy perennial | Shade or partial shade | Moist | Seed, division | Leaves | Medicinal |

*Rosa gallica* 'Officinalis'

# APOTHECARY'S ROSE

Fragrance alone would be justification enough for including some roses in the herb garden. But they also qualify on other counts. Rosewater is used medicinally and in cooking, rose petals can be crystallized or used fresh in salads and desserts, and the hips are made into teas and syrups. So have no qualms in planting plenty of roses to bring beauty and colour to your herb collection. However, try to restrict yourself to those that have been used traditionally as herbs or are a source of fragrant oils, such as the apothecary's rose. Others which should be considered are *R. × damascena* 'Trigintipetala' (a form of the damask rose much used for the production of attar of roses in Bulgaria), *R. × alba,*

and *R. × centifolia* (the cabbage or Provence rose). Modern hybrid roses should be avoided as they seldom look right in a herb garden.

If you have space for just one shrub rose, the apothecary's rose combines the qualities of beautiful blooms with intense fragrance, petals of substance that dry well and a good herbal pedigree. In England it is sometimes misleadingly called the damask rose; in America it is also called the French rose or rose of Provins. Whatever name it goes under, it makes a shrub 1–1.2 m (3–4 ft) tall with a similar spread. The semi-double flowers have crimson petals with a central cluster of golden anthers, and red hips in the autumn.

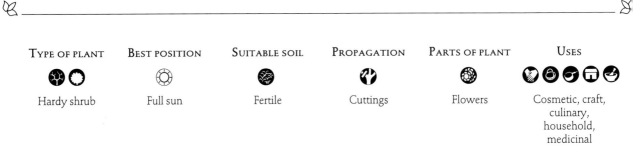

| Type of plant | Best position | Suitable soil | Propagation | Parts of plant | Uses |
|---|---|---|---|---|---|
| Hardy shrub | Full sun | Fertile | Cuttings | Flowers | Cosmetic, craft, culinary, household, medicinal |

# *Rosmarinus officinalis*
# ROSEMARY

Rosemary is a first-rate evergreen shrub, at home in the flower garden. This variety is 'Sissinghurst Blue'.

Rosemary is one of the essential culinary herbs and should be included in every garden. It is well worth planting purely as an ornamental shrub. The small grey-green leaves are evergreen, and simply brushing against them releases their distinctive resinous fragrance. The small flowers – which vary from dark blue to very pale blue or even white according to variety – nestle close to the stem among the foliage. The flowers sometimes begin to open in late winter in mild districts, though late spring is the main flowering period.

Rosemary varies considerably in size depending on the variety. Some remain compact at about 90 cm (36 in) or less, others like 'Fastigiatus' grow tall and erect. A plant of a tall variety can easily reach 1.8 m (6 ft). Some other species grow as prostrate ground-huggers.

Rosemary can be a centrepiece to a formal herb garden, form an informal dividing hedge or be planted in a decorative shrub border. It makes an elegant patio plant for a tub or large pot and, in a cold area, growing it in a container makes winter protection easier. Rosemary tolerates clipping, so you can keep it small and compact if necessary.

Although hardy in most areas, in a severe winter or in cold, exposed districts protection is worthwhile. Cuttings can be taken in summer.

| TYPE OF PLANT | BEST POSITION | SUITABLE SOIL | PROPAGATION | PARTS OF PLANT | USES |
|---|---|---|---|---|---|
| Hardy shrub | Full sun or partial shade | Light, well drained | Cuttings | Leaves | Cosmetic, craft, culinary, household, medicinal |

# *Rumex acetosa*
# SORREL

*Sorrel looks like a weed, so don't give it a conspicuous position.*

SORREL IS GROWN FOR the tangy flavour of its leaves. It is sometimes known as the broad-leaved sorrel as the leaves are up to 10 cm (4 in wide). The mature plant reaches about 90 cm (3 ft), but the leaves are best eaten before the spikes of small rusty-coloured flowers appear. The flavour is best if the soil is moist and cool. So in hot and dry areas apply a thick mulch around the plants after watering thoroughly. Pick the plants over frequently and remove flower buds to ensure a continuing supply of young succulent foliage.

Sorrel is a deep-rooted perennial plant that can be difficult to eradicate. If allowed to flower and set seed, the resulting self-sown seedlings will become a nuisance. Therefore to avoid these problems and because fresh young leaves have a more refined flavour, sorrel is best treated as an annual.

Sow in spring, where the plants are to grow, and thin the seedlings to about 30 cm (12 in) apart. Try to remember to remove the flowering stems before they can set seed.

Seeds can usually be bought from seedsmen specializing in herbs and wild flowers, and many herb nurseries sell established plants.

| TYPE OF PLANT | BEST POSITION | SUITABLE SOIL | PROPAGATION | PARTS OF PLANT | USES |
|---|---|---|---|---|---|
|   |  | | | | |
| Hardy perennial | Sun or partial shade | Fertile, moist | Division, seed | Leaves | Culinary, household, medicinal |

## *Rumex scutatus*

# BUCKLER LEAF SORREL

THIS PLANT PROVIDES PLENTY of spinach-like leaves that are milder in taste than some of the other sorrels. The pale green, distinctively shaped wavy leaves are about 10 cm (4 in) long and arise from ground level to form a clump. Insignificant small greenish flowers appear on stalks about 30–45 cm (12–18 in) tall in late spring or early summer.

Water the plants well in dry weather to encourage a plentiful supply of tender leaves. The flowering stems should be removed as soon as they appear to

*Sorrel lacks eye-appeal and is best grown in rows like spinach.*

help promote more leafy growth and also to avoid self-sown seedlings becoming a problem.

If you prevent flowering in this way, the plants will continue to flourish for several years. However, they are best divided and replanted after three years. Buckler leaf sorrel can also be raised easily from seed. Sow it in spring where it is to grow, or in seed trays to plant out later.

Slugs, snails and caterpillars also find the leaves make a succulent feast, so be prepared to control these pests.

| TYPE OF PLANT | BEST POSITION | SUITABLE SOIL | PROPAGATION | PARTS OF PLANT | USES |
|---|---|---|---|---|---|
| Hardy perennial | Full sun or partial shade | Fertile, moist | Division, seed | Leaves | Culinary |

## *Ruta graveolens*

# RUE

THIS SMALL EVERGREEN SUB-SHRUB looks more like a herbaceous perennial than a shrub. It grows about 60–75 cm (24–30 in) tall and is covered with attractive, rounded and divided foliage which is green or blue-green. The leaves have an acrid smell and in very cold areas the plant may lose some of them in winter. In summer it bears bright yellow flowers which some people prefer to remove.

A variegated rue with leaves flecked creamy white is available, but the most attractive varieties have bright glaucous-blue foliage. 'Jackman's Blue' is the one usually grown in Europe and 'Blue Mound' is popular in America.

Rue can be grown as single plants in a herb or herbaceous border, but a row planted as a low dividing "hedge" within the herb garden can look particularly decorative. Don't be afraid to clip the plants with shears in spring to encourage new bright foliage and compact growth.

Sow seeds in spring or cuttings of non-flowering shoots can be taken in summer.

WARNING    Take care when handling rue. The foliage can cause a very severe reaction in some people, especially if handled in sunshine. Particularly severe reactions can need hospital treatment. Use it with caution medicinally too – it can be toxic in high doses. Use it sparingly as a culinary herb, as the flavour is very strong.

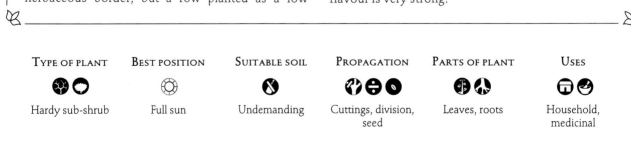

| TYPE OF PLANT | BEST POSITION | SUITABLE SOIL | PROPAGATION | PARTS OF PLANT | USES |
|---|---|---|---|---|---|
| Hardy sub-shrub | Full sun | Undemanding | Cuttings, division, seed | Leaves, roots | Household, medicinal |

*Salvia elegans*

# PINEAPPLE SAGE

THE SOFT, DOWNY LEAVES which smell strongly of pineapple are the main attraction of the plant. Where conditions suit, however, an attractive display of tubular red flowers on slender spikes is a bonus in late summer. These are attractive to many insects and also, in some countries, to humming birds in search of nectar.

This tender perennial never makes a large shrub and normally only reaches 60–90 cm (24–36 in). To encourage a bushy shape, pinch out the growing tips of the plants when they are small. It will grow happily in a tub or large pot. This makes the winter protection this shrub requires easy, as you can simply move the container into a greenhouse or

conservatory. However, where the winters are mild pineapple sage might survive outdoors protected by a sunny wall. It is always worth taking a few cuttings each year to overwinter in a frost-free place as an insurance against winter losses.

*Salvia rutilans*, also a tender perennial, has similar qualities and in Europe is also known as pineapple sage.

*Growing pineapple sage in a tub makes it easier to move to a frost-free place for the winter.*

| TYPE OF PLANT | BEST POSITION | SUITABLE SOIL | PROPAGATION | PARTS OF PLANT | USES |
|---|---|---|---|---|---|
| Tender perennial | Full sun | Well drained | Cuttings | Leaves | Culinary |

## *Salvia officinalis*

# COMMON SAGE/GARDEN SAGE

*Salvia officinalis*

*The useful sage can be surprisingly beautiful in flower.*

COMMON SAGE IS A classic culinary herb. It is also one of the most ornamental, particularly if one of the varieties with variegated or coloured foliage is chosen. It is a dwarf, semi-evergreen sub-shrub that usually grows no more than about 60 cm (24 in). In summer it forms a neat mound of aromatic foliage that looks equally good alongside herbaceous plants and shrubs as it does in the herb garden.

Decorative spikes of white, pink, or pale blue flowers usually appear in late spring and early summer, but you may prefer to remove them as this plant is primarily grown for its foliage. In any case sage is reluctant to flower unless the climate and conditions are favourable.

Although hardy in most places, sage often suffers damage in a harsh winter. In less than favourable areas it will look tatty at the onset of spring with

| TYPE OF PLANT | BEST POSITION | SUITABLE SOIL | PROPAGATION | PARTS OF PLANT | USES |
|---|---|---|---|---|---|
| Hardy sub-shrub | Full sun | Undemanding, well drained | Cuttings, seed | Leaves | Culinary, cosmetic, household, medicinal |

*Salvia officinalis 'Tricolor'*

*Salvia officinalis 'Purpurascens'*

many damaged leaves, and in very cold areas it may even be killed by winter cold. However, by early summer most plants will again be well clothed with fresh young leaves and in mild areas sage will come through the winter looking good.

After three or four years plants often begin to lose their compact shape and are then best replaced. The species itself can be raised from seed, but for variegated and coloured-leaved varieties you need to take cuttings. In any case it is always worth taking a few cuttings to overwinter in a cold frame as insurance against winter losses.

### SELECTED VARIETIES

The species itself has leaves that open pale green but harden to almost grey. This common sage, as it is known, is a perfectly acceptable foliage plant and looks pleasing in a herb garden. However, it has some outstanding varieties which should be seriously considered for any garden. Try to include one or two varieties of *S. officinalis* to add colour and interest to the herb garden, or grow them in beds and borders with other ornamentals. They look good in raised beds and in patio containers, where they will add summer-long colour and the leaves can be crushed to release the distinctive aroma.

The most popular varieties are listed below, but there are many others from which to choose, such as the white-flowered **'Alba'**, and golden-leaved **'Aurea'** and **'Kew Gold'**. Nurseries offer both broad-leaved and narrow-leaved forms of the common sage, but the one sold as narrow-leaved may be a distinct species called *S. lavandulifolia*.

**'Icterina'** Sometimes called 'Variegata', it is known as golden sage and has particularly bright colouration. The new foliage in spring is marbled primrose, gold and green, and it retains a good gold and green contrast throughout summer and into winter.

**'Purpurascens'** This is purple sage with velvety grey-green leaves suffused with purple. Violet-blue flowers may be produced in summer. It makes a splendid companion for yellow-leaved plants, with which it contrasts well.

**'Tricolor'** A compact variety with bright leaves that manage to combine green, cream, white, purple and pink. Although very attractive it tends to be less hardy than some of the others.

*The variegated sages are better garden plants, and can be used like plain sage. This one is 'Icterina'.*

*Salvia officinalis 'Icterina'*

*Salvia sclarea*

# CLARY

look good growing in front of shrubs, or you can include a few plants in the herbaceous border. It is probably at its best as a cottage-garden plant in an informal setting.

Clary is usually grown as a biennial, sown in late spring to flower the following year. But as it is the leaves and not the flowers that are used, you can treat it as an annual. This is useful in a cold area as otherwise the plant needs a warm, sheltered position to survive the rigours of a harsh winter.

Seed is usually available from specialist seedsmen, but be careful when buying from general seedsmen not to buy the ornamental *Salvia horminum*, also described as clary.

THE NAME CLARY IS sometimes applied to other salvias, but *S. sclarea* is the one usually grown in herb gardens. It is a striking plant with large, wrinkled leaves covered with white, woolly hairs. Pale pink or violet-flushed flowers with papery bracts appear in late summer and bring the plant to a height of about 90 cm (3 ft).

True clary is an imposing plant with its large leaves and striking flowerheads, but it is not an easy plant to place. Try it in a mixed herb border as it can

*Clary has large leaves that can make the plant look ungainly at first, but it's stunning in flower.*

| TYPE OF PLANT | BEST POSITION | SUITABLE SOIL | PROPAGATION | PARTS OF PLANT | USES |
|---|---|---|---|---|---|
| Biennial | Full sun | Undemanding | Seed | Leaves | Culinary, medicinal |

*Santolina chamaecyparissus*

# COTTON LAVENDER

COTTON LAVENDER, OR LAVENDER cotton, is more widely grown as an ornamental plant than as a herb, but its use as an insect repellent justifies its inclusion in the herb garden. It was once used to treat worms in children, but its medicinal applications have fallen into disuse.

The plant makes a small mound of finely cut, silvery white aromatic foliage that acts as a good foil to other plants. Like box, it is suitable as a dwarf hedge for use in knot gardens and as a divider in formal herb gardens. It can also edge a formal herb bed or a centrepiece containing a bay tree or rosemary.

Cotton lavender will grow to about 45 cm (18 in) as a foliage plant if pruned regularly, and about 60 cm (24 in) if allowed to flower. The masses of button-like yellow flowers in summer can be attractive on single plants, but where cotton lavender is grown as a hedge or edging, cut them off with shears to retain a neat and compact outline.

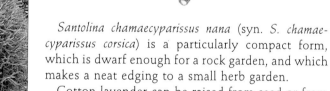

*This pleasing foliage shrub should not be confined to a herb garden.*

*Santolina chamaecyparissus nana* (syn. *S. chamaecyparissus corsica*) is a particularly compact form, which is dwarf enough for a rock garden, and which makes a neat edging to a small herb garden.

Cotton lavender can be raised from seed or from cuttings taken in summer.

| TYPE OF PLANT | BEST POSITION | SUITABLE SOIL | PROPAGATION | PARTS OF PLANT | USES |
|---|---|---|---|---|---|
| Hardy shrub | Full sun | Fertile, moist but well drained | Cuttings, seed | Leaves | Cosmetic, culinary, household |

## *Saponaria officinalis*
# SOAPWORT

Before commercial soap production started in the 1800s, soapwort was an important herb. The leaves produce a cleansing lather when crushed and rubbed in water, although it is the tough root that provides most of the saponins – the active ingredients. It was also once used medicinally, but now it is only used cosmetically and as a water-softener.

This perennial plant produces spreading shoots in spring which emerge from the fleshy roots, as thick as a finger. Delicate-looking, slightly fragrant, pinkish white flowers open over a long period during the summer. The individual flowers are about 2.5 cm (1 in) across, borne in loose heads on stems 30–90 cm (12–36 in) high. Double varieties with both white and pink flowers are also available.

Where the plant grows naturally it shows a preference for stream sides and damp woods, and in a moist position in partial shade it will grow taller and much better than in the dry, sunny conditions that many herbs prefer.

Soapwort mixes in well with cottage-garden plants grown informally to give a country-garden atmosphere. It needs plenty of space in order to grow well and to allow it to spread and flop about, and where conditions suit it will spread enthusiastically by runners. It can also be raised from seed sown in spring.

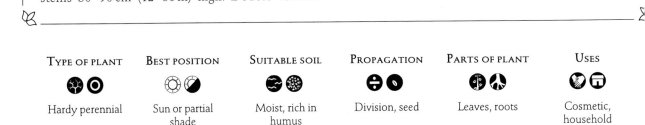

| Type of plant | Best position | Suitable soil | Propagation | Parts of plant | Uses |
|---|---|---|---|---|---|
| Hardy perennial | Sun or partial shade | Moist, rich in humus | Division, seed | Leaves, roots | Cosmetic, household |

*Satureja hortensis*

# SUMMER SAVORY

Summer savory is a small-leaved, rather modest annual, but pungently flavoured. Most cooks find the flavour of summer savory superior to that of the similar looking, but perennial winter savory.

Summer savory is a bushy, spreading plant that grows to about 30 cm (12 in) tall. It tends to be top-heavy as the season advances and if not supported is likely to flop over. The dainty pale lilac flowers bloom intermittently between mid summer and early autumn, but are too insignificant to make much of a show.

Sow the seed in spring where the plants are to grow and later thin the seedlings to about 15 cm (6 in) apart. Seed can also be started off under glass and the seedlings planted out, but the plant generally resents transplanting.

Reserve an area in the herb garden for summer savory as you can depend on a supply of self-sown seedlings in subsequent years, and the seedlings are less likely to become a nuisance among other plants. Summer savory also does well in containers such as pots and windowboxes.

*Summer savory is best grown in its own bed, where self-sown seedlings will not be a problem.*

| TYPE OF PLANT | BEST POSITION | SUITABLE SOIL | PROPAGATION | PARTS OF PLANT | USES |
|---|---|---|---|---|---|
|  Hardy annual | Full sun | Light | Seed |  Leaves |  Culinary, medicinal |

## *Satureja montana*
# WINTER SAVORY

Winter savory is an evergreen perennial, though it may shed its leaves in very cold areas or a particularly harsh winter. A slow-growing plant, it makes a neat mound about 30 cm (12 in) high and 20 cm (8 in) across. In late summer tiny pale lilac, white or pinky white flowers cover the plant. It is worth clipping over the tops of plants in spring to encourage a supply of fresh young leaves for picking. In addition the trim will keep the plant looking tidy and stimulate dense growth. This tolerance of clipping means that winter savory can be grown as a low hedge within the herb garden with plants spaced about 20 cm (8 in) apart.

Winter savory prefers a soil that is not too fertile, and provided it is given a sunny position is a trouble-free herb to grow. In cold areas it will benefit from winter protection by covering with a cloche or placing in a cold frame.

Try growing winter savory in a pot or other container. If the pot is small enough to be taken indoors and kept in a very light position you will be able to keep the plant cropping through the winter months. Pinch back the tips of the shoots regularly to prevent the plant becoming leggy.

Winter savory can be raised from seed and when allowed to flower it will self-seed. It can also be propagated from cuttings.

*Although it may shed its leaves in winter in very cold areas, winter savory is a useful evergreen.*

| TYPE OF PLANT | BEST POSITION | SUITABLE SOIL | PROPAGATION | PARTS OF PLANT | USES |
|---|---|---|---|---|---|
| Hardy evergreen sub-shrub | Full sun | Undemanding, well drained | Cuttings, seed | Leaves | Culinary, household, medicinal |

## *Stachys byzantina* (syn. *S. lanata, S. olympia*)

# LAMB'S EARS

THIS EXCELLENT ORNAMENTAL LOOKS good in the herb garden proper, combined with herbaceous plants or as a ground cover in front of shrubs. Some herb enthusiasts may challenge its place in a herb garden as it has no medicinal or culinary uses, but it is stocked by some herb nurseries as a cottage-garden plant and is listed in some herb books. It is used to enhance herbal wreaths, so let it enhance the beauty of your herb garden too.

The plant forms a dense, slowly spreading mat of soft, woolly, silvery grey leaves said to resemble a

*Don't confine this excellent ground cover plant to the herb garden. It's a first-rate general garden plant.*

lamb's ears. Its ground-hugging habit and light colour make it a particularly attractive plant during the summer. The foliage grows to about 23–30 cm (9–12 in), but the spikes of pink to purple flowers in mid summer bring the height to about 45 cm (18 in).

Many people find the flowers attractive, others prefer the low carpeting foliage alone. In the latter case "Silver Carpet" would be a good choice as it seldom flowers. For a carpet of pale yellow early in the year, try 'Primrose Heron'. The colour of the new leaves tones down during the summer and by winter the leaves are a silvery grey.

Although evergreen, the winter-damaged leaves of lamb's ears usually look untidy by the end of winter and should be cleared to make way for the new growth. The plant does best where winters are mild and it may die in cold areas.

| TYPE OF PLANT | BEST POSITION | SUITABLE SOIL | PROPAGATION | PARTS OF PLANT | USES |
|---|---|---|---|---|---|
| Hardy evergreen perennial | Full sun | Fertile, well drained | Division, seed | Leaves | Craft |

# *Symphytum officinale*
# COMFREY

Comfrey is decorative enough to include in the herbaceous border. Its trusses of mauvey pink, bell-shaped flowers begin to open in early summer and continue for many weeks. The flowers bring a touch of colour to what is otherwise a rather unassuming clump of leaves about 60 cm (24 in) tall.

It grows naturally in damp ground near river banks, so a moist, fertile soil will produce the tallest plants and yield the best crop of lush leaves.

Division is the easiest and quickest method of propagating this perennial. Plants grown from seed are often slow to mature.

Be prepared to protect the leaves from the ravages of slugs and snails if these are a problem in your garden or herb bed.

COMFREY HAS SUCH A tremendous reputation for its medicinal qualities that no herb garden would be complete without a clump. Even if you don't feel tempted to test its medicinal properties, you can use its foliage as a valuable addition to the compost heap. Many organic gardeners grow comfrey for this specific purpose.

*This medicinal herb does not look amiss in an herbaceous border, but it demands plenty of space.*

| TYPE OF PLANT | BEST POSITION | SUITABLE SOIL | PROPAGATION | PARTS OF PLANT | USES |
|---|---|---|---|---|---|
| Hardy perennial | Full sun or partial shade | Fertile, moist | Division, seed | Leaves, roots | Cosmetic, culinary, household, medicinal |

# *Tanacetum vulgare*
# TANSY

*Don't confine tansy to the herb garden. It is also a worthwhile herbaceous border plant.*

Tansy's bright yellow heads of button-like flowers show up well against its feathery dark green leaves which have a very pungent taste. The foliage is most attractive and worthy to cut for use in fresh or dried arrangements. The flowers can be dried for winter arrangements.

This hardy perennial herb is undemanding and easy to grow. It does well even in poor soil. In an exposed position it may become ragged and look untidy after strong winds. Inserting supports in late spring will help to overcome this minor drawback.

Tansy soon forms a dense clump about 1–1.2 m (3–4 ft) tall and spreads rapidly by underground rhizomes. It is advisable to divide and replant established plants every second or third year. Plants can also be propagated from seed.

WARNING   Tansy should not be eaten at any time during pregnancy.

| TYPE OF PLANT | BEST POSITION | SUITABLE SOIL | PROPAGATION | PARTS OF PLANT | USES |
|---|---|---|---|---|---|
| Hardy perennial | Full sun | Undemanding | Division, seed | Leaves | Craft, culinary, medicinal |

# *Taraxacum officinale*
# DANDELION

Many gardeners spend hours each year trying to eliminate dandelions from their garden, and it sometimes comes as a surprise to find it grown as a crop. In fact it has a long history of medicinal use – especially as a diuretic, hence the colloquial names piss-the-bed or French *pis-en-lis*.

Nowadays it is more likely to be grown for its culinary properties. The young leaves, rich in vitamins and minerals, can be used in salads or cooked like spinach. The roots are used to make a coffee-substitute, and home wine-makers use the flowers or the leaves. The quality of the leaves is improved by blanching like endive. Some roots can be lifted in the autumn and forced in the dark, like chicory, to supply crisp young leaves in the winter.

Dandelion seed can be bought from some seedsmen, and the selections they offer are likely to be superior to wild dandelions. But you may prefer to dig up and replant some roots from another part of the garden or collect them elsewhere. Bear in mind that the deep tap roots are difficult to lift without leaving some behind, which is why dandelions are so difficult to eradicate. Deadhead before it self-seeds.

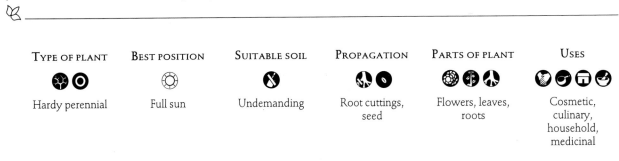

| TYPE OF PLANT | BEST POSITION | SUITABLE SOIL | PROPAGATION | PARTS OF PLANT | USES |
|---|---|---|---|---|---|
| Hardy perennial | Full sun | Undemanding | Root cuttings, seed | Flowers, leaves, roots | Cosmetic, culinary, household, medicinal |

## *Teucrium chamaedrys*

# WALL GERMANDER

Wall germander used to be grown for medicinal use, and a tea brewed from its leaves was a popular remedy for gout. Nowadays it is more often grown as an edging plant for a herb bed or border. It can also be used to form patterns in knot gardens and parterres. As the common name implies, it is a good plant to grow in a dry stone wall or at the edge of a raised bed.

A dwarf, aromatic, evergreen sub-shrub with creeping roots, wall germander forms a low, bushy plant about 30 cm (12 in) high. The small but dainty pink flowers are never spectacular but occur over a long period from mid summer through to early autumn. In cold areas, or during severe winters, it may drop its leaves, but normally it remains evergreen. In very cold regions it is worth mulching around the roots in the autumn to give some protection during winter.

The creeping roots make wall germander suitable for division, but take cuttings if you need a lot of plants, for instance to create an edging.

*Wall germander is a useful edging for a herb bed or border. It can also be grown in dry stone walls.*

| Type of plant | Best position | Suitable soil | Propagation | Parts of plant | Uses |
|---|---|---|---|---|---|
| Hardy evergreen sub-shrub | Full sun | Fertile | Cuttings, division | Leaves | Medicinal |

# *Thymus*
# THYME

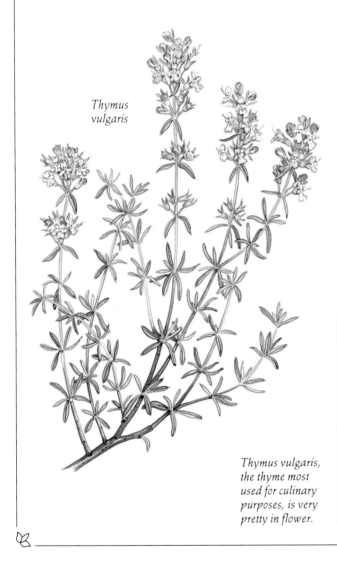

*Thymus
vulgaris*

No HERB GARDEN WORTH the name should be without some thyme. There are many species and varieties, all highly aromatic and attractive. If space permits, start a collection – there are dozens to choose from, all widely available. Most of them flower in mid and late summer.

The one most commonly used in the kitchen is *T. vulgaris* (English or common thyme), but many others can be used for culinary, medicinal and aromatic purposes. Some, such as golden and variegated lemon thyme, can be used for cooking, but the flavour is not as good as common thyme. Creeping, mat-like species, such as *T. pulegioides*, have tiny interwoven branches that have leaves too small to make the effort of harvesting worthwhile.

It makes sense to grow a few culinary varieties in greater numbers for harvesting, and a selection of

*Thymus vulgaris,
the thyme most
used for culinary
purposes, is very
pretty in flower.*

| TYPE OF PLANT | BEST POSITION | SUITABLE SOIL | PROPAGATION | PARTS OF PLANT | USES |
|---|---|---|---|---|---|
|  |  |  |  |  |  |
| Hardy evergreen sub-shrub | Full sun | Undemanding | Cuttings, layers, seed | Leaves | Cosmetic, culinary, household, medicinal |

*There are many varieties of thyme, with variations in flower and foliage colour. A collection of them makes a very pleasing feature.*

other thymes for their decorative effect. All the thymes described on the following pages are undemanding evergreen sub-shrubs that have the same cultural requirements.

They require little attention once established but tend to become straggly and untidy after a few years. Therefore it is best to propagate a few new plants every year to use as replacements. Layering is possible, but for more than one or two plants cuttings are a better proposition.

Although hardy in most areas, in very cold regions or exceptionally severe winters losses are not uncommon – another reason for overwintering young plants in a cold frame.

### Thyme in the Garden

Thymes are versatile plants to use around the garden. If you want to grow them purely as a crop to harvest, a massed group in a bed or herb garden is both practical and pleasing. You can, however, make more of a feature by growing thyme between paving slabs, as edging plants, for ground cover, or in containers.

**Scented thyme lawns** These are a practical proposition provided you consider using thyme as a grass-substitute for a small area seldom walked on, or for secondary paths within the herb garden.

The best thymes for a lawn or path are the creeping thyme (*T. praecox arcticus*, syn. *T. drucei*) and

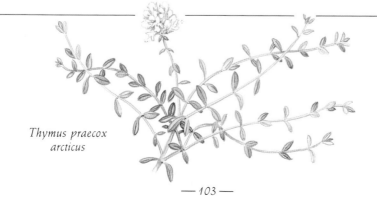

*Thymus praecox arcticus*

*Thymus
pseudolanuginosus*

the woolly thyme (*T. pseudolanuginosus*, syn. *T. languinosus*). Both are low creepers that grow about 5 cm (2 in) high; woolly thyme makes an especially low ground-hugging carpet. As selective weedkillers cannot be used on a thyme lawn, it is essential to make sure the ground is as weed-free as possible before planting. You will have to weed by hand.

**Between paving** The two thymes mentioned above are also a good choice to plant in the crevices between paving. But at the very edge of a path, which will have the least amount of wear, you can also grow varieties of *T. vulgaris*.

**Around the garden seat** Thyme is a delightful plant to grow between paving around a garden seat or in a raised bed where the leaves are conveniently close to be crushed to release their aroma. But remember, thyme attracts bees and wasps, so this idea may not appeal to everyone.

### IN CONTAINERS

Thymes are ideal for growing in a windowbox or other kind of container, either alone or together with other plants. To maintain a supply of leaves for the kitchen, plant a windowbox with *T. vulgaris* if you have no space in the garden, or no garden. Otherwise grow the more decorative thymes in containers. Good ones to use are the golden *T. × citriodorus* **'Bertram Anderson'** (syn. *'Anderson's Gold'*), variegated *T. × citriodorus* **'Variegatus'** (syn. *T. × '**Silver Posie'**) and good flowering varieties like *doerfleri* **'Bressingham Pink'**.

### AND INDOORS . . .

Thyme can be grown indoors by a very light kitchen window, but this is best regarded as a novelty venture or as a way of supplementing the garden supply. Kits can sometimes be bought with everything necessary: container, compost and seed. Unless light conditions are excellent, however, you would do better to buy a small plant from a garden centre and pot it up in an attractive container. Then when it deteriorates and ceases to be attractive or useful, plant it out in the garden to recover.

### SELECTED SPECIES AND VARIETIES

The following thymes are species and varieties worth including in a collection. Many other thymes will be obtainable from specialist nurseries.

The commonly used synonyms have been included in the following list. Plants may be sold

*Thymes are
small enough for
you to be able to
grow a collection
in a container.*

*Thymus ×
citriodorus
'Bertram
Anderson'*

*This group of thymes in a terracotta trough shows varieties grown for foliage and flowers. 'Bressingham Pink' sits next to a golden thyme.*

under any of the names given. Varieties of *T. drucei, T. serpyllum, T. vulgaris* and *T. × citriodorus* are often attributed to different species which can cause much confusion, but the varietal name should give a good indication as the identity of the plant.

*T. × citriodorus* (lemon thyme) Broader leaves than *T. vulgaris* and strongly lemon-scented when crushed; 23 cm (9 in).

*T. × citriodorus* 'Aureus' (golden thyme) Leaves edged yellow; less hardy and robust than most thymes; 20 cm (8 in).

*T. × citriodorus* 'Bertram Anderson' (syn. 'Anderson's Gold') A dwarf carpeter with bright golden foliage that holds its colour well even through the winter; 5 cm (2 in).

*T. × citriodorus* 'Golden King' Bushy, upright

*Thymus citriodorus 'Silver Queen' with a group of other thymes in a terracotta trough.*

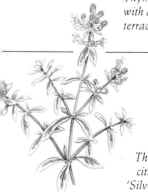

*Thymus × citriodorus 'Silver Queen'*

habit, with gold-edged leaves; 23–30 cm (9–12 in).

*T. × citriodorus* 'Silver Queen' Leaves edged cream; not as hardy and robust as most thymes; 20 cm (8 in).

*T. × citriodorus* 'Variegatus' (syn. 'Silver Posie') Silver-edged leaves and pinkish flowers – an attractive plant for a container; 15 cm (6 in).

*T. doerfleri* 'Bressingham Pink' Bright pink flowers; carpeting habit; 5 cm (2 in).

*T.* 'Doone Valley' Low mat-forming plant with

*Thymus
herba-barona*

dark green leaves heavily marked with gold; mauve flowers; 8 cm (3 in).

*T. herba-barona* (caraway thyme)  Forms a mat of dark green leaves with a strong smell of caraway seed; pinkish mauve flowers; 10 cm (4 in).

*T. praecox arcticus* (syn. *T. drucei*)  Low-growing, with small grey-green leaves, red or pink flowers; "Albus" has white flowers; 2.5 cm (1 in).

*T. pseudolanuginosus* (syn. *T. lanuginosus*) (woolly thyme)  Grows into a mat of minute woolly leaves; it seldom flowers; 5 cm (2 in).

*T. serpyllum* (creeping wild thyme)  Forms a flat green mat, with tiny pale lavender flowers; 5 cm (2 in).

*T. serpyllum coccineus*  A crimson-flowered variety of the above.

*T. serpyllum* 'Pink Chintz'  Loose cushions of soft, woolly leaves topped with pale pink flowers; 10 cm (4 in).

*T. vulgaris* (common, English or garden thyme)  More upright than the other thymes; usually mauve or purple flowers, but sometimes white; 15–25 cm (6–10 in).

Caraway thyme (*T. herba-barona*) is a ground-hugger that forms a mat of caraway-scented foliage.

*Thymus serpyllum
albus, a white form
of creeping thyme.*

*Thymus
serpyllum*

# *Trigonella foenum-graecum*
# FENUGREEK

THIS TENDER ANNUAL will grow into an erect plant 45–60 cm (18–24 in) tall if allowed to reach maturity. But it is usually harvested before it even becomes a seedling. This is because fenugreek is grown mainly as a "sprouting seed". However, the seeds are also an important ingredient in curry powder and they yield a yellow dye. The mature plant, as depicted in the illustration, has culinary and medicinal uses.

Use the sprouting seeds at the stage shown in the photograph to add a spicy tang to a salad or as a sandwich filling. The fully developed leaves are bitter and strong-tasting but can be used in some Indian dishes.

To grow fenugreek in the garden start the seed off under glass and plant out when there is no risk of frost, or sow directly outdoors in late spring.

*Fenugreek is usually grown as sprouted seeds, but you can grow it to maturity.*

To produce the curry-flavoured sprouts, germinate the seed on layers of moist paper towel in a light position indoors. Keep the towel moist, and harvest the seedlings when ready – which can be as little as six days. Wash, then drain. Special jars for sprouting the seeds are obtainable, or improvise with a glass jar, a piece of cloth and an elastic band – the trick is to keep the seeds moist but to drain off excess water so that they do not rot.

| TYPE OF PLANT | BEST POSITION | SUITABLE SOIL | PROPAGATION | PARTS OF PLANT | USES |
|---|---|---|---|---|---|
|  | | | |  |  |
| Tender annual | Full sun (outdoors) | Fertile, well drained | Seed | Leaves, seeds, sprouting seeds | Culinary, household, medicinal |

## *Tropaeolum majus*

# NASTURTIUM

This POPULAR ANNUAL IS easy to grow and a favourite with children. It is always worthy of a place in the herb garden. Both flowers and leaves are edible, and the seeds can be pickled as capers.

Nasturtium flowers are so bright and colourful that even one or two plants will enliven a part of the herb garden dominated by foliage plants. Although the climbing varieties can be used, they tend to smother other plants. The compact varieties that grow to about 60 cm (24 in) are more practical and are good container plants.

This is one plant that you don't need to feed or provide with very fertile soil – rich soil is positively detrimental. Too fertile a soil or too much watering will produce a mass of leaves but few flowers, most of which are likely to be hidden underneath the foliage. Poor conditions are needed to produce plants with compact growth and masses of flowers carried above the foliage.

Sow nasturtiums where they are to flower, or start them off in pots to plant out in late spring or early summer. Although usually described as hardy annuals, the seedlings are likely to be killed by the first sharp frost so avoid early sowing outdoors.

It is difficult to grow nasturtiums without attracting aphids and caterpillars. To avoid having to use an insecticide on an edible crop, pick off affected leaves at the first sign of attack.

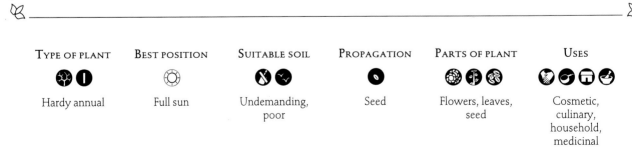

| TYPE OF PLANT | BEST POSITION | SUITABLE SOIL | PROPAGATION | PARTS OF PLANT | USES |
|---|---|---|---|---|---|
| Hardy annual | Full sun | Undemanding, poor | Seed | Flowers, leaves, seed | Cosmetic, culinary, household, medicinal |

# *Valeriana officinalis*

# TRUE VALERIAN

V ALERIAN WAS FORMERLY VALUED for its root, which was used for a number of medicinal purposes, but nowadays it is grown mainly as an ornamental plant. Although not the most attractive herb, it is useful at the back of a border. The finely divided blue-green leaves are attractive, and the white or pink flowers held on stiff, 1.2–1.5 m (4–5 ft) stems in spring have a pleasant vanilla-like fragrance.

When the plant is grown for its root, the flowers are usually removed so that all the plant's energy goes into the development of what is, in fact, the rhizome. If you are growing it simply as an interesting herb to have in your collection, let it flower – the tall spikes look especially attractive viewed against the dark background of a hedge. However, staking is prudent in an exposed position.

The plant can be raised from seed, and where conditions are suitable self-sown seedlings will usually be found if you need more plants. Clumps can also be divided.

The plant is attractive to cats . . . and to rats (it is reputedly the charm the Pied Piper of Hamelin used to lead the rats away).

*The true valerian is a tall plant best at the back of a herb border.*

| TYPE OF PLANT | BEST POSITION | SUITABLE SOIL | PROPAGATION | PARTS OF PLANT | USES |
|---|---|---|---|---|---|
| Hardy perennial | Full sun or partial shade | Moist but well drained | Division, seed | Roots | Medicinal |

## *Verbena officinalis*
# VERVAIN

Vervain is a herbaceous perennial with toothed leaves on branching stems that arise from spreading roots. It usually makes a clump about 90 cm (36 in) tall and 45 cm (18 in) across. It is primarily a leafy plant and the insignificant mauve flowers borne at the tips of the shoots from mid summer to mid autumn contribute little.

Use it as a "filler" in a border of mixed herbs rather than in a prominent place. Although it has no culinary use its inclusion in a practical herb garden can be justified. A tisane is made from the dried leaves which is said to be a mild sedative.

Vervain is easily grown from seed sown in spring, or from cuttings taken in summer. But division in

spring is the quickest and easiest method of propagation for just a few plants.

Although a perennial, vervain can be raised annually from seed and discarded at the end of the season. Seed will probably have to be bought from a specialist seedsman or nursery stocking herbs or wild flowers.

*Vervain is not a spectacular plant, but it does produce a show of small flowers from mid summer.*

| TYPE OF PLANT | BEST POSITION | SUITABLE SOIL | PROPAGATION | PARTS OF PLANT | USES |
|---|---|---|---|---|---|
| Hardy perennial | Full sun | Fertile, well drained | Cuttings, division, seed | Leaves | Medicinal |

## *Viola odorata*

# SWEET VIOLET

THE DELICATE FRAGRANCE OF sweet violets has won them a place in the hearts of most gardeners. The plant seldom grows more than 15 cm (6 in) tall, and the actual flowers – like pansies with a spur at the back – are diminutive, only about 12 mm (½ in) across. Early to mid spring is the main flowering time, but a few flowers may appear in a mild winter.

The most common colour is violet-blue, but there are other shades of blue, and white violets are not uncommon. Parma violets are probably hybrids, with *V. odorata* as a parent. These were once very popular, with collectors attracted to the larger,

*Sweet violets are one of the delights of spring. Cut some to enjoy their fragrance indoors.*

sometimes double, and more fragrant flowers.

Although violets are now grown primarily for their scent and delicate beauty, they have culinary uses too, and they were once widely used medicinally. They grow naturally in damp shady hedgerows and grassy banks in or near woodland. Although they will grow in a sunny position, they thrive in partial shade in moist and fertile soil. Plant them in drifts, like ground cover, as individual plants are easily overlooked. The front of a herb border would suit or near a hedge or wall, provided the soil is not too dry.

Sweet violets self-sow freely once established. Clumps can also be divided.

| TYPE OF PLANT | BEST POSITION | SUITABLE SOIL | PROPAGATION | PARTS OF PLANT | USES |
|---|---|---|---|---|---|
| Hardy perennial | Partial shade | Fertile, moist | Division, seed | Flowers, leaves, root | Cosmetic, culinary, medicinal |

# GROWING

# $\mathcal{H}$ERBS

# MAKING PLANS

Before you launch into anything more ambitious than buying a pot or two of culinary herbs to flourish on a kitchen windowsill, take stock of your garden, patio, terrace, balcony or even windowbox if that is the extent of your territory; your home interests and hobbies, and the time you have available or are prepared to give to tend and nurture the plants.

If you enjoy cooking and have only a small balcony but are prepared to give even a few minutes a day to the plants' care, then the world of herbs is your oyster. If your interest lies more strongly in home remedies, your garden is north-facing and largely unsheltered, and time is even more of the essence, then these factors will influence your choice of plants at the planning stage. The details given in the *Directory of Herbs* will be invaluable in helping you to assess the possibilities of achieving just the right balance between time and effort over results. Traditionally herbs were grown in geometrically formal knot gardens as found in monasteries and large estates established in medieval times or higgledy-piggledy in cottage gardens. Somewhere between these two extremes there is a level of growing herbs that is appropriate to each of us, whether it is a designated herb patch or a few herbs intermingled with other flowers and vegetables.

Before planting, it is important to take a critical look at your garden and helpful to draw up a scale plan. In this way you can be sure of making the closest possible match between the native environments of your chosen herbs and the situation you are about to offer them. You do not need to be a landscape architect to measure your plot and transfer the details onto graph paper. Draw in boundary walls and fences, paths and ponds, hedges, trees and screens, and any other existing features, such as raised beds and rock gardens, terracing and steps, and structures such as car ports, oil tanks and fuel storage tanks and bins. Indicate the north-south aspect of the garden and you will at once be able to identify and mark areas that receive maximum, medium and minimum amounts of light: those that receive the full glare of the noon-day sun, those that are partially shaded and those that never enjoy the benefits of direct sunlight.

Since many herbs originate from the warm and sunny

*Neatly clipped hedges outline a series of geometrical herb beds in the knot garden at Hatfield House, Hertfordshire.*

Scented-leaved
pelargonium and
sage grow side by
side with brightly
coloured flowers
and vegetables in
a backyard
garden.

climes of the Mediterranean region, a well-drained soil
plus a sunny aspect match up to the general
requirements of those such as basil, coriander, marjoram
and rosemary. But as the *Directory of Herbs* shows, all is
not lost if your garden has a largely shady character.
Among the herbs that would settle happily for such
conditions are mint, woodruff and sweet violet. And
you may be able to elevate sun lovers to a more
favourable spot, where the sun will reach them, on a flat
roof for example, by growing them in containers.
Water is another essential requirement for plant
development, and in this case, too, a plant's specific
needs are largely determined by its native habitat. Those
that originate from damp and temperate regions –
chiefly broad-leaved plants – have a higher requirement
and a higher tolerance of moisture than their
Mediterranean counterparts. If you have a patch in your
garden which is well drained but does not dry out
completely, even in summer, you can plant it with a
selection of moisture-tolerating herbs, such as valerian.
   Conversely, if your garden has a sandy soil which

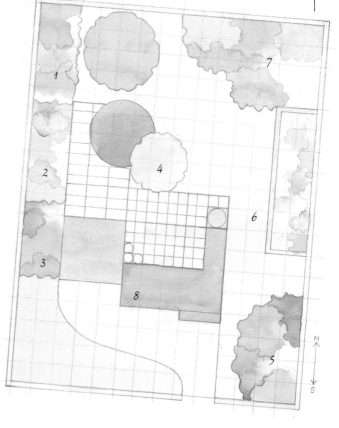

*Even in a small
garden you can
make room for a
wide variety of
herbs. Simply
create as many
different growing
conditions as
you wish.*

1   *North-facing – lavender*
2   *Fertile loam, sunny – catmint, clary*
3   *Partial shade – bee balm, yarrow*
4   *Moist and sunny – comfrey, soapwort*
5   *South-facing – oregano, tansy*
6   *Full sun, dry – borage, sage*
7   *Full sun, well drained –*
    *apothecary's rose, evening primrose*
8   *Container – sweet bay*

does not retain moisture and you wish to cultivate plants such as bergamot, marshmallow or meadowsweet which require a damp spot, then you can easily adapt your growing conditions to suit. Dig a broad trench or a patch of the required shape at least 30–45 cm (12–18 in) deep. Line it with a sheet of heavy-duty polythene pierced at intervals with holes and fill it with garden soil enriched with plenty of well-rotted manure or garden compost to retain moisture. The polythene will prevent the moisture from draining away quickly, yet ensure that the area does not become waterlogged. (Few herbs thrive if their roots are permanently in water.) In a dry spell, remember to keep the area damp by frequent watering.

# Preparing the ground

Most herbs are undemanding regarding soil type. Some of the most useful herbs, such as sages and thymes, naturally grow in poor or shallow soils that are often dry and impoverished.

It is seldom that you will have to abandon trying to grow a particular herb because of your soil, but you will achieve better results if you can try to give them the kind of soil conditions suggested for each herb.

When preparing the ground for a herb garden, concentrate on removing perennial weeds, and dig the soil to a depth of about 25cm (10in). For deep-rooting plants like horseradish and lovage, loosen the soil to twice this depth – using a fork to break up the lower level and adding plenty of compost or rotted manure.

Sandy soils are light to dig but because they are free-draining tend to dry out very quickly. If you want to grow herbs that prefer a moist, fertile soil, dig in humus-forming material – rotted farmyard manure,

garden compost or composted seaweed – then mulch the plants annually. As sandy soils are often impoverished, add a balanced general garden fertilizer before planting, following the manufacturer's recommended rates. If you want to grow herbs described as needing a fertile or rich soil, hoe or rake in a fertilizer annually.

Clay soils are heavy to dig, often becoming waterlogged in wet weather, and clumps stick together in a mass if you pick up a handful and squeeze it in your hand. A clay soil is usually slow to warm up in spring, can become almost hard in hot, dry weather, and is generally unpleasant to dig. The treatment suggested for sandy soil will also improve clay soils.

Loam soils are easy to dig and fairly rich in nutrients. Except for adding fertilizer annually for those herbs described as needing a fertile or rich soil, you should not have to add anything to the soil routinely.

## Soil testing

*A simple test which gives some indication of general soil types, known as the kitchen jar test, can be carried out as follows:*
*1 Put a few tablespoons of soil in a large jam jar, fill it with water and put on the lid.*
*2 Shake the jar vigorously and leave the soil and other material to settle for a day or two.*
*The table right provides an at-a-glance guide to soil types and the herbs best suited to them. However, don't be afraid to take a chance as most herbs are not fastidious.*

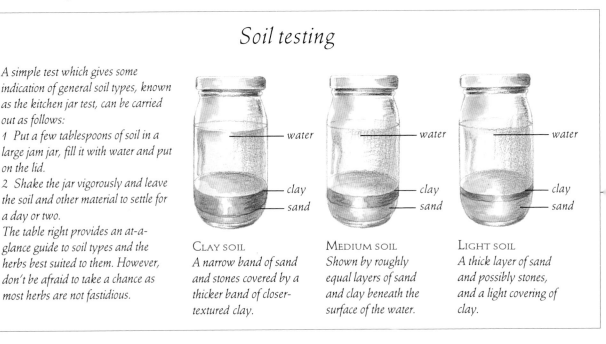

CLAY SOIL
*A narrow band of sand and stones covered by a thicker band of closer-textured clay.*

MEDIUM SOIL
*Shown by roughly equal layers of sand and clay beneath the surface of the water.*

LIGHT SOIL
*A thick layer of sand and possibly stones, and a light covering of clay.*

# Soil types and herbs – the perfect marriage

It is important to know what type of soil you have and whether it differs from one part of the garden to another. Soil type affects not only the water-holding properties but also the nutrients naturally available to the plants. Most herbs will survive and even thrive in a wide range of soil types, but for healthy plants, with abundant foliage and prolific flowering, it is best to grow them in soil which closely resembles that of their native habitat.

## SANDY SOIL

Water drains rapidly from a light sandy soil taking nutrients with it, but all the undemanding Mediterranean herbs will thrive in such soils.

| | |
|---|---|
| Borage | Borago officinalis |
| Chamomile | Anthemis nobilis |
| Coriander | Coriandrum sativum |
| Evening primrose | Oenothera biennis |
| Fennel | Foeniculum vulgare |
| Lavender | Lavandula |
| Tarragon | Artemisia dracunculus |
| Thyme | Thymus |
| Wild marjoram | Origanum vulgare |
| Winter savory | Satureja montana |

Lavender 'Hidcote'

## CLAY SOIL

Because this type of soil bakes solid in summer and is uncompromisingly sticky in winter, it is not a favourite with gardeners. Clay does, however, favour a number of herbs, predominantly those with deep roots. These will, incidentally, help to break up the large soil mass. Working generous amounts of garden compost into the top layer will make clay soils more suitable for the herbs listed under loam and moist loam.

| | |
|---|---|
| Bee balm or bergamot | Monarda didyma |
| Comfrey | Symphytum officinale |
| Mint | Mentha |
| Wormwood | Artemisia absinthium |

Bee balm, or bergamot

## MOIST LOAM

Poorly drained, medium loam can be improved by frequent forking over. It favours deep-rooted herbs and those which naturally occur on heavy soil.

| | |
|---|---|
| Angelica | Angelica archangelica |
| Bee balm or bergamot | Monarda didyma |
| Buckler leaf sorrel | Rumex scutatus |
| Lady's mantle | Alchemilla |
| Lemon balm | Melissa officinalis |
| Meadowsweet | Filipendula ulmaria |
| Mint | Mentha |
| Parsley | Petroselium crispum |
| Sweet Cicely | Myrrhis odorata |
| Valerian | Valeriana officinalis |

## WET SOIL

Most herbs dislike having permanently wet roots, but the following are worth a try in poorly drained soil.

| | |
|---|---|
| Angelica | Angelica archangelica |
| Bee balm or bergamot | Monarda didyma |
| Marshmallow | Althaea officinalis |
| Meadowsweet | Filipendula ulmaria |
| Valerian | Valeriana officinalis |
| Watercress | Nasturtium officinale |

Watercress

## LOAM

Usually rich in nutrients and well drained, this type of soil is ideal for most herbs.

| | |
|---|---|
| Basil | Ocimum basilicum |
| Bay | Laurus nobilis |
| Caraway | Carum carvi |
| Catnip | Nepeta cataria |
| Chervil | Anthriscus cerefolium |
| Chives | Allium schoenoprasum |
| Coriander | Coriandrum sativum |
| Dill | Anethum graveolens |
| Fennel | Foeniculum vulgare |
| Lady's mantle | Alchemilla |
| Lovage | Levisticum officinale |
| Parsley | Petroselium crispum |
| Rosemary | Rosmarinus officinalis |
| Rue | Ruta graveolens |
| Sage | Salvia officinalis |
| Thyme | Thymus |

# DESIGNING YOUR HERB GARDEN

Sun and soil are important considerations, since they affect the plants' chances of, at best, healthy development or, at worst, survival. Although such considerations have a bearing on garden planning, where and how you position your herbs is a matter of personal preference, too.

WALK ALONG ANY TOWN or village street and glance at any three or four neighbouring plots. They may be identical in size, shape and aspect and enjoy a similar soil type; in other words the ground plans are carbon copies. Yet the chances are that the preferences and even the personalities of the various owners will be evident in their widely different approach to garden planning. One garden may be laid out with neatly symmetrical beds, each planted with military precision. There may be meticulously straight rows of chives, sage, chamomile and lavender with never an intervening trail of orange-bright nasturtium to interrupt the geometry. Next door the garden may be planted with clumps and clusters of herbs and flowers, patches of cornflowers, pot marigolds, lady's mantle, purple sage and variegated

apple mint mingling with one another and, an added bonus, planted closely enough to deter weed growth.

Another garden may demonstrate a strong preference for roses, from centifolia and rugosa types to large-flowered modern hybrids, planted in random-shaped beds and borders and interplanted with vigorous herbs such as woodruff, marjoram and borage: truly a scented garden. Inspired perhaps by one of the great country-house gardens, a fourth plot may be given over to an all-white garden, using silver-foliaged plants as much for the characteristics they share as for those that separate them. There may be the brilliant yellow, tiny button-shaped flowers of cotton lavender next to the minute pink flowers of the woolly-leaved lambs' ears and the purple spikes of sage and lavender.

### A LOOK OF FORMALITY

If your own image of a herb garden or a herb patch runs along formal and well-defined lines, it may be a case of going back to the drawing board, or at least to the graph paper, to plot the outlines. The size of the patch is immaterial, as "formal" is in no way synonymous with "grand". It is possible to achieve a look of complete formality in the smallest of plots, or to create a formal island, perhaps in the shape of a diamond or a series of concentric circles, in the midst of an otherwise undisciplined garden.

Once you have allocated the space you wish to plant, and taken due note of the aspect and soil type, measure it accurately and draw the outlines on graph paper, allowing one centimetre to each ten centimetres (one

*The plants in this formal herb garden are well contrasted for height and leaf colour, with the low-growing ones spilling over onto the stone pathway.*

*The fragrance of honeysuckle, fennel, rosemary and nicotiana mingles with hemerocallis lilies and a delicate pink rose in this scented border.*

inch for each foot). The more formal and stylized you want the garden to be, the more important it is to ensure that the measurements and subsequent subdivisions you intend to make are precise. There is no room for the "rule of thumb" approach in geometrical layouts!

Whatever the overall shape you favour, it is important not to lose sight of the practicalities. Easy access is essential. All flower beds and borders need tending from time to time. Weeding, watering, trimming and pruning are all necessary tasks. Culinary herbs will also have to be harvested. A large part of the *raison d'être* of a herb bed is that you can have flavour at your fingertips: a

sprig or two of mint to enhance the new season's potatoes and peas or a few stalks of parsley, thyme and rosemary to tie into a *bouquet garni*.

Gathering herbs from your garden is always a pleasure, but somewhat less so if you have to put on wellington boots to reach the back of a wide border on a rain-soaked day, or tread perilously close to tender plants. It is therefore important to plan the herb beds with picking in mind. Divide large patches into two or more smaller beds separated for the sake of convenience and appearance by narrow paths or stepping stones. As a general rule to avoid having to step on to the beds,

## Traditional patterns for a formal herb bed

*Make rough drawings of some possible traditional designs within your proposed outline.*

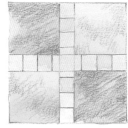

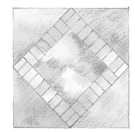

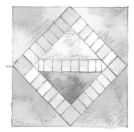

*Divide the herb garden by criss-crossing paths.*

*Diamond bed with a tri-angular bed at each corner.*

*A square or rectangular bed of six triangles.*

those that are accessible from only one side should be little more than 90 cm (3 ft) wide. (Such beds may be bordered on one side by a fence, a hedge, a screen or other structure which prevents all-round access.) Those that can be approached from all sides, an island bed for example, may be conveniently up to 1.5 m (5 ft) wide.

### PREFERENCE FOR PAVING

The choice of paving may be determined to a certain extent by local materials or simply by your own preference. Once the area has been thoroughly weeded, lay down dividing paths of bricks (laid in any one of a number of patterns, such as herringbone or circular), stone, gravel, granite chippings, wood chips or even chamomile. The latter is soft underfoot and has the advantage of adding fragrance to the garden. Choose dwarf and creeping varieties that would provide complete ground cover, but remember chamomile paths need more attention than those of other materials.

Whatever style of planting you envisage and whatever herbs you plan to plant it is important first to prepare the ground well to make sure that there is a hospitable balance between good drainage and adequate nutrients. If drainage is a problem, it may be necessary to dig out the designated area to a depth of about 30 cm (12 in) and fork over the bottom. Then half fill the trench with rubble, cover it with a 10 cm (4 in) layer of good loamy soil enriched with plenty of well rotted manure or garden compost and level it off with a layer of gravel or stone chippings.

*herringbone brick path*

*paving and gravel*

*granite chippings*

*chamomile*

Dark grey brick paving makes a dramatic background for golden- and silver-leaved plants.

# Formal herb gardens

*The red, weathered spokes of the cartwheel neatly divide low-growing herbs into wedge-shaped segments.*

AN ATTRACTIVE WAY OF achieving a formal-looking herb garden without any structural work is to use an old cartwheel, which you may be able to buy from country antique shops or farm sales. After preparing the ground in the way described above, position the wheel and plant dwarf varieties in the segments between the spokes. Those herbs with a neat and easily-restrained habit such as chives, dwarf lavender, santolina and sweet violets would all be suitable. To maintain the visual effect of the wheel it is important to keep the plants in order by trimming and pruning them so that the spokes are not concealed beneath a mass of foliage.

A wheel garden will have its own built-in central feature, a well-turned and well-ground hub, but other symmetrical herb garden layouts can be enhanced by a well-planned focal point. It is never too early to start looking out for an old weathered sundial partially covered with moss or stylish birdbath. If apiary happens to be a hobby of yours, a traditional straw bee skep would be an appropriate choice. There is an environmental link between a well-used hive and the surrounding bee-attracting plants found in herb gardens. Such features not only draw the eye to that section of the garden, but provide an interesting contrast of texture and tone to that of the foliage.

Plants, too, can hold centre stage in a similar way. Clip a standard bay tree to form a neat cone or characteristic ball shape; or train a weeping rose around

*This physic garden emulates the traditional cartwheel design using brick as dividers between medicinal and ornamental planting.*

*Brick "stepping stones" across the beds allow easy access to all the plants.*

a sturdy pole. Morning glory or clematis can be allowed to ramble up and over a wigwam structure of canes. Another equally colourful option would be a lead, stone or terracotta urn, or one of their look-alikes, planted with trailing nasturtiums, purple and white-flowering thyme and feverfew, cascading over the rim like a fragrant fountain.

### Creating an Effect

With the garden planned in outline, and perhaps a central feature in mind, it is time to decide on the overall style of planting you want to achieve. A garden or a plot planned on symmetrical lines need not be planted in a formal way. Take, for example, a diamond bed

sub-divided into four triangles and a square. You could plant each individual bed with neat clumps of herbs following the geometric outlines, or with rows of, say, compact lettuces, ornamental cabbages or other vegetables, each outlined with a different herb, for example thyme edging one bed, chives or oregano another. Any of these options would look neat and orderly provided you keep the beds well weeded and the herbs well trimmed.

A different approach to the same geometric layout is to plant each individual bed with one herb variety, which in this context can be as wayward and straggly as a cottage-garden plant. In a small plot you could plant one section with mints, secure in the knowledge that the confines of the bed would restrict their root development and prevent the colonization that can be a problem when this species is planted in a mixed bed. Plant one triangular section of variegated apple mint, others of eau de Cologne mint with its purplish flowers, plain-leaved apple mint with its rounded, woolly leaves and the fourth with the contrasting features of curly mint. The square bed in the centre could be planted with pennyroyal covering the ground around, say, a birdbath, or simply with a tall herb such as a clump of feathery bronze fennel.

A different approach to planting may be preferable where larger herb beds are planned, when for example each one is around 1.5 m (5 ft) across. This may be a case for the type of graduated planting that is popular for island beds planted with herbaceous plants, with the tallest in the centre, those of medium height around them and low-growing ones at the front, forming an edging. More specific ideas and details of planting schemes are given later in this section.

*Add definition with bright spikes of clary.*

*Neat areas and clumps define a diamond bed.*

# Informal herb gardens

SOMEWHERE BETWEEN THE DISCIPLINES of a geometric plan and the free-style planting of a cottage garden comes a chequerboard garden. This design, created by planting herbs between paving stones, is equally attractive in a town or a country setting. It is achieved by leaving squares of open soil between alternate paving stones. Each bed-in-miniature can be filled with a mixture of small herbs, or confined to a single plant type. Some squares can be left free for sowing annual herbs, or you can plant out nursery-grown ones, such as basil, borage and dill. Depending on the aspect of your garden, you could plant larger herbs, such as fennel, caraway, sweet Cicely and horseradish, in this way to form a screen from the prevailing wind, or where they would curtain off a utilitarian but unattractive corner of the garden, such as a compost heap.

From growing herbs between paving stones to growing them in gravel is a short visual step. In either case the plants can easily be tended and harvested, and are set off to good effect by a contrasting and sympathetic material. Herbs from the dry Mediterranean region will grow well in gravel and some will seed themselves freely. Make your selection from, among others, rosemary, sage, thyme, marjoram, summer and winter savory and pot marigolds.

Herbs tumbling over gravel, brick and stone paths conjure up images of cottage-style gardens, where herbs intermingle with other flowering plants and vegetables in a way that takes no account of horticultural demarcations. This concept of mixed planting has much to offer today, especially where a small plot is concerned. A clump of stately globe artichokes could grow alongside caraway and coriander, the yellowy

*Raised herb beds edged with fallen logs make light work of tending the plants.*

green flowers of the herbs contrasting strikingly with the grey-green foliage of the vegetables. Plant green- and bronze-leaved fennel among hollyhocks and foxgloves – the feathery leaves will give pleasure long after the flower spikes have faded. Hummocks of golden marjoram and thyme could cover the ground beneath sorrel and perpetual spinach, and purple sage interplanted with ornamental cabbage illustrates that this approach to planting recognizes no limitations.

*Lavender 'Twickle Purple' creates natural curves in the brick path.*

*Soften the lines and angles of square paving with clumps of low-growing herbs.*

# GROWING HERBS IN CONTAINERS

Where garden space is limited, or where your claim on the great outdoors begins and ends at the balcony or windowbox, you can create visual and literal feasts with herbs grown in tubs and troughs, pots, old stone sinks, barrels and wheelbarrows. In some Mediterranean countries, no doorstep or windowsill is complete without a flourish of basil, rosemary, oregano and thyme, and culinary herbs are proudly grown in used and often unpainted olive-oil cans.

EVERGREEN HERBS SUCH AS sweet bay and rosemary are also at their most effective when planted on their own in a container. A pair of clipped bay trees in troughs on either side of a doorway or flight of steps is a classic among herbal decorations. For a lesser degree of formality they could be underplanted with, for example, nasturtiums, lady's mantle or thyme.

A tall, urn-shaped, terracotta strawberry pot, purpose-made for the cultivation of alpine strawberries, is a perfect container for a collection of herbs. Those with a trailing habit such as thyme and nasturtiums are well suited to planting in the cupped holes around the sides and in the top, so allowing their stems to cascade gracefully. Reference to the *Directory of Herbs* will remind you of the variation of leaf and flower colour, and of aroma, that could be achieved by planting such a container only with various thymes.

Shallow containers such as stone sinks and terracotta troughs are suited to annual herbs such as sweet basil,

*Create a herb bed in a strawberry pot if you are short of space.*

dill, chervil and pot marigolds. In containers, as in open ground, it is advisable to separate annuals and perennials so that you do not disturb the long-term herbs when you plant or discard the annuals.

### ARTIFICIAL ENVIRONMENT

Whatever type of container you use, the first essential is to check that it has adequate drainage holes in the base. Without these, and a layer of broken crocks to cover them, plants will be in danger of becoming waterlogged and will soon perish. When planting a large container, cover the broken crocks with some bulky organic material such as one or two turves placed upside-down. Then fill with a soil-based potting compost, well firmed down to give the roots a good hold; peat-based compost, which dries out much more quickly, especially in terracotta pots, is not suitable.

Position pots of sun-loving plants where they will have at least five or six hours of strong light every day. If the aspect of your balcony or windowbox makes this impossible, concentrate on growing herbs such as bay, lemon balm, mint, parsley and thyme.

How often to apply water and how much to give container-grown herbs is a matter of fine judgement. The general rule is to water the pots when the top 2.5 cm (1 in) of compost has dried out – which it will do more rapidly in strong sunlight or windy conditions. To check for dryness in a terracotta pot, tap the side of the container; when it sounds hollow, it needs water. However, this test will not work for containers made of other materials, so you will need to feel or test the soil below the surface. It may be that herbs will need light watering every day or two, or even twice a day in very hot or windy conditions. They will also need feeding. Apply a liquid fertilizer every two or three weeks. Alternatively use a slow-release fertilizer; one application will keep plants going all summer.

*Container-grown herbs clustered together on a wooden deck are redolent of southern climes.*

*Plant a stone trough with dill, chervil and pot marigolds to make a herb corner on a patio.*

# GROWING HERBS INDOORS

Plants grown in containers on a balcony, patio or elsewhere may be brought indoors to create a special effect – perhaps a cluster of small pot-grown herbs to make an informal table decoration. A collection of scented geraniums can be used instead of pot pourri in a bedroom or conservatory, a trough of annual herbs in a window recess forms a seasonal focal point, and a rosemary bush in a large planter can seem like a living sculpture in a conservatory.

Whether or not one has a garden, growing herbs indoors has many practical and aesthetic advantages. Pots of culinary herbs basking in the sun on a kitchen windowsill can be conveniently harvested, a leaf at a time, whatever the weather. They form a verdant and fragrant link with the world outside, serve as environmental air fresheners and some, such as mint, may even deter insects.

Much of the advice given earlier for growing plants in containers applies to those cultivated indoors; only more so. If the herbs are not only to survive but flourish, they will need at least four to five hours' strong light each day or, if that is impractical, eight to ten hours of artificial light. Herbs do not take well to extreme temperature changes, and should not be positioned near radiators or in strong draughts. Container-grown herbs may be arranged in a group but should never be crowded as a free circulation of air between plants is essential, and will help minimize the incidence of pests and diseases.

Good drainage is another essential requirement, which clay or plastic pots with drainage holes covered with broken crocks will provide. Such pots, acceptable in the garden, may not always complement the interior decor, so they may be placed in a trough or tray, or in a ceramic, basketware, tin or other pot holder or *câchepot*. When herbs are planted direct in containers with no holes, for example in a ginger jar, a decorative bowl or a floor-standing urn, then special provisions for adequate drainage must be made. Before filling with compost, place a layer of gravel or pebbles in the base of the container – the depth of the layer will depend on the size of the pot – followed by a thin layer of broken charcoal to keep the compost "sweet". This will allow the compost to drain and avoid waterlogging.

## Good Growing Medium

The choice of the growing medium will also have an effect on water retention. Soil taken from the garden, no matter what its composition, is wholly unsuitable not least because it may contain disease organisms and

*Pots of herbs fill the foreground in this indoor arrangement of shaped and clipped shrubs.*

pests which would flourish in the warmer indoor environment. Two types of compost are suitable. The first, soil-based type, is composed of sterilized loam blended with fertilizer, lime and sand. The other, soilless compost, may be all-peat or a mixture of peat and sand. The latter is heavier and especially suited for use in large containers. Soilless composts also have fertilizer added. This is normally adequate to nourish the herbs for the first few weeks after planting.

Indoor herbs should be watered only when the top centimetre or so (1 in) has dried out. The frequency will vary according to the temperature and humidity of the room. In a centrally-heated room kept at a high temperature watering could be necessary every day or two, and feeding every week or fortnight after planting.

Indoor herbs will rarely be as vigorous or prolific as those grown in the open, so show restraint when harvesting since the plants will have more difficulty in restoring growth. Pluck off a few leaves or a small side shoot rather than denuding or cutting off the main stem, and the herbs will crop over a longer period.

*Herbs grown indoors should be placed near a window so that they receive direct light. For best effect, arrange a variety of herbs in attractive containers.*

# SELECTING YOUR HERBS

Before you start selecting the herbs you want to grow, first decide what purpose they are to serve. Do you want them primarily to enhance the appearance of your garden? Do you want large quantities for culinary, medicinal and cosmetic preparations? Or perhaps you wish to grow plants to sweeten the air and improve the quality of the environment. The chances are that you will want to achieve all these aims, and with even a small selection of herbs it is possible to do so.

TRADITIONALLY SOME HERBS HAVE been grown with other plants to the benefit of one or all. Chives are said to prevent black spot on roses, and garlic to encourage more prolific flowering. Rosemary and sage are thought to be ideal companions and of mutual benefit. Some fragrant herbs such as chives, hyssop, marjoram, parsley, sage and thyme are believed to improve the production of vegetables. Tarragon is held to strengthen the growth of all the vegetables and flowering plants in its vicinity, which seems reason enough for its inclusion.

Many herbs have powerful bee- and butterfly-attracting properties, and a list of these plants is given right. Some have an especially strong fragrance. Choose from anise, lavender, lemon balm, lemon verbena, pineapple sage, rose, sweet violet and wormwood to create an open-air pot pourri.

While the majority of herbs have relatively small flowers, some have blooms which are decidedly showy. Bright red bergamot, citrus yellow and orange pot marigolds and nasturtiums, deep golden tansy and yarrow and pale lemon evening primrose are fine examples of flowering herbs. Attractive companion plantings can be achieved by mixing and mingling these "extroverts" with others that are admired more for their foliage, and by contrasting neighbouring foliage colours and shapes. Purple sage with its long spikes of deep mauve flowers emphasizes the fluffy delicacy of yellow-green lady's mantle; bergamot towers brilliantly above salad burnet; clumps of marjoram seem all the brighter when placed next to yellow-leaved feverfew.

Whenever space allows, it is a good plan to plant each herb type in small groups or rows so that its characteristics can be fully appreciated. In a formal setting this means spacing the plants so that they are seen to be separated by soil when they are fully grown. In an informal setting, on the other hand, herbs are planted so that at maturity they are closely blended, without being overcrowded.

# Bee- and butterfly-attracting herbs

The brilliant red flowers of bergamot (Monarda 'Lodden Crown') are among the showiest blooms in the herb garden.

| | |
|---|---|
| Anise | *Pimpinella anisum* |
| Basil | *Ocimum basilicum* |
| Bee balm or bergamot | *Monarda didyma* |
| Catnip | *Nepeta cataria* |
| Chicory | *Cichorium intybus* |
| Chives | *Allium schoenoprasum* |
| Comfrey | *Symphytum officinale* |
| Dandelion | *Taraxacum officinale* |
| Evening primrose | *Oenothera biennis* |
| Fennel | *Foeniculum vulgare* |
| Hyssop | *Hysoppus officinalis* |
| Lavender | *Lavandula* |
| Lemon balm | *Melissa officinalis* |
| Marjoram | *Origanum* |
| Marshmallow | *Althaea officinalis* |
| Meadowsweet | *Filipendula ulmaria* |
| Peppermint | *Mentha × piperita* |
| Rosemary | *Rosmarinus officinalis* |
| Sage | *Salvia officinalis* |
| Thyme | *Thymus* |
| Valerian | *Valeriana officinalis* |
| White horehound | *Marrubium vulgare* |
| Yarrow | *Achillea millefolium* |

Butterflies cover the blossom of low-growing marjoram.

Lavender in flower is an important source of pollen for bees.

# SEEDS VERSUS PLANTS

It is up to you to decide whether to take charge of the whole growing cycle and start from seed, or come in partway through the operation. You can buy small plants from a nursery or other specialist grower, or you can propagate the new plants yourself by stem cuttings, layering, root cuttings or division. The methods suitable for each plant are given in the *Directory of Herbs*.

*Pots of rosemary, bay and sage stand in moist gravel in a greenhouse.*

For most gardeners, a mixture of the two approaches proves most suitable. Some herbs either do not set seed, or the seed does not grow reliably to type, and so starting from scratch is not an option. Foremost among such herbs, especially for the enthusiastic cook, is French tarragon which, unlike the inferior Russian tarragon, rarely produces seed. So if bottles of home-made tarragon vinegar and deliciously flavoured fish dishes are in your sights, it will be necessary to buy plants, or propagate from cuttings or pieces of root provided by a friend. Other herbs best bought as plants include mints, most of which are hybrids, and the decorative forms of thymes and sages. These can also successfully be grown from cuttings or divisions.

*For best results, buy your seeds each year from a reputable seed merchant and follow the directions on the packet.*

# Growing from seed

PROPAGATING HERBS FROM SEED is what Nature does all the time. Once you have an established herb garden, or some herbs intermingled with other plants, you can rely on the process of self-seeding to increase your stock. Many species, caraway, dandelion, lady's mantle and pot marigold among them, seed themselves prolifically, although not always just where you might have chosen. The tiny parachute-like seeds of dandelion, so readily borne on the wind, are likely to emerge as vigorous little plants far from the parent, and so frustrate the best-laid garden plans. But as self-sown plants are usually more rugged than those raised from collected seed, they can be transplanted while young to form a new colony elsewhere. However some seedlings, like those of caraway, do not transplant successfully.

In order to germinate successfully, most seeds have certain basic requirements – the appropriate levels of moisture, warmth, air and light, although most seeds will germinate in the light or the dark. These conditions are usually best provided by sowing seed under glass or indoors, in trays or pots, although larger seeds may be successfully sown outside. Once germination has taken place light becomes essential for healthy growth.

Most seeds get off to the best start if they are sown in spring, when there is likely to be a steady rise in temperature and in daylight hours. However, some seed needs to be sown as soon as it ripens. Some annual

*Dandelion, with its wind-borne seedhead "clock".*

herbs, such as chervil, may be sown in the autumn and will overwinter satisfactorily. Seeds of biennial herbs like caraway and clary are best sown in late spring to flower the following year. A few types, those which rely on extreme cold to break down their seed coats and end their period of dormancy, are better sown in autumn. Prominent among these are sweet Cicely and angelica. Reference to the *Directory of Herbs* will indicate the preferred sowing time of each herb.

## *Sowing seed outdoors*

*Careful preparation of the seedbed is all-important when sowing seed outside. The soil should be free of large stones and all weeds, and raked until it is fine and crumbly, a texture known as a fine tilth. In order to* *satisfy the temperature requirements for germination it is essential to delay sowing until there is no longer any danger of frost, and preferably to wait until the soil has been warmed by a few days of sunshine. You can bring* *forward the time of sowing by placing cloches over the seedbed a week or two before planting, to trap all the available heat.*

*hoe to a fine tilth*

*cover seeds with cloches to protect*

# Sowing seed indoors

*By sowing seed indoors or in a greenhouse or cold frame, you can advance the date of sowing by three weeks or more, thereby getting seedlings well established before planting out.*

1  *Sow seed in seed trays filled to within 12–14 mm (½ in) of the top with a proprietary seed compost. Level the surface, firm it down with a block of wood.*

2  *Water thoroughly, using a watering can with a fine rose.*

3  *Sow the seeds thinly and sift over more compost to cover to the required depth, two to three times its diameter. Lightly water – the compost should never become waterlogged.*

4  *Label the tray with the relevant details, the type of seed and, for future reference and comparisons, the date it was sown.*

5  *Place a piece of glass over the tray, cover with a sheet of paper and move to a shaded spot. Check the tray every day until germination begins.*

6  *Once the seedlings appear, remove the paper and the glass covering and move the tray to a lighter position, but out of full sun.*

# Pricking out

WHEN THE FIRST TRUE leaves appear after the seed leaves, it is time for the seedlings to be transferred, or "pricked out", into pots containing soil-based compost. Lift each tiny seedling out gently with a round-bladed knife or a wooden lollipop stick eased under the roots. Hold the seedling carefully by a leaf tip between thumb and forefinger and lower it into a hole in the soil made by a pointed wooden tool known as a dibber. Firm the soil around the stem with your fingers or the dibber, and give the soil a light watering. Check daily to ensure the seedlings do not dry out.

The seedlings can be left to develop in the pots until their root systems begin to grow through the bottom – a sure sign that it is time for them to move on again. At

*Potting compost needs to be firmed around the stems of delicate seedlings.*

this stage you can introduce the plants to outdoor conditions by opening the cold frame wide during the day, or by standing the pots in the garden, on a balcony, or in front of an open window during the day and either bringing them in or covering them with a cloche at night and in bad weather.

After two or three weeks of "hardening off", or conditioning in this way, the herbs will be ready for planting out in their permanent site. This may be a tub or trough on the balcony, or a prepared site in the garden. Whatever the case, it is important to minimize the effect of the transition by planting out when conditions are most favourable.

*Herbs grown from seed and transferred to larger pots can be grown on under cover or planted outdoors.*

# Taking stem cuttings

Most herbs with woody or semi-woody stems, such as hyssop, lavender, rosemary, sage, scented-leaved pelargoniums, marjoram, thyme and winter savory, can be readily propagated by taking stem cuttings, known as softwood cuttings, in late spring and early summer. This is when the new shoots are soft and the sap is still rising. Trim off about 5–10 cm (2–4 in) of new growth just below a leaf node. Remove the lower leaves and stipules (present on the stems of pelargoniums), and dip the base of the cutting in a hormone rooting compound. Cuttings of some woody herbs, such as lavender and southernwood, give better results if they are pulled off

with a "heel" of older wood. This heel needs to be trimmed with a knife before the cutting is prepared as described above.

Fill a pot with potting compost or an equivalent that is low in nutrients, well drained and well aerated, such as John Innes potting compost No. 1. Insert the cuttings around the edge of the pot, about 2.5 cm (1 in) into the compost, and firm it in with your fingers. Lightly spray the soil with water and place the pots in a covered propagating case. Alternatively cover the individual pots with a polythene bag held in place with a rubber band around the rim, or with an upturned glass jar to keep the soil moist. Place the propagating case or pots in a shady situation, taking care to avoid full sun. Once they start to root and show signs of growth give them regular foliar feeds.

When the cuttings are well rooted, pot them on into small individual pots filled with a general-purpose compost. Then treat them as the young healthy plants they are, and condition or harden them off before planting them out to their permanent site.

You can continue to take cuttings of semi-ripe wood of lavender and rosemary during the summer months. Treat them in a similar way to softwood cuttings, but leave them to overwinter in a cool greenhouse or unheated room, then prick them out in spring.

# Layering

Some hardy perennials, sub-shrubs and shrubs can be grown from layered stems, for example sage. In fact some plants like mint spread naturally by means of runners, creeping stems that root at intervals to produce new plants.

You can encourage less vigorous subjects to form roots by selecting a leggy shoot and, without severing it from the parent plant, make slanting cuts at intervals

along the length, using a sharp knife. Peg the shoots in the soil with pieces of bent wire or staples and cover with a thin layer of sifted soil. If the layered shoots are pegged out in a wheel formation around the parent plant a healthy clump of herbs will soon be established. Once new young plants with well-developed root systems have formed along the cut stem, they can, if you wish, be cut from the parent and transplanted.

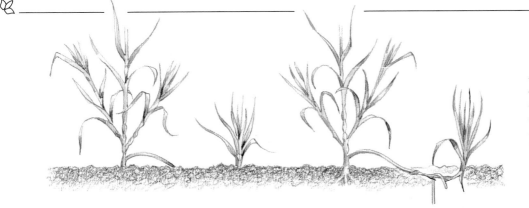

*For layering, pin down a vigorous shoot and cover. Separate from the parent plant when well rooted.*

# Root cuttings

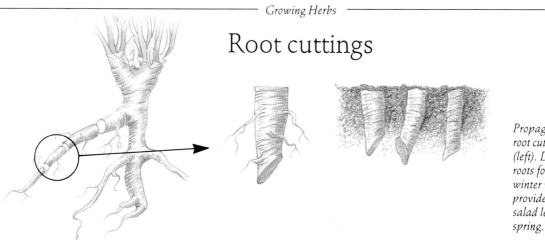

*Propagation by root cuttings (left). Dandelion roots forced in winter will provide early salad leaves in spring.*

MINT AND LICORICE CAN be raised from root cuttings taken at the end of the growing season to produce new young plants and fresh leaves throughout the winter. Expose some roots and cut them into 10 cm (4 in) lengths. Lay them in a box of general-purpose potting compost, cover them lightly with more compost, water them and bring them indoors. They will soon send out shoots and provide new leaf growth.

Fleshy roots such as horseradish and orris root can also be propagated from sections of root, or rhizome in the case of orris. Lift a section of root/rhizome carefully and cut it into short sections – a straight cut across the top, a slanting cut across the bottom. Plant these out the correct way up in a large pot or into prepared ground.

# Division

CLUMP-FORMING PERENNIALS THAT that have been established for at least two years can be propagated by division. Indeed, most will benefit from the procedure.

Divide the plants in spring or autumn, using a knife or a spade blade to cut through the centre of the clump. Carefully ease the individual plants apart and replant them, or a small part of the clump, in prepared ground.

# CARING FOR YOUR HERBS

Maintaining a herb garden should be a pleasurable hobby: pulling up any weeds that threaten to overcome young plants; watering and feeding the plants from time to time; staking up any herbs that are becoming straggly, and pruning unruly shoots at the end of the growing season. Sounds like hard work? Not when you consider that every time you brush against a plant, or spray it lightly with water, you will release and savour the fragrance for which you chose it in the first place.

## Watering and feeding

THE MANY HERBS THAT originate from hot, dry Mediterranean regions do not need a rigorous watering routine. Indeed, they can survive long, dry spells with no water at all. However, regular, light watering is beneficial. It not only helps to keep the plants, annuals especially, fresh-looking, but helps to maintain their fragrance. It is important not to over-water, particularly those plants with soft stems. These cannot readily dry out, and excessive moisture can lead to fungus growth. In a region where heavy rainfall is likely to be a problem, giving the plants space for air to circulate around them is essential.

However, other herbs, particularly those with fleshy roots like marshmallow and meadowsweet, require a moist spot and benefit from watering in dry summers.

Herbs growing in open ground make few demands in terms of nourishment. Well-rotted garden compost dug into the soil before planting, and at the end of every growing season, will provide most of the nutrients the plants need. An occasional dressing of an organic fertilizer may be applied, particularly if plants begin to look sickly. Herbs in containers benefit from feeding.

---

### *Pest and disease control*

*Pennyroyal and nasturtiums are known to repel ants, rosemary to repel carrot fly, and basil, sage and chamomile (which is known as "the plant's physician") to keep harmful insects at bay. Mint discourages flies, and chives will help preventing scab on apple trees and black spot on roses. Thyme plants will lure slugs away from other species, causing the pests to congregate in specific locations, for easy eradication each evening.*

*Aphids tend to be the main pest problem on herbs. If you have an inadequate colony of ladybirds or hoverflies, the larvae of which eat them, spray the plants with derris dust or your own organic pesticide made from an infusion of elder leaves. And make a note to plant more dill and fennel which attract hoverflies.*

*Derris dust is helpful, too, in eradicating leaf scale, which frequently affects bay trees. Regular spraying when the mites emerge should restore the leaves to their normal condition. Rust on mint, another unsightly problem, takes more perseverance to overcome.*

*Destroy the affected plants or remove the damaged parts, then dig up the plants. Soak the roots in hot water, then replant them in a different, uncontaminated, situation.*

PLANNING AHEAD
*At the end of the growing cycle it is time to start planning the following year's planting. Make a note to include more of the herbs which are bee-attracting – borage, coriander, lemon balm and summer savory among them – to be sure of a high pollination level.*

# Pruning

TAKE STOCK OF YOUR herbs at the end of the growing season. When it is time to pull out and discard the annuals (having first saved the seed), the time is right to see how the perennials are shaping up.

Use sharp secateurs to cut back any dead stems, and

*Lavender before pruning*          *After pruning*

*Lemon verbena is pruned in the growing season to remove the dead flowers and straggly or woody stems.*

to cut off long, straggly growth. Vigorous and woody plants like lavender, rue, sage and thyme should be cut back hard (but in the case of lavender not back to the old wood) to reshape the plant and encourage fresh, tidy growth. With the exception of rue, do not consign the clippings to the compost heap, but throw them on a wood fire or a bonfire to enjoy the last of their fragrance. Such plants are perennial but not everlasting, and there will come a time when they will no longer regain or retain an attractive shape and a concentration of growth. That is when it is time to propagate.

# Staking

MANY HERBS HAVE A naturally dwarfing habit, and others are bred specially to form low-growing hummocks. Even the tallest herbs like angelica, evening primrose and fennel are usually able to stand their ground, even in high winds, especially if you have taken the precaution of planting them in a reasonably sheltered part of the garden.

If plants do start to flop and sprawl, then assist them to stay upright by inserting stout bamboo canes, positioning three at intervals around a clump, tying round with green twine.

*Stake tall plants as they grow to prevent damage to the long stems and flowers.*

# HERBS IN

ACTION

# PRESERVING HERBS

Timing is everything when you are harvesting herbs for preserving and storing. Whether you intend to use herbs for medicinal purposes or for cooking, it is important to gather them at the point in their growing cycle when their volatile oils are most concentrated, and at the time of day when there is no unnecessary moisture on them. To obtain maximum benefit from herbs, treat them with great care, preserve them without delay and store them away from the light.

## Gathering herbs

Leaves are at their most fragrant, and richest in volatile oils, before any flowers have opened. Flowers are harvested as soon as they have fully opened. Seeds should be captured as soon as they are ripe, while roots need to be left in the ground until the end of the growing season, when they will have the greatest concentration of stored nutrients.

Aerial parts of the plants –

flowers, leaves, seeds and stems – should be harvested early on a dry day, as soon as the dew has dried. By noon, when the sun is at its height, the volatile oils will have dissipated. Always use sharp secateurs or florists' scissors to cut stems, to avoid damaging the plants. Shake off any insects, pick off damaged or discoloured leaves and flowers and put straight into water. Keep the plant material

away from strong light, which will draw out the volatile oils.

Harvest seedheads each day, as they ripen, tying a piece of muslin over them to catch any seeds as they fall. Do not use a plastic bag, as condensation could rot the seeds.

## Drying herbs

Drying requires free circulation of warm, dry air and the absence of strong light, especially sunlight. Herbs can be dried over several days in a cool room, more quickly in a warm atmosphere, but never hang them in a steamy kitchen or bathroom. Leaves are best dried on the stalk, though large ones such as borage may be separated and dried

on a rack. Seed heads should be hung up to dry inside a paper bag to collect the seeds as they fall. Flowers for drying should be cut from their stems. Roots must be brushed clean and then cut into 2.5 cm (1 in) slices.

Separate stems into small bunches to allow the warm air to circulate freely around them, and

hang bunches well away from a wall. Spread loose plant material in a single layer on a suitable drying rack, or place on baking trays and dry in a cool oven with the door slightly ajar, to allow the moisture to escape. Turn the herbs frequently. Flowers and leaves are dry when they are crisp and rattly, roots when they are woody.

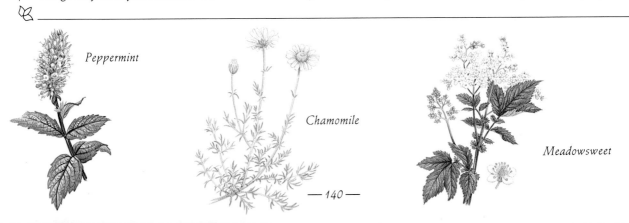

*Peppermint*

*Chamomile*

*Meadowsweet*

# Storing dried herbs

Gradually strip leaves from their stalks and crumble them lightly between your fingers. Pull marigold petals from the flower centres. Untie the bags covering seedheads and carefully collect the fallen seeds.

Store dried herbs separately in lidded glass or pottery (not plastic) jars, and label. Dark-coloured jars or pots are ideal since they exclude the light, or store clear glass jars in a dry, cool place. Keep a small "working jar" handy in the kitchen, replenishing it from time to time. This saves exposing a large jar of herbs to the air and light.

# Freezing herbs

You can open-freeze herbs on the stem, or strip off the leaves and freeze them whole. In either case, spread the herbs in a single layer on a baking tray or large plate and freeze them uncovered. Once they are frozen, pack them into lidded containers – they will be too fragile and brittle to hold their shape in polythene bags. Alternatively crumble them lightly between your fingers to obtain the frozen equivalent of chopped herbs. The crumbled herbs are best stored in small, lidded containers. Be sure to label each herb.

Another method is to pack chopped herbs into ice-cube trays and top up with water. When frozen, turn out into labelled plastic bags. These herbed ice cubes can be added to soups and casseroles straight from the freezer.

Small sprays of herbs or edible flowers can be frozen in ice-cubes, or in fancy-shaped biscuit cutters wrapped round with foil and filled with water. Match herb fragrance to the drink – lemon verbena with lemonade – or choose flavour contrasts – scented pelargonium-leaf cubes in a cup of chilled chamomile tea.

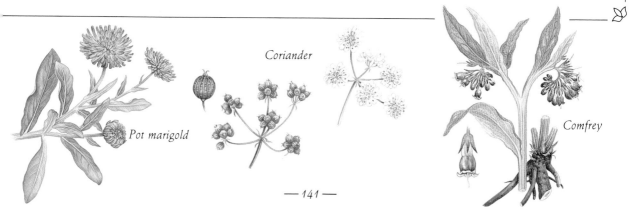

*Coriander*

*Pot marigold*

*Comfrey*

# COOKING

Although these days we tend to think that the herbs added to our meals are there purely to provide flavour, in the past they were regarded as far more functional. Many are good gastric stimulants, making it easier to digest strong, rich meats like pork or game. Others were used to balance the meal and prevent illness: Culpeper tells us that in the 17th century all housewives cooked fish with fennel because fish – coming from the sea – were damp and so could cause stomach upsets, while fennel was a dry, hot herb to provide balance. Herbs are also ideal to add flavours to replace over-dependence on salt or sugar.

| FOOD TYPE | HERB | SERVING SUGGESTIONS |
|---|---|---|
| Soups | | |
| *Clear/light* | Chervil | Enhances consommés |
| | Tarragon | Good with chicken broth soups |
| *Fish* | Dill | Use seeds with strong fish; leaves with lighter varieties |
| | Lemon balm | Can replace grated lemon rind |
| | Tarragon | Good with strong-flavoured fish |
| *Lentil* | Caraway/Dill seed/Fennel | Use ground seeds |
| *Rich/meaty* | Coriander seeds | Use ground early in cooking |
| | Lovage | Chopped stems can thicken soups and broths |
| *Vegetable* | Chervil | Enhances flavours |
| | Dill seed | Use ground seeds |
| | Fennel | Use ground seeds or finely sliced bulb of Florence fennel |
| | Lovage | Stems can replace celery |
| | Oregano | Adds Mediterranean flavour |
| | Sage | Use sparingly as quite strong |
| *Pea* | Coriander | Use ground seeds |
| | Cumin/ Fenugreek | Ground seeds add spicy flavour |
| | Ginger | Use fresh chopped root |
| | Turmeric | Use ground and sparingly |
| Starters | | |
| *Rich pâtés* | Bay | Good with all game dishes |
| | Parsley | Italian/flat-leaved has a stronger flavour |
| | Sage | Good in pork/rabbit dishes |
| Main dishes | | |
| *Fish-fat/rich* | Basil | Use with mackerel/shellfish |
| | Dill seeds | Ideal for salmon |
| | Tarragon | Use in rich cream sauces |
| | Thyme | Good with strong-flavoured fish |

| FOOD TYPE | HERB | SERVING SUGGESTIONS |
|---|---|---|
| *Fish – white* | Chervil | Combine with lemon balm in light fish dishes |
| | Dill weed/ Fennel | Use young sprigs finely chopped |
| | Lemon balm | Can replace lemon |
| *Beef* | Coriander | Use for an oriental flavour |
| | Dill seeds | Good with veal |
| | Hyssop | Good in casseroles |
| | Lovage | Adds celery flavour, thickens |
| | Marjoram/ Thyme | Use in stews and casseroles |
| *Lamb* | Garlic | Combine with lavender for young roast lamb |
| | Rosemary | Classic for roast lamb and lamb casseroles |
| *Pork* | Chervil/ Marjoram | Use in stuffings and sauces for roasts |
| | Fennel | Good in casseroles/pâtés |
| | Sage | Use for stuffings |
| | Summer savory | Good with ham dishes |
| *Chicken/ poultry* | Coriander | Adds oriental flavour |
| | Lemon balm | Rub with leaves before stir-frying or roasting |
| | Sage/Summer savory | Add to casseroles and stir-fried dishes |
| | Tarragon | Ideal with baked chicken and light casseroles |
| Cheese dishes | Chervil | Chop into omelettes and quiches |
| | Dill weed/ Marjoram | Add freshly chopped to cream cheese |
| | Mint | Add freshly chopped to cream or cottage cheese |
| | Oregano | Ideal for vegetarian dishes |
| | Sage | Add to cooked sauces or cheese and potato dishes |

# Classic fresh herb mixtures

*The right combinations of herbs complement each other and enhance the foods they season.*

### FINES HERBES
*equal amounts of chevril, chives, parsley and tarragon*

### BOUQUET GARNI
*3 stalks parsley, 1 bay leaf and 1 sprig thyme*

### HERBES DE PROVENCE
*oregano, rosemary, thyme, savory, marjoram and French lavender*

### BEEF MIX
*equal amounts of rosemary, thyme savory, orange peel and parsley*

### LAMB MIX
*equal amounts of rosemary, thyme, savory, mint and parsley*

### PORK MIX
*equal amounts of sage, thyme, and marjoram*

### POULTRY MIX
*equal amounts of parsley, thyme, majoram, tarragon and bay leaf (juniper berries for game birds)*

### SEAFOOD MIX
*equal amounts of dill, tarragon and lemon peel*

| Food type | Herb | Serving suggestions |
|---|---|---|
| Egg dishes | Basil/Chervil/ Dill weed/ Thyme | Add chopped to omelettes and other dishes |
| | Tansy | Use for sweet puddings |
| Pasta | Basil | Use fresh with tomato sauces |
| | Marjoram/ Oregano | Tends to taste stronger when dried |
| | Nutmeg | Use grated with Parmesan |
| Salads | Basil | Use chopped leaves from different coloured varieties |
| | Borage/ Marigold | Sprinkle flowers/petals on salads as a garnish |
| | Chives | Chop finely for a mild onion flavour |
| | Coriander/ Lemon balm | Add two or three leaves to green salads |
| | Nasturtium | Use both flowers and leaves |
| | Salad burnet | Gives a taste of cucumber |
| | Sorrel | A little perks up lettuce |
| Vegetables Tomatoes | Basil | Gives all tomato dishes the classic taste of Italy |
| | Oregano | Use fresh in Greek salads |
| Rice | Fennel | Add a bag of seeds to boiling rice or use finely sliced Florence fennel |
| | Saffron | Classic for oriental dishes |
| Beans/peas | Chervil/ Summer savory | Great flavour enhancers |
| | Dill seeds | Add to broad beans/peas |
| | Mint | Add fresh to young peas |
| Cabbage family | Caraway seeds | Good with all cabbage dishes and sauerkraut |
| | Fennel seeds | Add to Brussels sprouts |
| | Marjoram | Good with broccoli |
| | Thyme | Add a sprig to boiled/ steamed cabbage |

| Food type | Herb | Serving suggestions |
|---|---|---|
| Root | Dill seeds | Cook whole with carrots and parsnips |
| | Fenugreek | Good with carrots |
| | Garlic | Add to baked potato dishes |
| | Paprika | Enhances carrots/turnips |
| | Sage | Add a sprig to boiling carrots/potatoes |
| Lentils/pulses | Caraway/ Fennel seeds | Use ground |
| | Ginger | Adds spice to lentil loaf |
| | Hyssop | Good with quick dishes |
| | Marjoram | Add to lentil loaf and casseroles |
| Onions | Caraway | Add to tarts |
| | Oregano | Use in quiches and soups |
| Desserts | Bergamot | Add flowers to fruit salads |
| | Mint | Use chopped in fruit salads and stewed pears/apples |
| | Rose petals | Use to flavour ice cream, junkets, or crystallize |
| | Scented perlagoniums | Use to flavour ice cream or sherberts, or as a garnish |
| | Sweet Cicely | Cook with rhubarb/apples to replace sugar |
| | Sweet violets | Crystallize for decoration |
| Cakes & Beads | Caraway seeds | Sprinkle onto breads and crackers |
| | Dill seeds | Use ground in crackers |
| | Fennel seeds | Use ground to flavour bread |
| | Ginger | For spicy biscuits and shortbread |
| | Mint | Add to white cakes |
| | Tansy | Use in Easter cakes |
| Pickles & relishes | Dill | Use for pickles and to accompany fish |
| | Mint | Ideal with lamb/cold cuts |
| | Mustard seed | Use with gravad lax and strong-flavoured dishes |

# SOUPS & STARTERS

Fresh green herbs and pungent spices demonstrate a versatility of ways to begin a meal, from tangy sorrel soup or creamy garlic soup to a robust game pâté. Accompanied with herb scones or breads, any one of these dishes would make a light luncheon.

## Hare pâté

*If you prefer a less rich mixture, use rabbit or chicken in place of the hare in this country pâté.*

1 kg (2¼ lb) hare joints
450 g (1 lb) belly of pork, skinned
1 onion, roughly chopped
2 cloves garlic, roughly chopped
3 tbsp chopped parsley
2 tsp chopped sage
salt and black pepper
100 ml (4 fl oz) red wine
40 g (1½ oz) butter, melted
3 bay leaves

Remove the meat from the joints and cut it into pieces. Trim the pork and cut it into cubes. Combine the hare, pork, onion and garlic in a food processor and process to make a smooth paste. Stir in the parsley and sage, season with salt and pepper and stir in the wine.

Pack the mixture into a 1.2 litre (2 pt) loaf tin or baking dish and level the top. Cover with foil and stand the dish in a roasting pan with water to come halfway up the dish. Bake in the oven (170°C/325°F/gas mark 3) for one and a half hours.

Pour off any excess fat and allow the pâté to cool. Arrange the bay leaves on top and pour over the melted butter to cover. Chill until the pâté is set.

*To serve 6 to 8*

## Chilled garlic soup

*This elegant soup has a subtle flavour with no more than a hint of garlic.*

12 blanched almonds
6 cloves garlic, peeled
2 tbsp olive oil
2 thick slices white bread, crusts removed, cut into small cubes
600 ml (1 pt) clear chicken stock
150 ml (¼ pt) dry white wine
salt and white pepper
2 tbsp snipped chives

Process the almonds and garlic to a paste in a blender or food processor, or pound them with a pestle and mortar. Heat the oil in a small pan and fry the garlic paste and bread cubes over medium heat until the bread is golden brown.

Pour the chicken stock and wine into a blender or food processor, add the garlic and bread mixture and season with salt and pepper. Process until the soup is smooth.

Stir in the chives, and chill for at least one hour. Before serving, taste and adjust seasoning if necessary. Garnish with croutons.

*To serve 4*

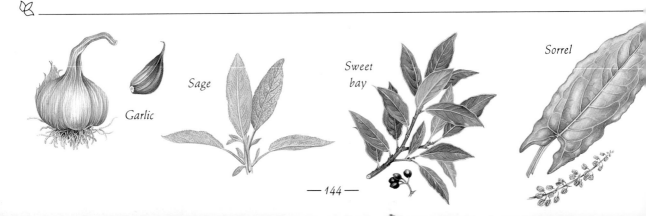

Garlic

Sage

Sweet bay

Sorrel

# Sorrel soup

*Deep, deep green with a sharp lemony tang, this soup can be served hot or cold.*

450 g (1 lb) sorrel
50 g (2 oz) butter
1 onion, roughly chopped
600 ml (1 pt) chicken stock
salt and black pepper
1 tbsp lemon juice
1 tbsp flour
4 tbsp single cream
1 tsp grated lemon rind, to garnish

Wash and drain the sorrel and tear off and discard the stalks. Melt 25 g (1 oz) of the butter in a large pan and sauté the onion over medium heat until translucent but not coloured. Add the sorrel and stir until it has collapsed. Add the stock, season with salt and pepper, cover and simmer for 15 minutes. Purée in a blender or food processor. Rinse out the pan.

Melt the remaining butter and stir in the flour to make a roux. Gradually pour on the sorrel purée, stirring all the time. Add the lemon juice, taste the soup and adjust the seasoning if necessary. Reheat the soup to serve it hot. If you wish to serve it cold, allow it to cool, then chill it for at least one hour.

To serve, swirl one tablespoonful single cream over each portion and sprinkle on the grated lemon rind.

*To serve 4*

# Spiced pea soup

*Fragrant with the aroma of a medley of ground spices, this golden soup is garnished with glistening raisins.*

150 g (6 oz) dried yellow split peas, soaked for at least one hour
600 ml (1 pt) chicken stock
25 g (1 oz) butter
1 tsp ground cumin
1 tsp ground coriander
½ tsp ground ginger
½ tsp ground turmeric
large pinch of ground fenugreek
pinch of sugar
salt
2 tbsp seedless raisins, to garnish
coriander leaves, to garnish

Bring the split peas to a boil in a large pan of unsalted water and cook, covered, for 30 to 45 minutes, until they are tender. Drain them and discard the liquid. Reserving two tablespoons of the cooked peas, purée the remainder with the stock in a blender or food processor.

Melt the butter in a large pan and fry the ground spices over medium heat for two minutes, stirring. Add the reserved peas, the pea purée and sugar. Season with salt and bring to simmering point.

To serve, stir in the raisins and garnish with the coriander leaves.

*To serve 4*

VARIATION
For an even more pungent flavour, you can use whole cumin, coriander and fenugreek seeds, pounding them in a pestle and mortar.

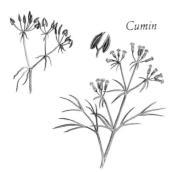

*Cumin*

# HERB SAUCES, OILS & VINEGARS

Salmon steaks brushed before grilling with tarragon oil; beef for pot roasting marinated in oregano oil and vinegar; spring vegetables tossed in aromatic herb butter, and rainbow trout pan-fried and served with a spoonful of green salsa – such herb flavourings and sauces can lift the plainest of dishes into the gourmet class, and keep alive the fragrance of the herb garden in spring.

## Aromatic herb butter

*Serve this butter as a dressing for grilled chops, steak and fish, toss with plain or green pasta, or drizzle over young spring vegetables.*

*100 g (4 oz) unsalted butter, at room temperature*
*1 clove garlic, finely chopped*
*4 tbsp chopped parsley*
*1 tbsp snipped chives*
*salt and black pepper*
*1 tsp lemon juice*

Beat the butter with the garlic, parsley and chives. Season with salt and pepper and gradually beat in the lemon juice, a few drops at a time. Shape the butter into a roll, wrap it in foil or film and chill it in the refrigerator. Cut it in slices, or pats, to serve.

*To make 100 g (4 oz)*

VARIATIONS
For watercress butter, especially good with grilled or poached salmon, use one small bunch of finely-chopped watercress leaves in the place of the parsley and chives. For other aromatic butters add chopped fennel, lemon balm, mint, summer savory or wild marjoram.

## Green salsa

*This piquant sauce is served principally with fried or grilled fish. To preserve the freshness of the herbs, make just before serving.*

*2 cloves garlic, crushed*
*2 tbsp capers, rinsed and drained*
*4 anchovy fillets, finely chopped*
*1 tbsp chopped basil*
*3 tbsp chopped flat-leaved parsley*
*1 tsp whole-grain mustard*
*3 tbsp lemon juice*
*3 tbsp olive oil*
*black pepper*

Beat all the ingredients together until they are well blended. Taste the sauce and adjust the seasoning if necessary. If you find it a little too strong or salty, add one or two teaspoonsful of double cream or plain yoghurt.

*To serve 4*

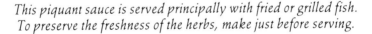

*French tarragon*

# Herb oils

*Use these fragrant oils to dress salads, in sauces and marinades, or brush on meat and fish for grilling. Use them, too, when making casseroles and soups.*

*6 tbsp chopped herb such as basil, mint, oregano, tarragon, thyme or wild marjoram*
*600 ml (1 pt) olive oil*
*1–2 sprigs of the herb*

Pound the herb to a paste in a pestle and mortar or mixing bowl. Stir in a few drops of the oil, mix until it is well blended, then add the remainder. Pour the mixture into a dry, sterilized jar, cover and set it aside for two weeks, shaking or stirring once or twice a day. Strain the oil into sterilized bottles, add the herb sprigs, seal and store in a cool dark place.

*To make 600 ml (1 pt)*

# Herb vinegars

*Add piquancy to salads, sauces, marinades and casseroles.*

*10 tbsp chopped herb, such as basil, mint, oregano, tarragon, thyme or wild marjoram*
*600 ml (1 pt) white wine vinegar*
*1–2 sprigs of the herb*

Pound the herb to a paste and transfer it to a heatproof jug. Pour the vinegar into a glass or enamel pan, bring it to the boil and pour it over the herb. Stir well and leave to cool. Pour the herb and vinegar into a sterilized jar, cover and set aside for three weeks, shaking or stirring once or twice a day. Strain the vinegar into sterilized bottles, add the herb sprigs and put on the caps and store in a cool dark place.

*To make 600 ml (1 pt)*

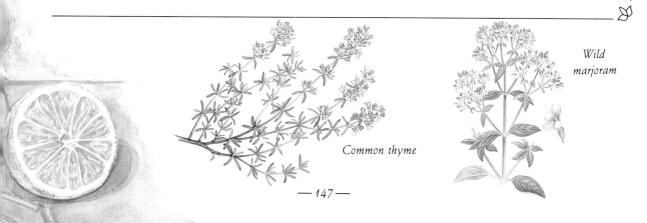

*Common thyme*

*Wild marjoram*

# MEAT & FISH DISHES

The use of herbs to flavour and offset the richness of meat and fish has its origins in ancient times, and cultures all around the world have absorbed classic combinations into their cultural heritage. Lamb studded with slivers of garlic and baked with rosemary sprigs; raw salmon wrapped in dill leaves before being marinated in salt and preserving spices for gravlax; cubes of lamb, pork or beef tossed in cumin, fennel and coriander seeds for Malaysian satay. These and the recipes that follow illustrate some of the culinary bonds between aromatic plants and protein foods.

## Meatballs in dill sauce

*A traditional Greek egg and lemon sauce is flavoured with dill to complement these meatballs, which are poached in a herb-flavoured stock.*

*350 g (12 oz) lean pork, cut into cubes*
*1 small onion, roughly chopped*
*40 g (1½ oz) fresh white breadcrumbs*
*2 tbsp chopped chervil (or you can use parsley)*
*salt and black pepper*
*large pinch of grated nutmeg*
*1 egg yolk, lightly beaten*
*flour, for dusting*
*900 ml (1½ pt) chicken stock*
*5 or 6 parsley stalks*
*2 egg yolks*
*4 tbsp lemon juice*
*2 tbsp chopped dill*
*dill leaves, to garnish*
*lemon wedges, to serve*

Process the meat and onion in a food processor or blender until it forms a smooth paste. Stir in the breadcrumbs and chervil, and season with salt, pepper and nutmeg. Stir in the egg yolk and mix until well blended. Cover and chill for at least one hour.

Dust your hands with flour and shape the mixture into walnut-sized balls.

Pour the stock into a large saucepan, add the parsley stalks and, when it is boiling, add the meatballs. Return the stock to simmering point, half cover the pan and simmer for 10–15 minutes. Remove the meatballs with a spoon and arrange them on a heated serving dish. Keep them warm while you make the sauce.

Strain the stock and measure 300 ml (½ pt) into a rinsed-out pan.

Bring to just below simmering point over a medium heat. Beat the egg yolks with the lemon juice, stir in the dill and season with salt and pepper. Pour a few spoonfuls of the hot stock into the egg and lemon mixture and stir well. (On no account allow the stock to boil, or it will curdle the mixture.)

Tip the sauce mixture into the pan and heat it gently over low heat, stirring constantly. As soon as the sauce thickens remove it from the heat, taste and adjust the seasoning.

Pour the sauce over the meatballs, garnish the dish with dill leaves and serve with lemon wedges. Green salad, and pasta shapes tossed in cream and chopped fresh herbs go well with this dish.

*To serve 4*

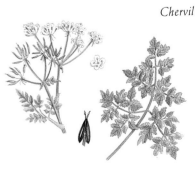

*Chervil*

# Baked sea bream

*The fish is cooked in a rich, colourful and aromatic sauce and can be
served fisherman-style, straight from the cooking dish.*

*1 sea bream, about 1.5 kg (3½ lb)*
*juice of 1 lemon*
*salt and black pepper*
*3 bay leaves*
*6 tbsp olive oil*
*1 medium onion, sliced*
*2 cloves garlic, chopped*
*150 ml (¼ pt) white wine*
*1 tbsp white wine vinegar*
*225 g (8 oz) chopped tomatoes*
*2 tbsp tomato purée*
*5 tbsp chopped flat-leaved parsley*
*8 tbsp dry white breadcrumbs*
*75 g (3 oz) feta cheese, crumbled*
*12 black olives, to garnish*

Ask the fishmonger to gut and clean the fish. Wash it well, sprinkle it inside with lemon juice and season with salt and pepper. Tuck the bay leaves inside. Heat the oil in a pan and fry the onion over medium heat until it is transparent. Fry the garlic for one minute, then add the wine, wine vinegar, chopped tomatoes, tomato purée and parsley and season with salt and pepper. Stir well and bring to the boil.

Pour half the sauce into a shallow baking dish – a cast-iron one is traditional – and place the fish on top. Pour on the remaining sauce and scatter on the breadcrumbs. Bake the fish, uncovered, in a pre-heated oven at 190°C (375°F or gas mark 5) for 35–40 minutes, until it is firm. Then sprinkle on the crumbled cheese, garnish with the olives and serve.

*To serve 6*

# Herb-coated chicken

*Chicken breasts, marinated in a spicy mixture, are sautéed to give a
delicious crispy coating.*

*4 small chicken breasts, or chicken
supremes, skinned*
*2 tbsp Dijon mustard*
*1 tbsp made English mustard*
*2 egg yolks, lightly beaten*
*3 tbsp double cream*
*salt and black pepper*
*100 g (4 oz) dry white breadcrumbs*
*3 tbsp chopped French tarragon (or
coriander or flat-leaved parsley)*
*plain flour, for dusting*
*oil, for shallow frying*

Pat the chicken breasts dry. Mix the mustards, egg yolks and cream in a shallow bowl, season with salt and pepper. Combine breadcrumbs and chopped herb on a large plate or a piece of greaseproof paper.

Dip each chicken breast in flour to coat it on all sides, then in the mustard mixture, turning it to coat it evenly. Drain off any excess, then turn the chicken in the crumb mixture until it is well coated.

Cover and chill for at least four hours. During this time the flavours will penetrate the meat and the coating will set.

Heat oil in a large, heavy frying-pan. Fry the chicken joints for about 10 minutes on each side, until golden brown. To test that the meat is cooked, pierce the thickest part with a fine skewer; the juice should run out clear.

New potatoes and sorrel are suitable accompaniments.

*To serve 4*

*Sweet bay*

*Flat-leaved
parsley*

*French tarragon*

# VEGETARIAN DISHES

Cooking for vegetarians has never been more imaginative or exciting, and using a wide range of herbs makes it even more so. A rich wholemeal pastry with the aroma of caraway seeds, a vegetable crumble pepped up with a hint of ground ginger, a warming hotpot flavoured with a cluster of spice seeds; these recipes will appeal to a much wider audience than convinced vegetarians.

## Carrot and broad bean crumble

*Fresh spring vegetables complemented by the fragrance of herbs make a delicious lunch or supper dish.*

450 g (1 lb) carrots, trimmed and sliced
225 g (8 oz) shelled broad beans, fresh
or frozen
15 g (½ oz) butter
1 tbsp chopped marjoram
1 tsp clear honey
½ tsp ground ginger
3 tbsp reserved vegetable stock

FOR THE CRUMBLE
25 g (1 oz) wholewheat flour
25 g (1 oz) wholewheat breadcrumbs
½ tsp ground ginger
1 tbsp sunflower seeds
1 tbsp sesame seeds
salt and white pepper
5 tbsp vegetable oil

Steam the carrots and broad beans until they are just tender. Reserve the stock. Toss the vegetables in the butter and stir in the marjoram, honey and ginger. Turn the mixture into a baking dish and sprinkle on the three tablespoons of reserved vegetable stock.

To make the crumble, mix together the flour, breadcrumbs, ground ginger, sunflower and sesame seeds and season to taste with salt and pepper. Stir in the oil and spread the mixture over the vegetables.

Bake in the oven (190°C/375°F/gas mark 6) for 20 to 25 minutes, until the topping is golden brown.

*To serve 4*

# Onion and caraway tart

*A hint of caraway in both the pastry and the filling gives this
vegetable tart an unusual piquancy.*

150 g (6 oz) wholewheat flour
85 g (3½ oz) butter, grated
1 tsp caraway seeds, lightly crushed
salt
1 egg yolk mixed with 2 tbsp water

FOR THE FILLING
40 g (1½ oz) butter
675 g (1½ lb) onions, thinly sliced
1 tbsp olive oil
2 eggs
2 egg yolks
150 ml (¼ pt) single cream
1 tsp caraway seeds
salt and black pepper

To make the pastry, mix together the flour and the butter and rub in the fat with the fingers. Stir in the caraway seeds and salt. Stir in the egg yolk and water and mix to a stiff dough. Wrap in film or foil and chill for at least 30 minutes.

Roll out the pastry to line a 20 cm (8 in) flan case. Trim the edges and prick the base. Cover the base with foil or greaseproof paper and weight with dried beans. Bake the pastry "blind" in the oven (200°C/400°F/gas mark 6) for ten minutes. Remove the beans and paper and bake the pastry case for a further five minutes. Reduce the oven heat (180°C/350°F/gas mark 4).

To make the filling, melt the butter and oil in a pan and fry the onions over low heat until they are soft and just beginning to colour. Remove from the heat.

Beat together the eggs, egg yolks and cream, stir in the caraway seeds and season with salt and pepper. Pour over the onions and stir with a wooden spoon. Pour the mixture into the partly-baked flan case and bake in the oven for 25 minutes, until the custard has set. Serve warm or cool.

*To serve 4 to 6*

# Tagliatelle with parsley sauce

*Serve with a colourful salad of grilled red and yellow peppers, or
tomatoes sprinkled with chopped basil and sunflower seeds.*

450 g (1 lb) fresh green tagliatelle
3 tbsp olive oil
6 spring onions, thinly sliced
4 cloves garlic, finely chopped
350 g (12 oz) button mushrooms, thinly sliced
1 cup chopped curly-leaved parsley
salt and black pepper
grating of nutmeg
150 ml (¼ pt) crème fraîche
225 g (8 oz) feta cheese, crumbled

Cook the tagliatelle in boiling, salted water until it is just tender. Drain and keep warm.

Meanwhile, heat the oil in a pan and fry the onions over medium heat until translucent. Add the garlic and cook for a further one minute. Add the mushrooms, stir well, cover and simmer over a low heat for five minutes. Carefully stir in the parsley, to avoid breaking up the mushrooms, and season with salt and pepper and nutmeg. Add the *crème fraîche* and heat through.

Turn the tagliatelle into a warm serving dish, pour on the sauce and toss well. Sprinkle on the cheese. Serve with crusty bread.

*To serve 4*

Caraway

Garlic

Curled parsley

# VEGETABLES & SALADS

Vegetables and salads that grow side-by-side with herbs in gardens have a natural affinity with them at the table, too. Add a sprig or two of herbs to the water when steaming vegetables. If you deep-fry vegetables in a crisp batter, toss them in chopped herbs before serving, and pep up a "plain" green salad with a sprinkling of mixed herb leaves.

## Apple and mint sambal

*Made in moments, this sharp, crunchy fruit dish is good served
ice-cold with grilled meat or fish.*

2 lemons
4 large dessert apples, cored
and thinly sliced
4 tbsp chopped mint
salt

Halve the lemons and cut two very thin slices. Reserve. Grate the rind and squeeze the juice from the remainder.

Put the apples in a bowl and immediately (to prevent them from discolouring) add the lemon juice and grated rind. Just before serving, stir in the mint and season with salt. Serve chilled, decorated with the lemon slices, cut in half.

*To serve 4*

## Fenugreek carrots

*This is a quick and easy way to add a little zest to carrots served
as an accompanying vegetable.*

675 g (1½ lb) small carrots, trimmed
4 tbsp olive oil
1 onion, finely chopped
1 clove garlic, finely chopped
1 tsp ground fenugreek seeds
1 tbsp red wine vinegar
2 tbsp orange juice
4 tbsp water
large pinch of paprika
salt and black pepper
1 tbsp orange rind
1 tsp chopped chervil

If small carrots are unavailable, cut the vegetable into 7.5 cm (3 in) slices. Heat the oil in a pan and sauté the onion over medium heat until translucent. Stir in the garlic and fenugreek seeds, add the carrots and cook for two minutes. Add the wine vinegar, orange juice and water, and season with paprika, salt and pepper. Cover the pan and simmer very gently for 15 minutes, until the carrots are just tender.

Shake the pan occasionally and make sure that it is not drying out.

Sprinkle with the orange rind and chopped chervil, and serve hot.

*To serve 4*

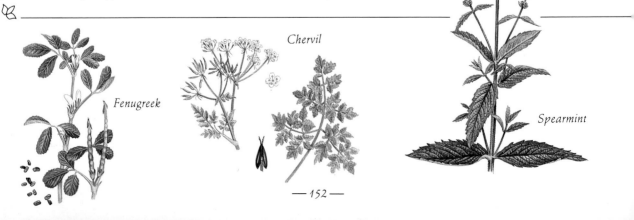

*Chervil*

*Fenugreek*

*Spearmint*

# Nasturtium-flower salad

*Use dramatic red, yellow and orange nasturtium flowers as
"containers" for a creamy salad.*

225 g (8 oz) cream cheese
6 tbsp crème fraîche
40 g (1½ oz) red lumpfish roe
1 tsp grated orange rind
1 tbsp orange juice

2 tbsp chopped lemon balm
1 tbsp snipped chives
12 nasturtium flowers, washed and
dried and stamens removed
salad leaves, to serve

Beat together the cream cheese and
crème fraîche. Fold in the lumpfish
roe, orange rind, orange juice and
herbs. Spoon into the flowers.

*To serve 4*

# Cous-cous and coriander salad

*The cous-cous grains absorb the flavour of the herb dressing and form
the base for the other principal ingredients.*

150 g (6 oz) pre-cooked cous-cous
juice of ½ orange
3 tbsp olive oil
3 tbsp chopped coriander leaves
salt and black pepper
300 ml (½ pt) boiling water
2 oranges
7.5 cm (3 in) piece of cucumber
4 tomatoes, quartered
3 eggs, hard-boiled and quartered
can of anchovy fillets, drained and
halved lengthways
12 black olives
1 tbsp pine nuts
coriander sprigs, to garnish

FOR THE SAUCE
150 ml (¼ pt) Greek-style yoghurt
juice of ½ orange
2 cloves garlic, crushed
3 tbsp olive oil
2 tbsp chopped coriander
large pinch of ground coriander
salt and pepper

Line a sieve with muslin, tip in the
cous-cous and run through with
cold water. Drain well and transfer
the cous-cous to a large bowl.

Mix together the orange juice,
the olive oil and chopped coriander
and season well with salt and
pepper. Pour the dressing over the
grains and mix well. Pour on the
boiling water and stir gently as the
grains swell. Stir frequently as the
grains double in size. Transfer the
cous-cous to a large serving dish.

Peel and slice the oranges. Thinly
slice cucumber and arrange the
slices and oranges over the cous-
cous, then arrange the tomato and

egg wedges, the anchovies and the
olives. Sprinkle with the pine nuts,
cover and chill.

To make the sauce, mix together
the yoghurt, orange juice, garlic,
oil, chopped coriander and ground
coriander and season to taste with
salt and pepper.

To serve, garnish the salad with
the fresh coriander and serve the
sauce separately.

*To serve 6 to 8*

Nasturtium

# DESSERTS & SWEET TREATS

Take a basket into the garden or reach out to the windowbox and gather the youngest, freshest herbs to flavour creamy desserts and syrups. Pick the most perfect flower specimens of sweet violets, marjoram and borage to turn into edible sugar-frosted decorations.

## Rose-petal junket

*Junket, or "swaying cream" as it was also known, was as popular in the eighteenth century as yoghurt is today.*

*600 ml (1 pt) full-cream milk*
*1 tbsp rose-petal caster sugar (see page 159)*
*1 plain junket tablet, powdered*
*2 tbsp triple rosewater*
*250 ml (8 fl oz) crème fraîche*
*crystallized rose petals, to decorate (see page 156)*

Heat the milk and sugar to 37°C (98°F), stirring once or twice. Remove from the heat and stir in the powdered junket tablet and the rosewater. Pour into a pretty glass dish and leave, uncovered, for about 30 minutes, until the dessert is just set. Once the junket is set,

carefully spread the *crème fraîche* over the top and decorate with crystallized rose petals.

The dessert is delicious served with fresh raspberries or strawberries, or with lightly cooked blackcurrants.

*To serve 4*

## Bergamot fruit salad

*The fragrant leaves of this versatile herb flavour the syrup and the bright red, shaggy flowers decorate the dish.*

*75 g (3 oz) caster sugar*
*150 ml (¼ pt) water*
*juice of 2 oranges*
*4–6 bergamot leaves*
*225 g (8 oz) blackcurrants, stripped from stalks*
*225 g (8 oz) strawberries, hulled*
*225 g (8 oz) raspberries, hulled*
*2 or 3 bergamot flowers, to decorate*
*scented pelargonium leaves, to decorate*

Put the sugar, water, orange juice and bergamot leaves into a pan over low heat. Stir occasionally until the sugar has dissolved, then bring to the boil for five minutes to reduce the syrup. Discard the bergamot leaves, add the blackcurrants and return to the boil. Simmer for 5 minutes. Remove from the heat and set aside the solution to cool.

Stir in the strawberries and raspberries, pour into a decorative glass dish and decorate with the bergamot flowers and scented pelargonium leaves.

*To serve 4–6*

Wild marjoram

Sweet violet

Bergamot

# Citrus icebox dessert

*Lemon-scented geranium leaves add a subtle flavour and fragrance
to this quick and easy dessert, which may be served frozen or chilled.*

*grated zest and juice of 2 oranges*
*grated zest and juice of 1 lemon*
*3–4 lemon-scented geranium leaves*
*150 g (6 oz) unsalted butter, at room
temperature*
*150 g (6 oz) caster sugar*
*3 eggs, separated*
*16 sponge finger biscuits*

Line a 450 g (1 lb) loaf pan. Infuse the zest and juice of the oranges and lemon in a bowl with the scented geranium leaves for 30 minutes.

Whisk the butter and sugar until light and foamy, then whisk in the egg yolks one at a time. Discard the herb leaves and gradually whisk the fruit juice into the egg mixture. Whisk the egg whites until stiff, then fold them into the mixture. Arrange alternating layers of sponge fingers and fruit mixture in the pan, finishing with sponge fingers. Wrap in foil and freeze for at least 3 hours. Serve the dessert frozen, or remove it to the refrigerator for 1 hour, and serve it chilled. Decorate the top with scented geranium leaves.

*To serve 6*

*Scented-leaved
pelargoniums*

*Apothecary's
rose*

# BAKING DAY

Chopped fresh herbs and pungent seeds impart their fragrance to baked goods – from wholewheat bread and scones to crisp, crunchy savoury cookies. And for a delectable tea-time treat, try rose-petal preserves. These are a few of the many and various ways herbs can add interest to baking day.

## Ginger shortbread

*Chopped crystallized ginger in melt-in-the-mouth shortbread*
*creates a delicious variation of this traditional tea-time favourite.*

*350 g (12 oz) flour, plus extra*
*for dusting*
*1 tsp ground ginger*
*salt*
*175 g (6 oz) butter*
*50 g (2 oz) icing sugar*
*3 rounded tbsp set honey*
*100 g (4 oz) crystallized*
*ginger, finely chopped*
*golden caster sugar, for dusting*

Sift together the flour, ground ginger and salt. Rub in the butter and stir in the sugar. Mix in the honey and chopped crystallized ginger and form it into a stiff dough. Knead lightly in the bowl.

Halve the dough and roll out each piece on a lightly floured board to make a 20 cm (8 in) circle. Transfer the rounds to baking sheets, mark each one into eight wedges and prick the top with a fork.

Bake (160°C/325°F/gas mark 3) for 15 to 20 minutes, until crisp and golden brown. Sprinkle with caster sugar and leave to cool slightly. Transfer to a wire rack to cool completely.

*To make 16 slices*

## Crystallizing flowers, petals and leaves

*Select only flowers that you know are edible – borage, pot marigold, sweet marjoram, thyme, sweet Cicely, elder flower, sweet violet and rose are examples – and decorative herb leaves such as lemon balm, mints, lemon verbena and sweet Cicely.*

*Cut clustered flowers such as those of marjoram into small sprays. Pull off each rose petal separately and cut all individual flowers from their stalks. Cut herbs into small sprays or pull off individual leaves. Whisk an egg white until it is just frothy and, with a small camel-hair paintbrush, paint every part of every surface of the plant material, to cover it completely and exclude the air. Lightly sprinkle on caster sugar, again to cover the surface completely.*

*Spread the sugared flowers, petals and leaves on waxed or greaseproof paper and leave in a warm, dry place to dry for at least two hours. Store in single layers between paper in an airtight tin.*

# Dill-seed cookies

*To make these savoury cookies even more spicy, substitute cumin
seed or caraway seeds for the milder dill.*

*50 g (2 oz) flour, plus extra for dusting
25 g (1 oz) butter, plus extra for greasing
salt
pinch of cayenne pepper
1 tsp dill seeds
75 g (3 oz) Cheddar cheese, grated
1 egg yolk, lightly beaten
1 tbsp iced water*

Sift the flour into a bowl and rub in the butter. Stir in the salt, cayenne, dill seeds and grated cheese. Stir in the egg yolk and mix to a soft but firm dough with the water. Wrap in foil or plastic film and chill for at least one hour.

Roll out the dough on a lightly floured board to a thickness of about 3 mm (⅛ in) and cut into rounds with a 4 cm (1½ in) pastry cutter. Gather up the trimmings, roll out again and cut out more rounds. Place well apart on a greased baking sheet and bake (200°C/400°F/gas mark 6) for seven minutes, until golden brown. Leave to cool slightly on the baking sheet, then transfer to a wire rack to cool.

*To make about 20 cookies*

# Fennel bread

*There is nothing to beat the smell of fresh baked bread, except when
the bread has the added fragrance of herbs.*

*1 litre (1¾ pt) tepid water
1 tbsp dried yeast
1.5 kg (3¼ lb) wholewheat flour, plus
extra for dusting
3 tbsp salt
40 g (1½ oz) butter, plus extra
for greasing
3 tbsp chopped fennel
milk, for brushing
3 tbsp fennel seeds, for topping*

Pour 300 ml (½ pt) of the water into a bowl and sprinkle on the yeast. Leave in a warm place for about ten minutes, until it is frothy.

Sift the flour and salt into a large mixing bowl and tip in any bran remaining in the sieve. Rub in the butter until the mixture resembles fine breadcrumbs, and stir in the chopped fennel. Gradually pour on the yeast liquid and the remainder of the warm water, stirring constantly, and mix until the dough leaves the sides of the bowl. Turn the dough on to a floured board and knead until it is smooth and elastic; or use the dough hook of an electric mixer.

Divide the dough into three equal parts. Press it into three greased 1 kg (2¼ lb) loaf tins and cover with greased foil or plastic film. Leave in a warm place for 60 to 90 minutes, until the dough has risen to the tops of the tins.

Brush the tops of the loaves with milk and sprinkle with the fennel seeds. Bake in the oven (220°C/425°F/gas mark 7) for 40 minutes, until the bread is brown and well cooked. It should sound hollow when the tins are tapped on the underside.

Turn the bread out of the tins and cool on a wire rack.

*To make three 1 kg (2¼ lb) loaves*

*Dill*

*Borage*

# AROMATIC PRESERVES

This selection from the many jams and jellies, syrups and cordials, pickles and other preserves that capture the characteristics of both sweet and pungent herbs includes flavoured sugars and a Victorian favourite, violet honey.

## Dill pickles

*Serve these sweet-and-sour pickled cucumbers with grilled fish such as herring and mackerel, or with bread and cheese, or pâté, ploughman's-style.*

2 ridge cucumbers
300 ml (½ pt) cider vinegar
75 g (3 oz) sugar
½ tsp salt
6 black peppercorns
4 cloves
½ tsp mustard seeds
1 tsp dill seeds
2 sprigs dill leaves

For the spiced vinegar, put vinegar, sugar, salt, peppercorns, cloves, mustard and dill seeds in a glass or enamel pan, bring slowly to the boil and boil two to three minutes. Cover, set aside for two hours.

Trim the cucumbers and cut them into 6 mm (¼ in) slices. Pack them into cooled, sterilized jars.

Return the pan to the heat, bring the vinegar to the boil, cool it slightly and strain it over the cucumbers. Put one sprig of dill into each jar. Close the jars with vinegar-proof lids, label and store in a cool place. The pickle will be ready to eat after about seven days.

*To make 900 g (2 lb)*

## Violet honey

*Flower-scented honey was popular in Victorian times. You can use it as a spread, to flavour sauces, or stir into yoghurt.*

225 g (8 oz) clear honey
½ cup sweet violet petals

Pour the honey into the top of a double boiler, or a bowl over a pan of simmering water. Stir in the violet petals, cover and heat for 30 minutes. Remove from the heat, and leave to infuse for seven days.

Reheat the flavoured honey – it will then be easier to pour – and strain it back into the jar.

*To make 225 g (8 oz)*

VARIATION
Rosemary honey, made in a similar way, by infusing three or four sprays of rosemary leaves, makes a delicious breakfast-time preserve.

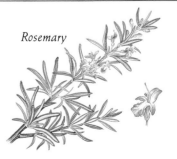

*Rosemary*

# Sage and cider jelly

*Brush this sweet-and-sour preserve on ham, pork or duck to glaze the
meat before cooking, or serve it as an accompaniment to roast or grilled meats.*

*1 kg (2¼ lb) cooking apples, sliced
juice of 1 lemon
750 ml (1¼ pt) water
750 ml (1¼ pt) medium cider
6 sprays sage leaves
775 g (1½ lb) sugar approximately (see
method)
5 tbsp chopped sage*

Put the apples, lemon juice, water
and cider into a large pan, add the
sprays of sage and bring slowly to
the boil, stirring occasionally until
the sugar has dissolved. Boil for 25
minutes or until the apples are
tender. Strain the fruit and liquid
through a jelly bag and leave it to
drain for several hours. Do not
squeeze the bag to hasten the
process, or the jelly may be cloudy.

Measure the strained fruit juice
and weigh 800 g of sugar to each 1
litre (1 lb sugar to each 1 pint). Pour
the fruit juice back into the pan,
add the sugar and stir occasionally
over low heat until it dissolves.
Increase the heat, bring to the boil
and fast-boil for ten minutes. Skim
off any scum that rises to the top.

To test for set, put a little of the

preserve on to a cold saucer and
leave it to cool. It should wrinkle
when pushed with a finger. When
the preserve has reached setting
point, remove the pan from the
heat, stir in the chopped sage and
leave for about five minutes. Then
stir the preserve again, and pour it
into warm, sterilized jars. Cover
with waxed discs and transparent
paper covers, or with screw or
clip-on lids, label and store in a
cool, dry place.

*To make about 1.5 kg (3¼ lb)*

VARIATIONS
Using apple jelly as the "carrier"
you can make a variety of herb
jellies in a similar way. You can, if
you wish, replace some of the cider
with water.

## Flavoured sugars

*Keep a range of granulated, caster and
icing sugars in small, lidded jars and
flavour them with, variously, rose
petals, rosemary sprays, bay leaves,
lavender flowers, scented pelargonium
leaves and sprigs of thyme. The
amount of herbs you use will depend
on the volume of sugar, and the
intensity of flavour you require.
Experimenting to "find your level" is
one of the joys of the kitchen!*

*Before use sieve sugar that may
contain, for example, fallen lavender
flowers.*

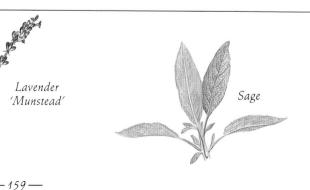

Lavender
'Munstead'

Sage

# COSMETICS

In the 17th and 18th centuries, every large household had its still-room for making perfumes and potions, scents and soaps, scented washballs and skin lotions. Many of these recipes gained world renown – like the famous Hungary water for whitening and cleansing the skin. Herbal cosmetics are simple to make at home and can be just as effective as and cheaper than commercial products.

*An infusion of marigold petals used as a hair rinse can lighten fair hair.*

*Store herbal cosmetics in dark containers or away from damaging light.*

| APPLICATION | HERB | PART USED | HOW TO USE |
|---|---|---|---|
| Baths | Chamomile | flowers | Relaxing – add an infusion |
| | | oil | Add a few drops |
| | Dandelion | leaves | Cleansing – add an infusion |
| | Eucalyptus | oil | Add a few drops for muscle aches |
| | Jasmine | oil | Add a few drops for stimulating baths |
| | Lavender/ | oil | Add a few drops for relaxing baths |
| | Marjoram | flowers | Use in tincture as body splash |
| | Lemon balm | leaves | Add an infusion for a relaxing bath |
| | Marigold | petals | A cleansing and astringent infusion |
| | Oats | meal | Add a sachet filled with oatmeal |
| | Peppermint | leaves | Add an infusion for a stimulating bath |
| | Rosemary | oil | Add to stimulating baths |
| | | leaves | Use infusion in bath water |
| Cleansers | Chamomile | flowers | In facial steam baths or lotions |
| | | oil | Add drops to oatmeal face packs |
| | Lavender | flowers | In facial steamers |
| | | flower water | As lotion |
| | Lovage | seeds | Use infusion as a wash and also as deodorant |
| | Oats | meal | Use as a facial scrub |
| | Peppermint | leaves | In facial steamers |
| | Thyme | leaves | In facial steamers |
| | | essential oil | Add a few drops to lotions or in steamers |
| | Sweet violet | flowers/ leaves | In facial steamers or infusion as wash |
| | Yarrow | flowers | In creams and lotions |
| Falling hair | Southernwood | leaves | Infusion as rinse for hair loss |
| Hair conditioners | Birch | leaves | Infusion |
| | Elder | berries | Strained decoction |
| | Marjoram | aerial parts | Infusion |
| | | oil | Add a few drops to water or sweet almond oil; rinse hair well |
| | Nettles | tops or root | Infusion or decoction, rub in well |
| | Marshmallow | leaves | Use the infusion for dry hair |
| | Rosemary | leaves | Use the infusion |
| | | oil | Add a few drops to water or sweet almond oil; rinse hair well |
| | Thyme | leaves | Use the infusion |
| | | oil | Add a few drops to water or sweet almond oil; rinse hair well |

| Application | Herb | Part used | How to use |
|---|---|---|---|
| Hair rinse | Chamomile | flowers | Use the infusion for fair hair |
| | Lavender | rinse | Use the infusion for greasy hair |
| | Lemon | juice | Use the infusion for fair hair |
| | Nettles | leaves/tops | Use the infusion for dandruff |
| | Peppermint | leaves | Use the infusion or decoction with vinegar for greasy hair |
| | Rosemary/ Sage | leaves | Use the infusion for dark hair and dandruff |
| Hand cream | Chamomile/ Elder/Lavender | flowers | Use for creams and lotions |
| Herbs for dry skin | Chamomile | flowers | Use in creams |
| | | oil | Add to creams |
| | Comfrey | leaves | Use in creams and infused oils |
| | Marigold | petals | Use in creams and infused oils |
| Herbs for oily skin | Agrimony | leaves | Use infusion as lotion |
| | Fennel | seeds | Use infusion as lotion with witch hazel |
| | Lady's mantle | leaves | Use infusion as lotion with witch hazel |
| | Marigold | petals | Use infusion as lotion |
| Moisturisers | Chamomile | flowers | Combine infusion with almond oil to make emulsion |
| | | oil | Add a few drops to almond oil and cocoa butter base |
| | Rose | petals | Use in creams |
| | | flower water | Mix with almond oil or glycerin |
| Scented water cologne | Lemon balm | leaves | Use the tincture or infusion |
| | Orange | rind | Use the infusion |
| | | flower water | Use undiluted or combine with other scented oils |
| | Rose | petals | Use the infusion |
| | | flower water | Use undiluted or combine with other scented oils |
| | | oil | Add a dew drops to water or alcohol |
| | Rosemary | leaves | Use the infusion |
| | | oil | Add to water or alcohol |
| Shampoo | Nettle | leaves | Add to any shampoo to treat dandruff |
| | Rosemary | leaves | Add to any shampoo |
| | Soapwort | leaves | For dry hair or as a basis for soap mixtures |
| Toners | Agrimony | leaves | Use the infusion as a face wash |
| | Fennel | seeds | Use the infusion as a face wash |
| | | essential oil | Add a few drops to skin lotions |
| | Lady's mantle | aerial parts | Infusion as face wash |
| | Lavender | flower water | Combine with witch hazel |
| | Marigold | petals | Use the infusion as a face wash |
| | Mint | leaves | In vinegars/infusions as face wash |
| | Peppermint | oil | Add drops to face wash |
| | Witch hazel | distilled extract | Combine with rose- or lavender-water |
| | Yarrow | flowers | Combine infusion with distilled witch hazel |
| Anti-wrinkle | Comfrey | leaves | In creams or infused oils |

*Cucumber slices can revitalize tired eyes.*

*A pestle and mortar are as useful in the bathroom as they are in the kitchen.*

# BATH PREPARATIONS

Taking a bath can be all things to all people. Depending on your choice of herbs a bath or shower can help you face the rigours of the day or relax afterwards. Not only that, a bath can soften the skin and assist the body's natural oils to replenish.
By making your own bath products you can be sure of using only pure ingredients, and also match the herbs to your needs. Keep a range of bath oils and gels, soap and sachets in the bathroom cupboard and make your selection day by day.

## Herbal bath splash

*Midway between a bath oil and a soap, splashes are made by blending a herbal infusion with grated pure Castile soap.*

*1 handful of blackberry or eucalyptus leaves*
*1 litre (1¾ pt) soft water, rainwater if possible*
*5 tbsp grated Castile soap*

Put the leaves into a pan, pour on the water, bring to the boil, cover and simmer for 15 minutes. Remove the pan from the heat and leave to infuse for two hours.

Strain the infusion, discard the leaves and return the liquid to the pan. Bring to the boil and whisk in the grated soap. Whisk until it has dissolved, then remove from the heat and set aside to cool.

Pour into bottles, cover, label and store in the refrigerator. Use as a soft soap.

*To make about 1 litre (1¾ pt)*

## Floral bath gels

*These are made with fresh or dried flowers such as lavender, thyme and chamomile ground to a paste or powder.*

*3 tbsp fresh or dried flowers, picked from the stalks*
*150 ml (¼ pt) water*
*12 tbsp grated Castile soap*
*3–4 drops oil of lavender or thyme (optional)*

Pound the flowers with a pestle and mortar until they form a paste or powder. Put the water into a small pan, bring to the boil and whisk in the grated soap until the soap has dissolved, then remove pan from the heat. Stir in the flowers and, if you wish, the oil.

Leave to cool, then pour into bottles, cover, label and store in the refrigerator. Use as a soft soap.

*To make about 250 ml (8 fl oz)*

*Lavender 'stoechas'*

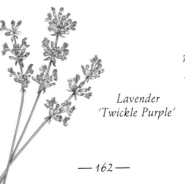

*Lavender 'Twickle Purple'*

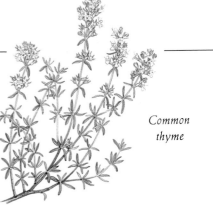

*Common thyme*

# Frothy bath oil

*This is the ultimate in bath preparations which will feed, soothe
and moisturize the skin.*

2 eggs
250 ml (8 fl oz) olive oil
150 ml (¼ pt) corn oil
150 ml (¼ pt) almond oil
2 tbsp clear honey
250 ml (8 fl oz) milk
100 ml (4 fl oz) vodka
1 tbsp mild soap flakes
3 drops essential oil, to choice

Whisk together the eggs, vegetable oils and honey. Add the milk, vodka, soap flakes and essential oil, still whisking. Pour into bottles, cover, label and store in the refrigerator.

Add one tablespoonful under the tap when running the water for a warm bath.

*To make about 1 litre (1¾ pt)*

BATH OILS AND VINEGARS
Herbal oils and vinegars (see page 146) can usefully travel between kitchen and bathroom. Add about one tablespoonful of oil or up to half a cupful of vinegar flavoured with mint, thyme, wild marjoram, or what you will, to a warm bath. And then luxuriate in its toning and restorative effect.

*Bowles mint*

*Variegated
apple mint*

*Wild
marjoram*

# Honey and herb soap

*If you don't want to make your own soap – a messy procedure – add
your individual choice of herbal oils to pure Castile soap.*

10 tbsp grated Castile soap
½ tsp olive oil
2 tsp clear honey
2–3 drops essential oil, such as
rosemary

Put the grated soap in the top of a
double boiler, a bowl over a pan of
simmering water, or a bowl in the
microwave set on low power. Melt
the soap. Stir in the olive oil, a drop
or two at a time. Stir in the honey
and essential oil, then remove from
the heat. Continue to stir until

the mixture is well blended.
   Pour into moulds such as waxed
paper cake cases, cover and leave
undisturbed to become hard – this
may take up to two weeks.
Unmould and wrap in greaseproof
paper to store.
   *To make 1 tablet of soap*

# Elizabethan washballs

*Surely one of our most evocative links with the past, individual
soaps perfumed with roses.*

150 g (6 oz) grated pure Castile soap
150 ml (¼ pt) rosewater, plus extra for
brushing

Melt the soap over simmering
water (*see Honey and herb soap*) and
stir in the rosewater. Whisk until
the mixture is well blended.
Remove from the heat, cool slightly
and, using a teaspoon, form into

small balls. Dry on greaseproof
paper in a warm place.
   Moisten a ball of cotton wool
with rosewater and polish the soap
balls once they are hard.
   *To make about 250 g (10 oz)*

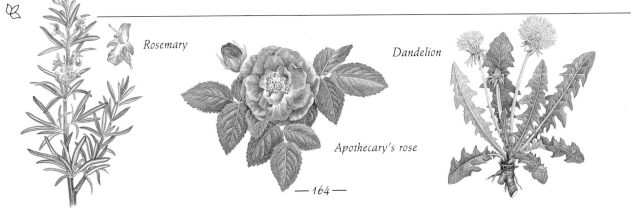

*Rosemary*

*Dandelion*

*Apothecary's rose*

## Herbs to use in the bath

*Infuse a handful of leaves or flowers in 1 litre (1¾ pt) boiling water, then add to a warm bath.*

| PLANT | PART OF PLANT | EFFECT |
|---|---|---|
| Blackberry | Infusion of leaves | Soothing to the skin |
| Chamomile | Infusion of leaves and flowers | Soothing |
| Comfrey | Infusion of leaves or decoction of root | Healing |
| Dandelion | Infusion of leaves | Cleansing |
| Elder | Infusion of leaves | Healing and stimulating |
| Eucalyptus | Infusion of leaves | Cleansing and soothing |
| Horsetail | Infusion of leaves | Healing |
| Lady's mantle | Infusion of leaves | Soothing |
| Lavender | Infusion of flowers | Cleansing and deodorizing |
| Lemon verbena | Infusion of leaves | Stimulating |
| Lovage | Infusion of leaves | Cleansing and deodorizing |
| Mint | Infusion of leaves | Healing and cleansing |
| Nettles | Infusion of leaves | Cleansing |
| Pot marigold | Infusion of leaves | Healing, especially thread veins and varicose veins |
| Rosemary | Infusion of leaves | Stimulating |
| Thyme | Infusion of leaves and flowers | Stimulating and cleansing |
| Yarrow | Infusion of leaves | Astringent and cleansing |

# Bath sachets

*Resist the temptation to toss a handful of aromatic herbs into the bath. You will emerge with bits and pieces clinging to your body.*

If you like the hands-on approach of using fresh or dried herbs, rather than an infusion, it is better to tie the leaves or flowers into a piece of muslin or cheesecloth and suspend the sachet beneath the hot water tap. Another way, a development of the medieval pomander principle, is to pack the herbs into a perforated tea infuser and swish under the hot tap.

*Lady's mantle*

*Lovage*

# COSMETIC TREATMENTS

Making your own skin preparations is itself a pleasurable pastime. Just to stir a handful of pot marigold petals into a bowl of steaming water is both invigorating and calming, an indirect form of aromatherapy. You may wish to perfume cleansing, moisturizing and nourishing creams with a herbal infusion or oil, to pamper and soothe your skin. This section suggests many cosmetic and therapeutic recipes using a blend of aromatic herbs to help you care for your skin, or just to allow a little self-indulgence.

## Lavender cleansing cream

*Lavender refreshes and feeds the skin. Suitable for dry skin, this rich cleansing cream helps replenish natural oils.*

*6 tbsp almond oil*
*10 tbsp grated white wax*
*3 tbsp lavender water*
*½ tsp cider vinegar*
*1 drop oil of lavender (optional)*

Melt the oil and wax in the top of a double boiler or a bowl over a pan of simmering water. Remove from the heat, cool slightly, then whisk in the lavender water, cider vinegar and oil of lavender if you use it. Pour the cream into a lidded jar. Do not refrigerate.

Smooth the fragrant milk over your face and neck, avoiding the area around the eyes, and remove with cotton wool.
*To make about 250 ml (8 fl oz)*

## Chamomile cleansing milk

*With its lemon juice content, this preparation is especially suitable for normal and oily skins.*

*150 ml (¼ pt) buttermilk*
*2 tbsp lemon juice*
*3 tbsp chamomile tisane*

Whisk the ingredients together until well blended. Pour into jars and store in the refrigerator.

Soak a pad of cotton wool in the preparation and wipe it lightly over your face and neck, avoiding the area around the eyes.
*To make 225 ml (7 fl oz)*

*Chamomile*

*Lavender 'stoechas'*

# Rose-petal cold cream

*Use this as a moisturizing night cream. It is suitable for all skin types.*

*1½ cups approximately of damask or
other scented rose petals
6 tbsp olive oil
1½ tbsp purified beeswax
about 1 tsp distilled water*

Pick over the rose petals and discard any blemished ones. Put the olive oil in the top of a double boiler or in a bowl over a pan of simmering water, and heat gently. Stir in as many rose petals as the oil can take up. Remove from the heat. Cover and infuse for seven days.

Strain the oil through a nylon sieve, pressing the petals against the sides to extract as much of the oil as possible.

Melt the beeswax in a bowl over simmering water then gradually stir in the fragrant oil. Remove from the heat and add the water, drop by drop, until the cream has the consistency you like. Pour the cream into a pot, cover and label.

*To make 120 ml (4½ fl oz)*

# Floral hand gel

*Lavender flowers and chamomile flowers have similar and beneficial
properties, to cleanse, soothe and soften the skin. Apply this hand gel
sparingly, rubbing it well into the skin.*

*300 ml (½ pt) petroleum jelly
2 tbsp lavender flowers,
stripped from the stalks
1 cup chamomile flowers,
approximately*

Heat the petroleum jelly in a double boiler or a bowl over a pan of simmering water. Stir in as many of the flowers as the jelly can take up. Cover and simmer for one hour, stirring occasionally. Remove from the heat, and leave to cool.

Strain through a nylon sieve, pressing the flowers against the sides to extract as much of the volatile oils as possible.

Pour the fragrant jelly into pots, cover and label.

*To make 300 ml (½ pt)*

## *Massaging oils*

*Create your own scented oils using a
combination of these vegetable oils and other
herbal products.*

Almond oil
Apricot oil
Avocado oil
Beeswax, purified
Cocoa butter, melted
Coconut oil (a
  saturated oil
  which sets hard)
Corn oil
Glycerin
Lanolin
Maize oil
Peach oil

Peanut oil
Safflower oil
Soya oil
Sunflower oil
Wheatgerm oil

# Lavender-flower lotion

*Splash on this gentle toning lotion to tauten and refresh the skin.*

5 tbsp lavender water
5 tbsp witch-hazel
5 tbsp lemon juice, strained
through muslin
2–3 drops oil of lavender

Pour all the ingredients into a bottle, close it with a cap or cork and shake it vigorously. Shake well before use.

*To make 225 ml (7 fl oz)*

# Mint astringent

*This gentle astringent soothes the skin and helps improve the complexion.*

2 tbsp chopped mint
4 tbsp cider vinegar
600 ml (1 pt) distilled water

Put the mint and vinegar in a lidded jar, cover and leave to infuse for seven days. Strain and pour on the distilled water. Mix well.

Bottle the astringent, cover and label. Shake well before using.

*To make 600 ml (1 pt)*

# Dandelion oil

*This old country recipe employs the volatile oils in dandelion leaves to bleach freckles and other skin blotches. Use no more than twice a day.*

6 young dandelion leaves, chopped
6 tbsp castor oil

Place chopped leaves and oil in a small glass or enamel pan over low heat, bring to simmering point and simmer for 15 minutes. Remove from heat, cover and infuse four or

five hours. Strain through a nylon sieve, pressing the leaves against the sides to extract as much oil as possible. Bottle, cover and label.

*To make 6 tbsp*

## *Herbs for the skin*

*This chart will help you to select the most beneficial herbs to use as infusions and in lotions.*

| Herb | Effect |
|------|--------|
| Chamomile | Cleansing, cooling, soothing |
| Comfrey | Emollient |
| Dandelion | Bleaching, drying |
| Fennel | Astringent |
| Horseradish | Bleaching, drying |
| Horsetail | Astringent |
| Lady's mantle | Astringent |
| Lavender | Antiseptic, stimulating, toning |
| Marigold | Astringent, cleansing, toning, healing |

| Herb | Effect |
|------|--------|
| Marshmallow | Emollient |
| Mint | Astringent, cleansing, soothing |
| Parsley | Lightening |
| Rosemary | Cleansing, stimulating |
| Thyme | Cleansing, antiseptic, toning |
| Violet | Cleansing, emollient |
| Witch-hazel | Astringent, healing |
| Yarrow | Cleansing, toning |

# Facial steam

*Choose the herb according to your skin type. This fragrant steam will
be helpful in cleansing both dry and greasy skins.*

*2 cups fresh herb or 1 cup dried herb,
such as lavender, peppermint or thyme
hot water (not boiling)*

Place the herbs in a bowl, pour over
the hot water and stir well. Drape a
towel over your head to trap the
steam, and steam your face for five
minutes.

If your skin is dry, nourish it by
massaging in a little moisturizing
cream after steaming.

*To make one facial steam*

# Herbal face pack

*Spread this soothing face pack over the skin, avoiding the area
around the eyes and mouth. Place a slice of cucumber over each eye and rest
for ten minutes. Wash off with warm water, or a herbal infusion.*

*2 tbsp plain yoghurt
2 tbsp finely chopped herb leaves or
flowers, selected according to skin type
1–2 tbsp fine oatmeal*

Stir the yoghurt and herbs together
until they are well blended. Stir in
just enough of the oatmeal to form
a soft paste and mix well.
  If you need to store the paste,

spoon it into a pot, cover, label and
store in the refrigerator.

*To make about 5 tbsp*

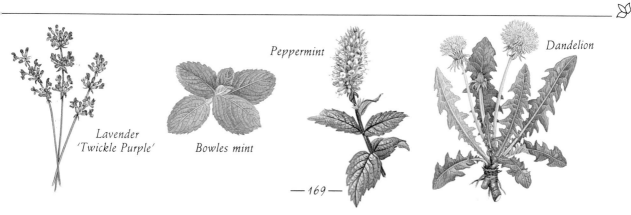

Lavender
'Twickle Purple'

Bowles mint

Peppermint

Dandelion

# FLORAL WATERS & COLOGNES

The image of the "mistress of the pot pourri", familiar to us through paintings and engravings, is one of daylight hours spent in the still-rooms of the great estates, where exotic and alluring fragrances were created.

Although our modern kitchens may lack the specialist equipment used in those days, our gardens are a rich source of fragrant leaves and flowers, and herbalists' shelves are well stocked with essential oils to add more concentrated aromas.

## Lavender water

*This reviving floral water can be used as a body splash after bathing or – as it was in the nineteenth century – sprinkled on a handkerchief and inhaled.*

*2 cups lavender flowers*
*1 litre (1¾ pt) distilled water, boiling*
*2 tbsp vodka*

Put the lavender flowers into a heatproof container, pour on the boiling water and stir well. Cover and leave to infuse for about 48 hours, stirring occasionally.

Strain the liquid through a nylon sieve, pressing the flowers against the sides to extract the maximum fragrance. Stir in the alcohol, pour into bottles, cover and label.

*To make 1 litre (1¾ pt)*

## Floral splash

*This "splash" has a pungent, heady aroma. You can vary the fragrance by substituting other essential oils.*

*4 drops rosemary oil*
*4 drops bergamot oil*
*2 tbsp rosewater*
*300 ml (½ pt) vodka*

Stir all the ingredients together, pour into a bottle, cover and set aside for at least six weeks, shaking every day if possible.

*To make about 300 ml (½ pt)*

*Rosemary*

*Lavender 'Hidcote'*

# Floral toilet fragrance

*Create the fragrance of your choice by using a single flower type or blending two or more.*

4 cups fragrant flowers or petals,
such as chamomile, lavender,
pot marigold, rose, violet
600 ml (1 pt) white wine vinegar
300 ml (½ pt) distilled water

Place the flowers or petals in a heatproof container. Heat the vinegar and water to boiling point, pour over the flowers and stir well. Cover and leave in a warm place for three weeks, stirring at least once a day if possible.

Strain through a nylon sieve, pressing the flowers against the sides to release the maximum fragrance. Pour into bottles, cover, label and store.

*To make 900 ml (1½ pt)*

# Lemon balm and rosemary cologne

*Fresh herbs add a contrasting fragrance to the rosewater and alcohol in this refreshing splash cologne.*

3 tbsp lemon balm
3 tbsp rosemary
strip of thinly-pared orange rind
300 ml (½ pt) rosewater
6 tbsp vodka

Put all the ingredients into a screw-topped jar, cover and shake vigorously. Leave to infuse for two weeks, shaking at least once a day. Strain through a nylon sieve,

pressing the herbs against the sides to extract the maximum fragrance. Pour into a bottle, cover and label. Store in a cool, dark place.

*To make about 400 ml (14 fl oz)*

# Rosewater

*True rosewater is the delightfully fragrant by-product of distilling roses, the process by which rose oil, or attar of roses, is extracted.*

10 cups fragrant rose petals,
traditionally those of damask roses
600 ml (1 pt) distilled water
1 tsp liquid storax
1 tsp tincture of benzoin

Put the rose petals and water into a pan which has a tightly-fitting lid, or cover the pan tightly with foil. Bring the water slowly to the boil, lower the heat and simmer very slowly for two hours. Remove from the heat and leave to infuse for about 48 hours.

Bring the water and the petals to

the boil again, simmer for a further hour, and leave to cool. Strain through a nylon sieve, pressing the petals against the sides to extract the maximum fragrance. Stir in the storax and tincture of benzoin. Pour into bottles, cover and label.

*To make about 450 ml (¾ pt)*

*Chamomile*

*Pot marigold*

*Sweet violet*

# HAIR CARE

A glance along the hair-care counter in a chemist's or drug store will confirm that the practice of using herbs in shampoos, conditioners and tonics is as alive and well today as it has ever been. Folklore abounds with herbal recommendations for hair lighteners and darkeners, strengtheners and improvers; chamomile rinse for fair hair and rosemary for dark tresses are probably among the best known of the country-lore prescriptions. The following recipes use different herbs to suit varying hair types and conditions.

## Horsetail shampoo

*This all-in-one shampoo and conditioner combines the cleansing properties of soapwort root and the conditioning ability of horsetail, sometimes known as the "hair gloss herb".*

*7 tbsp snipped horsetail stems*
*7 tbsp grated dried soapwort root, soaked overnight and drained*
*2 litres (3½ pt) soft water*

Put the horsetail and soapwort into a pan, pour on the water and stir well. Bring to the boil. Cover and boil for 15 minutes. Remove from the heat and leave the mixture to infuse for one hour.

Strain the liquid into bottles, cover and label. Use about 300 ml (½ pt) of the shampoo each time.
*To make 2 litres (3½ pt)*

### Herbs for the hair

| Hair type | Herb |
|---|---|
| Dry | Comfrey, marshmallow |
| Greasy | Lavender, peppermint |
| Dull and lifeless | Fennel, parsley, rosemary, stinging nettle tops, garlic |
| Fair | Chamomile flowers |
| Dark | Comfrey, rosemary, sage, thyme |
| Auburn | Pot marigold petals |
| To treat dandruff | Eau de Cologne mint, elder flowers, parsley, sage, southernwood, thyme |
| General conditioners | Birch leaves, horsetail stems, marjoram, rosemary, thyme, stinging nettle tops |

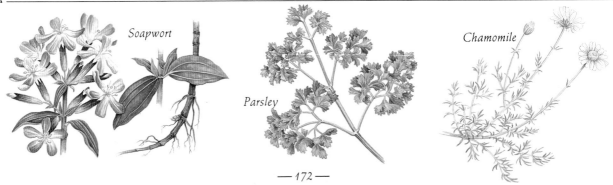

*Soapwort*

*Parsley*

*Chamomile*

# Controlling lotion

*This solution may be just what is needed for all those who say they cannot do a thing with their hair.*

10 tbsp herbal tisane (chosen according to hair type)
1 tbsp eau de Cologne
1 tbsp glycerin

Pour the herbal infusion and eau de Cologne into a bowl and add the glycerin drop by drop, whisking all the time. Pour the lotion into a bottle, cover and label.

Rub a little into the scalp, or comb it through the hair.
*To make 180 ml (5½ fl oz)*

# Garlic conditioner

*With its strong antiseptic properties garlic is a useful aid to healing scalp conditions, and can put the sheen back into dull, lifeless hair. Shampoo your hair with your favourite fragrance after this treatment!*

10 large cloves of garlic, crushed
150 ml (¼ pt) castor oil, hot

Stir the garlic and castor oil thoroughly, cover and infuse for two days. Strain into a bottle, cover and label.
Massage the oil into the scalp,

wrap the head in a towel and leave it for about an hour, then shampoo thoroughly.
*To make about 150 ml (¼ pt)*

# Peppermint rinse

*This aromatic hair rinse is especially beneficial for greasy hair.*

10 tbsp chopped peppermint leaves
1 litre (1¾ pt) soft water
1 litre (1¾ pt) cider vinegar

Put the peppermint leaves in a pan, pour on the water and bring slowly to the boil. Simmer for 15 minutes, remove from the heat and infuse for one hour. Strain the infusion and stir in the vinegar. Pour into bottles, cover and label.
Use about 300 ml (½ pt) of the rinse after shampooing.
*To make about 2 litres (3½ pt)*

*Garlic*

*Peppermint*

# REMEDIES

For many of the world's people, herbs are – even today – the only available medicine, and folk healers still prepare their remedies following centuries-old traditions. In the West, we are more likely to use herbal medicines in the form of chemical extracts – like aspirin, which was originally derived from willow bark, or ephedrine, originally found in the Chinese plant *Ma-huang*. Whole plants can, however, be just as effective as many of these patented extracts: they're gentler, too, with fewer side effects, though caution must be observed.

*Marshmallow's medicinal uses date from ancient times.*

| Ailment | Herb | Application |
|---------|------|-------------|
| Blackheads | Comfrey | Root poultice mixed with marigold infusion; leaf infusion as face wash |
|  | Marigold | Diluted tincture from petals in compress |
| Breath fresheners | Caraway/ Cumin/ Fennel/ Fenugreek/ Lovage | Chew the seeds fresh or dry |
|  | Mint/Parsley | Chew the fresh leaves |
| Bruises | Comfrey | Leaf infusion in compress |
|  | Witch hazel | Distilled extract in compress |
| Burns | Marigold | Dilute petal tincture in compress |
|  | Lavender | Use essential oil diluted in compress or add to St. John's wort infused oil |
|  | St. John's wort | Made from flowering tops, use dilute tincture in compress; apply infused oil directly |
| Colds & flus | Eucalyptus/ Hyssop/ Thyme | Use the essential oil in chest rub/steam inhalation |
|  | Ginger | Decoction of fresh root |
|  | Peppermint | Inhale a few drops of essential oil |
|  | Yarrow | Make an infusion from leaves/flowers |
| Coughs | Angelica | Leaf infusion/tincture |
|  | Garlic | Syrup, steam inhalation |
|  | Hyssop | Dilute essential oil to make chest rub |
|  | Licorice | Root decoction/syrup |
|  | Marshmallow | Use leaves and flowers to make syrup or infusion |
|  | Onion | Syrup from fresh vegetable |
|  | Oregano | Steam inhalation from essential oil |
| Cuts & grazes | Garlic | Poultice from cloves |

| Ailment | Herb | Application |
|---------|------|-------------|
| Abscesses & boils | Comfrey | Root poultice mixed with comfrey-leaf tea |
|  | Fenugreek | Poultice of mashed seeds |
|  | Marshmallow | Root poultice – on its own or combined with slippery elm |
|  | Slippery elm | Poultice made from bark |
| Aches & pains | Birch | Use oil/sap for external massage |
|  | Celery | Infusion from seeds for rheumatism/arthritis |
|  | Lavender | Use flowers or essential oil to make external massage oil |
|  | Rosemary/ Thyme/ Wintergreen | Use leaves or essential oil to make external massage oil |
| Acne | Chamomile | Use flower infusion/tincture as face wash |
|  | Garlic | Rub with fresh clove |
|  | Marigold | Use petal infusion/tincture as face wash |
|  | Rose | Apply a rosewater lotion |
|  | Sage | Make a lotion using leaves |
|  | Witch hazel | Lotion using distilled extract |

| Ailment | Herb | Application | Ailment | Herb | Application |
|---|---|---|---|---|---|
| Cuts & grazes cont. | Marigold | Petal infusion/dilute tincture on compress | Eyes, tired/ irritated | Chamomile | Flower poultice/cold teabag on the eye |
| | St. John's wort | Cream or infused oil from flowering tops | | Cucumber | Raw slices applied |
| | | | | Eyebright | Infusion of whole plant in sterilized eyebath |
| Depression | Jasmine/ Neroli/Rose | Essential oil diluted as massage oil or inhalant | | Fennel | Seed poultice/cold teabag |
| | Lemon balm/ St. John's wort | Aerial parts used in infusion/ tincture | Headaches & migraine | Feverfew | Fresh leaves in sandwich or as infusion/tincture |
| Digestive problems | Catmint | Use aerial parts in an infusion—especially for children | | Lavender/ Peppermint/ Rosemary | Dilute essential oil as a massage for temples |
| | Chamomile | Flower infusion for flatulence | Insect bites & stings | Eucalyptus/ Lavender | Essential oil diluted and applied to sting |
| | Dill/Fennel | Seed infusion for flatulence/ indigestion | | Feverfew | Leaf infusion as wash |
| | Fenugreek | Seed infusion for stomach cramps and upsets | | Lemon balm/ Sage | Fresh leaves applied to sting |
| | Lemon balm | Leaf infusion for nervous stomach upsets | | Onion | Apply slices to sting |
| | Licorice | Root decoction for ulceration/inflammation | | Witch hazel | Apply lotion of distilled extract |
| | Parsley/Sage | Leaf infusion as a stimulant | Mouth & gum disorders | Sweet Cicely | Use diluted tincture as mouthwash |
| | Peppermint | Leaf infusion for flatulence | | Rosemary/ Sage/Thyme | Leaf infusion as mouthwash |
| | Rosemary | Leaf infusion as a bitter stimulant | | | |
| | Thyme | Leaf infusion/tincture for diarrhea | Nervous tension | Catmint/ Lemon balm/ Vervain | Use aerial parts in infusion or tincture |
| Earache | Lavender | Dilute essential oil and massage outer ear | | Chamomile/ Lavender | Use flowers in infusion or tincture |
| | St. John's wort | Use infused oil on cotton wool as ear plug | Sprains | Rosemary | Leaf infusion in compress |
| | | | | Thyme | Dilute essential oil as massage or in compress |
| Eczema | Chamomile/ Elder | Flowers in infusion as skin wash or in creams | Throat, sore | Eyebright | Use infusion of whole plant as gargle/mouthwash |
| | Evening primrose | Seed oil in capsules or in ointment | | Sage/Thyme | Leaf infusion as gargle |
| | Marigold | Use petal infusion as wash/ tisane; creams and ointments | Toothache | Cloves | Apply essential oil to gum area |
| | Stinging nettle | Infusion of aerial parts as internal cleanser | | | |

*Use a pot kept specially for the purpose to make your delicate tisanes.*

# HERBAL TISANES

Herbal tisanes, or teas, are the most widely used of home remedies, and among the simplest to prepare. They are made by infusing the aerial parts of a herb, the fresh or dried leaves or petals, in boiling water just long enough to release the active constituents contained in the volatile oils. The infusion may then be enjoyed soothingly hot and, as a matter of choice, sweetened with honey, or refreshingly cold and sharpened with a slice of lemon or lime. If the tisane is administered to someone with a fever, then the tea should be drunk lukewarm.

### MAKING A TISANE

Herbal tisanes have a delicate and in some cases almost elusive flavour, and should be made in a glass or china pot, the prettier the better, kept specially for the purpose. The residue of the tannin left in a pot used for infusing tea leaves could both mask the flavour and detract from the feel-good factor induced by taking herbal tisanes.

Allow one level teaspoon of dried herbs or one level tablespoonful of fresh herbs for each cup. Place the herb in a warmed pot, measure and pour on the required amount of boiling water, and cover. Leave the infusion to steep for 10 to 15 minutes – no longer – before straining. It is not advisable to increase the infusion time in the hope, for example, of intensifying the flavour, since prolonged exposure to heat causes a loss of volatile oils through evaporation.

Herb tisanes, unlike tinctures, which are made with alcohol, have a relatively short shelf-life. If you wish to serve a tisane ice-cold, or to make it in larger quantities, cool and strain the liquid, pour it into a lidded jar and store for up to 24 hours in a refrigerator. You can then reheat the tisane without boiling in a glass or enamel pan if a warm drink is wanted.

Once you have become accustomed to the benefits of herbal tisanes, you can learn to become your own tea blender. By mixing two or more types of aromatic leaves and flowers it is possible to create innumerable permutations of flavours, and to benefit simultaneously from the perceived healing properties of more than one plant. For example, an infusion of lemon balm and rosemary leaves with hawthorn blossoms, when available, can be helpful in relieving stress and nervous tension; a blend of yarrow, elder flowers and peppermint makes a tea that has become a classic remedy for fever, and, without peppermint, the combination of yarrow and elder flowers may be taken to alleviate the effects of a hangover.

## TAKING HERBAL TISANES

Herbal tisanes made in the proportion suggested are mild medicines which may be taken to relieve symptoms over a period of four to eight weeks. If during this time additional symptoms develop, or the condition worsens, then medical help should be sought. When tisanes are taken for medical rather than social reasons, the normal frequency is two or three times a day, after meals; taking tisanes before meals, as a medicinal aperitif, is not recommended, as they can dilute the gastric juices and upset the digestion.

Whilst some herbal remedies can bring almost instant relief, when they are taken to ease a headache, for example, others take time to strengthen and stimulate the body systems. And so when chronic conditions such as rheumatism are being treated, patience is a virtue.

# *A guide to herbal tisanes and their attributes*

| HERB | USE TO EASE |
| --- | --- |
| Basil | flatulence, nausea |
| Chamomile flowers | insomnia |
| Caraway | flatulence |
| Catmint | feverishness, insomnia |
| Elder flower | chills, fever |
| Hyssop | mucus on chest |
| Lady's mantle | menstrual problems |
| Lavender flowers | headache, nervousness |
| Lemon balm | headache, insomnia, depression |
| Marigold petals | indigestion, gall bladder problems |
| Marjoram | flatulence, nausea, asthmatic complaints |
| Meadowsweet | acidity in the stomach |
| Mint | digestive disorders |
| Parsley | indigestion |
| Peppermint | flatulence, nausea, colic |
| Rosemary | indigestion, poor circulation, nervousness |
| Sage | coughs, sore throat, indigestion |
| Thyme | colds, indigestion, asthmatic complaints |
| Wormwood | indigestion |
| Yarrow | flatulence, indigestion |

# DECOCTIONS, COMPRESSES AND TINCTURES

Decoctions are made by simmering the roots, rhizomes, or woody parts of plants in liquid to extract the bitter principles and mineral salts. The strained liquid may then be drunk, or added to compresses and applied to the skin, when the beneficial elements will be quickly absorbed. Or, herbs may be steeped in spirits to make a tincture.

COMPRESSES AND POULTICES
Compresses and poultices, which are particularly effective in the treatment of bruises, strains and inflamed areas, help the body to absorb beneficial herbal compounds through the skin.

A compress is made by soaking a piece of clean cloth such as lint, linen, cotton or gauze in a decoction or infusion and applying it as hot as can be tolerated. When the compress has cooled, it can be soaked again and again in the reheated liquid and reapplied until the condition has been relieved.

Poultices, which have been widely used in self-help medicine for centuries, consist of parts of the herb itself, rather than a decoction or infusion and are applied directly to the skin, or made into a paste and wrapped in sterile gauze.

Among the most widely used poultices, which are particularly effective in the localized treatment of abscesses and boils, are those made of powdered marshmallow root, comfrey root or slippery elm, all of which are available from herbalists. The poultice is made by mixing one tablespoon (15 ml) of the powder to a thick paste with hot chamomile or comfrey-leaf tea, hot cider vinegar, or hot water. The paste is spread between two pieces of gauze and applied hot to the affected area. A hot-water bottle pressed against the poultice will keep the heat in for as long as possible. Once it cools it should be changed and another, as hot as possible, applied in its place.

Other forms of poultice can be made with fresh herbs. The application of fresh parsley leaves or marigold petals moistened with a little hot water can help to relieve styes, the inflammation of the glands at the base of the eyelashes.

A well-known way of relieving tired and strained eyes is to apply a slice of chilled cucumber to each eye. Puffy eyelids can be relieved and the swelling reduced by the application of grated raw potato. In each case it is probable that resting in a quiet room with closed eyes adds to the beneficial effects of the poultice.

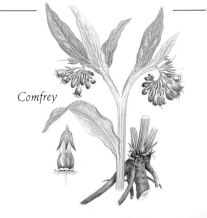

*Comfrey*

## Culpeper says . . .

*Nicholas Culpeper, the seventeenth-century herbalist, attributed the delightfully scented herb southernwood (Artemisia abrotanum) with powerful healing and restorative properties. He claimed that, "boiled with barleymeal, it removes pimples and wheals from the face or other parts of the body . . . The ashes mingled with old salad oil, helps those that are bald, causing the hair to grow again." The herb has been known by the popular names of garde-robe, because it was hung as a moth repellent, old man, boy's love, and maiden's ruin.*

# Decoctions

*A decoction of valerian is an example of a classic herbal medicine which may be used, for a limited period only, to relieve nervous disorders.*

25 g (1 oz) roots or woody
part of plant
600 ml (1 pt) water

Put the plant material into a glass or enamel pan and add the cold water. Bring to the boil, lower the heat and simmer for 15–20 minutes. Strain the decoction through a nylon sieve, and press the material against the sides with a spoon to extract the moisture. Allow to cool. The decoction can be stored in a lidded jar in the refrigerator for up to 24 hours. If it is to be taken or applied hot, slowly reheat.

# Tinctures

*Tinctures, which are usually bought from herbalists, may be taken undiluted or in hot drinks, or added to skin applications.*

100 g (4 oz) herb
600 ml (1 pt) spirit such
as vodka

Put the herb in a screw-topped jar and pour on the spirits. Seal the jar, shake well and leave in a warm, dark place for 14 days, shaking once or twice a day. Strain into a dark-glass bottle, store in a cool, dark place.

To take in a drink, measure out undiluted tinctures in dropfuls. Tinctures may also be mixed with compresses and ointments, or added to a bath.

Curled parsley

Pot marigold

Marshmallow

# SKIN PROBLEMS

It should be possible to treat skin problems, acne, eczema, abscesses and boils included, in two ways, in the short term to alleviate any irritation or inflammation of the skin, and in the longer term to reinforce the body's own immune system and its ability to function healthily.

Poor diet or nutritional deficiency may contribute to such complaints. A gradual movement away from animal and other saturated fats and sugar and other refined carbohydrates will almost certainly bring about a noticeable improvement in general health.

Fresh fruits and vegetables have a positive part to play in a healthy routine, and the increased use of herbs in cooking and salads adds more than nutritional value. These aromatic plants add interest and flavour to dishes of all kinds. Some vegetables and salad leaves are particularly rich sources of the vital chemicals or electrolytes potassium, iron and sulphur. Among them are carrots, celery, radishes, spring onions, spinach and green peppers, and herbs including dandelion leaves, parsley and watercress. Inclusion of these, especially, in your diet should help clear up skin problems.

## Eczema

*Eczema, which may be caused by fatigue, stress or an allergy,
notably to dairy products, can be relieved by taking evening primrose oil.*

Gamma linolenic acid – GLA – the active constituent of oil of evening primrose, has proved beneficial to many eczema sufferers. Capsules and ointments are available from healthfood shops and herbalists.

### Floral tisanes
A tisane made from marigold can also help. Make the tisane by infusing one teaspoon of dried flowers or one tablespoon of fresh flowers in a cup of boiling water for 10 minutes. The infusion may be drunk hot three times a day.

### Grasping the nettle
Wearing rubber gloves or thick gardening gloves, gather young leaves of stinging nettles where they will not have been contaminated by pollutants. Make them into a purifying tea, using a handful of leaves to 600 ml (1 pt) of boiling water.

### Herbal washes
To tackle the problem of dry, flaky skin from the outside, make a tisane in the usual way from the leaves of comfrey or the flowers of chamomile or elder, and use it, refreshingly cool, as a face wash.

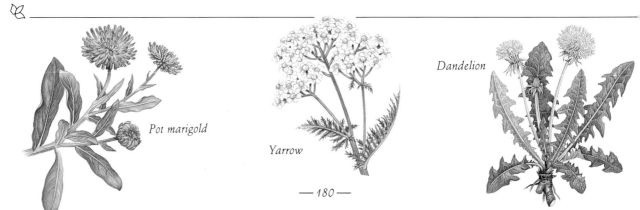

*Pot marigold*

*Yarrow*

*Dandelion*

# Acne

*Acne, caused when the sebaceous glands of the face and neck become blocked, has a demoralizing effect on teenage sufferers.*

Scrupulous cleanliness is essential, with natural herb soaps and cleansing creams preferred to synthetically perfumed products. Herbal tonics, face washes, poultices and tinctures can help, with marigold (calendula), chamomile, sage leaves and witch-hazel among the most beneficial plants.

### HERBAL TONIC
Mix equal parts of witch-hazel and rosewater (not triple rosewater) and keep it in a stoppered bottle in a cool place. Dab it on your skin after washing or cleansing.

### HERBAL FACE WASH
Fresh or dried flowers infused in boiling water can be used as a soothing and cleansing face wash. Elder flowers, chamomile, lavender and yarrow flowers are all suitable. Infuse a handful of flowers in 600 ml (1 pt) boiling water for 10 minutes, cool, strain and keep in a stoppered bottle in the refrigerator. Splash on the affected areas, or dab on generously with cotton wool.

### COMFREY POULTICE
For a "drawing out" poultice, mix one teaspoon powdered comfrey root to a paste with hot comfrey tea or hot water and spread it over the affected areas. Gently remove it by dabbing with cold comfrey tea, made by infusing the dark green leaves in boiling water. The plant contains allantoin, which can help stimulate healing.

### MARIGOLD COMPRESS
Benefit from the healing and soothing properties of marigold by mixing one teaspoon calendula tincture (available from herbalists) with 200 ml (6 fl oz) distilled water. Apply it to affected areas, or use the mixture as a face wash. Store it in a stoppered bottle.

# Boils and abscesses

*A tendency to boils or abscesses is an indication that something is wrong internally. It is wise to seek medical advice.*

These localized infections often occur in people who suffer from a general malaise or poor nutrition. Stimulating and healing remedies should be accompanied by adequate exercise and a healthy diet.

### LEMON LORE
When it comes to bringing boils to a head, the answer is a lemon.

Squeeze out the juice and use it to soak a piece of sterilized lint, held or bandaged against the eruptions. Alternatively, bind a thin slice of lemon directly on the affected site.

Country folk used to put their faith in baked or boiled onions. Cook an onion until it is soft, skin it and bind it, as hot as can be tolerated, over the affected area.

### TEA TIME
Fenugreek tea has internal and external applications. Crush one teaspoon of dried seeds, and boil them in a cup of water for 10 minutes. Strain, and drink the infusion hot. Reserve the seeds, wrap them in sterilized gauze and use them as a poultice.

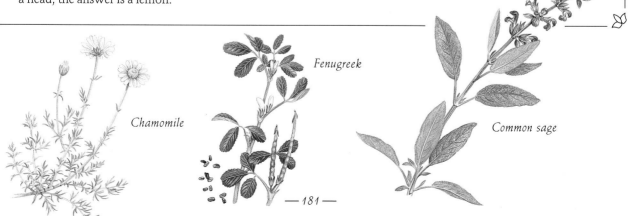

*Chamomile*

*Fenugreek*

*Common sage*

# NERVOUS DISORDERS

Nervous tension, anxiety and depression may be caused by a wide range of personal and psychological problems, and can be the cause or the effect of widely differing physical disorders, too. A lack-lustre approach to life, a state of permanent tiredness, loss of energy and severe physical pain may all be experienced.

## The case for hops

John Gerard, the sixteenth-century surgeon and apothecary to King James I, made a convincing case for hops as a tranquillizer when he wrote in his herbal that beer was more of a medicine than an ordinary drink.

To enjoy the benefits of hops in other ways, infuse three fresh or dried heads in a cupful of hot water for 10 minutes and drink the tisane hot. To reinforce the effect, take a warm bath to which a strong hop infusion has been added, and retire to bed with a sleep pillow filled with dried hops.

As more is understood about the interrelationship of mind and body, so it is realized that depression, one of the most widespread of nervous disorders, can have a variety of causes, not all of them psychological. In some people depression may be symptomatic of an allergy to certain foods, chemical food additives or petrol or other fumes. It can be an after-effect of an illness such as influenza or liver complaint and thus prove a severe hindrance to complete recovery, or it can be a sign of a vitamin deficiency. And as is well known, many women suffer post-natal depression, a condition that can have far-reaching effects on family life. When an acute or severe form of depression is experienced, from whatever cause, it is imperative to seek medical advice at once.

Some drugs, too, can have depressant side effects, especially when a high dosage is taken. Among these are some antibiotics and painkillers, and tranquillizers that may themselves be prescribed

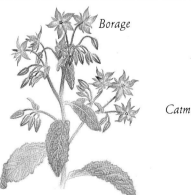

*Borage*

*Catmint*

*True valerian*

to treat nervous disorders.

For anyone suffering from a mild nervous complaint some herbs offer a gentle non-addictive means of toning, strengthening and nourishing the nervous system, and of easing day-to-day stress and tensions. Tisanes made from borage, catmint, chamomile, lemon balm, rosemary, valerian and vervain especially have been taken as mild tranquillizers for centuries. Now recent scientific experiments have proved what exponents of folk medicine and young readers of Beatrix Potter have long known; that chamomile, one of the mildest herbs, has relaxant and sleep-inducing properties. Peter Rabbit's mother, it will be recalled, put him to bed with a cup of chamomile tea after his anxious encounter in a nearby garden.

The tisanes may be made from fresh or dried herbs, in the ways described on pages 184–5. Dried chamomile flowers can be bought in health-food shops and from herbalists, and are among many herbs available in powdered form and sold as teabags, an up-to-date way of taking age-old remedies.

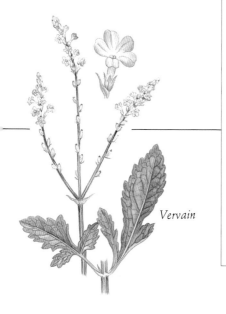

Vervain

## Quick tips

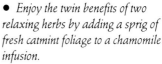

- *Enjoy the twin benefits of two relaxing herbs by adding a sprig of fresh catmint foliage to a chamomile infusion.*

- *Lemon balm tea, another long-standing self-help medicine, is usually drunk cool. As an anti-depressant it is especially effective taken at bedtime.*

- *To make chamomile tea from dried flowers, infuse a heaped teaspoon in a cup of boiling water for 10 minutes, and drink it hot.*

- *Add a pinch or two of lavender flowers to chamomile tea, or to any other relaxing tisane, to increase its effectiveness.*

- *Valerian is an example of an old belief – if a medicine tastes foul, it must be good for you. You can buy the powdered root from herbalists to make a decoction. Stir in a few lemon balm or peppermint leaves and a spoonful of honey to help make the three-times-daily dosage a more pleasant experience.*

- *Some essential oils, which you can buy from herbalists, can be diluted with a vegetable oil and used for a healing massage to relieve depression. Among the most effective are bergamot, jasmine, neroli, orange and rose.*

- *Rosemary may help you to see the brighter side of life following an illness. It is high in calcium and has been found to be effective in relieving post-illness depression. Drink rosemary tea hot and sweetened with honey, if you wish.*

# RESPIRATORY DISORDERS

From the common cold to laryngitis, respiratory disorders are always irritating and may be temporarily disabling. In mild forms, when the patient is disinclined to consult a doctor, their effects can be minimized by self-help medicine. Other related disorders including tonsillitis, bronchitis and asthma, may call for urgent medical attention.

## Common cold

*At the first signs of a cold – which may be sore eyes, a tickly nose or a sore throat – resort to the folk medicine principle of sweating out the cold with the following infusions.*

Soothing herbs such as marshmallow ease respiratory problems. Others can help in specific ways. Those which have antibiotic volatile oils include eucalyptus, hyssop, lavender, rosemary and thyme. Among the herbs which can, for example, help to dry up mucus, are agrimony, eye bright and elder flowers.

### ELDER-FLOWER AND YARROW TEA
Infuse one teaspoonful each elder flowers and yarrow flowers in a cup of boiling water for 15 minutes. Strain, sweeten with honey if you wish, and drink hot every two or three hours, especially at bedtime.

### AROMATIC INFUSION
Slice 25 g (1 oz) fresh root ginger and put it in a small glass or enamel pan with a crumbled stick of cinnamon, six cloves, one teaspoon coriander seeds and half a lemon, sliced. Add 600 ml (1 pt) boiling water, cover and bring to the boil. Simmer for 15 minutes, strain and drink hot, sweetened with honey if you like, every two or three hours, and especially at bedtime.

### STEAM HEAT
Put eight to ten drops of lavender, thyme and eucalyptus oils – any one or a mixture of two or three – into a bowl and pour on 600 ml (1 pt) boiling water. Cover your head with a towel and inhale.

### CATARRH MIXTURES
The build-up of mucus that results from the irritation of the mucous membranes can be relieved by gently sniffing a warm infusion up the nostrils. Effective mixtures are the juice of half a lemon in a cup of warm water, and fenugreek tea which is also a soothing drink.

### FENUGREEK TEA
Lightly crush one teaspoon fenugreek seeds and simmer them in a cup of water for 15 minutes. Strain, cool and sniff gently up the nostrils. Sweeten the remainder with honey, and drink hot.

### VAPOUR RUB
An old remedy valued more for its antiseptic and bactericidal properties than for its aroma, a chest rub of crushed garlic cloves and Vaseline can be helpful, especially at bedtime. Crush six large garlic cloves and put them into a small glass or enamel pan with one tablespoon petroleum jelly. Heat just until the jelly melts, then pour it into a sterilized jar and cool. Rub on the chest and back.

*Hyssop*

*Anise*

*Fenugreek*

# Sore throats

*Sage, thyme, vinegar, lemon and honey are the ingredients to keep on hand to ease sore throats. Gargles, infusions and compresses also relieve the discomfort of tonsillitis.*

HERBAL GARGLE
Choose between the combinations of sage and vinegar or thyme and lemon juice to make a soothing gargle, which is also helpful in cases of laryngitis. Infuse one teaspoon fresh herb leaves in a cup of boiling water for 10 minutes. Add one teaspoon vinegar or lemon juice depending on the herb. Gargle with a little of the infusion and drink the remainder.

Tonsillitis is a condition that calls for medical attention. Herbal gargles may soothe the burning sensation. Sage or thyme infusions may be used as compresses and held against the throat.

# Coughs

*Coughing dislodges the excess mucus produced when the membrane lining the throat or airways becomes irritated or infected (as in bronchitis). Blended tisanes help soothe and heal.*

COUGH MIXTURE
A combined decoction and infusion makes an effective three-way cough medicine. Simmer one teaspoon lightly crushed aniseed seeds and one tablespoon powdered licorice root (available from herbalists) in 600 ml (1 pt) water for 20 minutes. Pour the decoction over one teaspoon each dried coltsfoot flowers and dried thyme leaves, cover and infuse for 10 minutes. Strain through muslin and drink one cupful, hot, three or four times a day.

KITCHEN REMEDY
Peel a large onion, slice it into rings and put it into a bowl. Pour on three tablespoons clear organic honey, a powerful antiseptic and expectorant. Cover and leave it overnight. Strain and take one dessertspoon four times a day.

GARLIC ELIXIR
The antiseptic properties of garlic and honey come together in a country remedy for bronchial coughs. Chop eight garlic cloves, put them in a jar and cover them with four tablespoons clear organic honey. Enjoy one teaspoon of the elixir at two-hourly intervals.

EUCALYPTUS TEA
The tough leaves of this medicinal plant need to be boiled briefly before infusing. Place 25 g (1 oz) of dried leaves in a glass or enamel pan, add 600 ml (1 pt) water and bring to the boil. Cover and infuse for 15 minutes. Strain and drink hot every three hours.

BREATHE IN!
The essential oils of herbs such as lavender, oregano and thyme are effective as inhalants. Sprinkle one or two drops on a handkerchief, as Victorian ladies used to do, or add about six to eight drops of one of the oils to a bowl containing 600 ml (1 pt) of boiling water. Cover your head with a towel and breathe in. Alternatively, and less sweetly, crush three large cloves of garlic and add them to the steaming water.

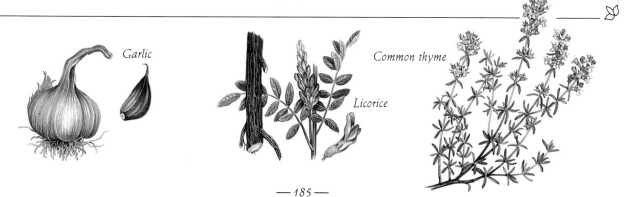

*Garlic*

*Common thyme*

*Licorice*

# ACHES & PAINS

The aches and pains that can make daily life an uphill struggle range from the inflammation of muscles and joints that result in rheumatic pain to the nervous conditions or food allergies that can trigger the debilitating headache and sickness of migraine.

## Headaches and migraine

*The first question to ask when one has a headache is why? There are a number of causes, indigestion, high blood pressure, tension, fatigue, too low blood sugar and menstrual problems among them.*

Frequent or recurring headaches should always be reported to a doctor. Those brought on by nervous tension may be relieved by any of the infusions suggested on page 183.

### HERBAL RUBS
Massaging the temples with an oil such as peppermint or rosemary, diluted with a vegetable oil, can be helpful. An alternative is to sprinkle one or two drops of oil on a handkerchief, rest in a darkened room and inhale the aroma.

### FEVERFEW TEA
Infuse one teaspoonful of the dried leaves or one heaped tablespoon of fresh leaves in a cup of boiling water, in the usual way, and drink it hot, not more than two cups each day. It will almost certainly be necessary to sweeten the infusion with honey.

### SWEET LAVENDER
Lavender is especially helpful in the relief of nervous headaches. Sprinkle two or three drops of tincture of lavender on a lump of sugar and dissolve it slowly in your mouth, or rub the oil into your temples. Sipping a cup of warm, sweetened lavender tea, made with the flowers, is a third option from this plant.

### MIGRAINE
Any of the remedies suggested for tension headaches may help relieve the throbbing and often one-sided migraine. Recent research has given migraine its own herbal remedy, feverfew, a medicinal herb now known to have an action similar to that of aspirin. The bitter leaves are made more palatable by spreading them, two or three at a time, in honey sandwiches.

## The case for feverfew

In his Herball *in the sixteenth century, Gerard said that feverfew "is very good for them that are giddie in the head or with the turning called Vertigo".*

*Scientific research has taken his assertions further. Extracts of feverfew have been found to inhibit the production in the body of substances called prostaglandins, which play a part in causing inflammation and pain. The herb is now used in the treatment of migraine and for rheumatism and arthritis.*

*Peppermint*

*Rosemary*

# Sprains

*Sprains and suspected fractures require professional attention, but
minor cases respond to herbal compresses and ointments.*

Treat sprains with a compress of sterilized lint soaked in hot comfrey tea, or comfrey root ground to make a poultice.

Mix two tablespoonsful of dried comfrey root powder (available from herbalists) to a thick paste with boiling water. Simmer very gently for 15 minutes, moistening the paste by adding water a little at a time if necessary.

John Wesley in his book of home remedies, *Primitive Physick*, prescribed comfrey for strained tendons: "Boil comfrey roots to a thick mucillage or jelly and apply this as a poultice, changing it twice a day." A modern version of the "jelly" can be made by boiling three tablespoons dried comfrey root powder with 250 g (8 oz) petroleum jelly. Cool and strain through muslin into a small pot. Rub on the affected parts.

# Muscle and joint pain

*Minor muscle strain or fatigue caused by over-exertion can be eased
by gentle massage with a herbal oil. It is more effective if the area to
be treated is first bathed in hot water.*

It is advisable to consult a doctor or herbal practitioner to find the underlying cause of the rheumatism, which may include stress, inadequate diet, and arthritis which may be a result of injury.

To make a soothing oil, put 300 ml (½ pt) olive oil in a small pan and add two tablespoons lavender flowers, dried rosemary or thyme leaves, or a few sprigs of the fresh herbs. Warm the oil gently, turn off the heat and leave it to steep for 10 minutes, strain the oil and use it warm, to ease the affected muscles.

### A STINGING REPLY

The young tops of stinging nettles can be gathered freely in spring and summer and are rich in vitamins and minerals and highly alkaline, which can counteract excessive acidity and ease rheumatic aches and pains. You can also buy them dried out or, conveniently, as teabags to make nettle tea.

### CELERY MILK

An old country medicament for the treatment of rheumatism and arthritis is celery milk, made by chopping three large sticks of celery and simmering them in 300 ml (½ pt) milk for 20 minutes. The resulting mixture, which was also known as "celery mess", is taken warm as a soup.

Celery seeds, too, have a high alkaline content and can be used to make a helpful infusion. Lightly crush one teaspoonful of the seeds and simmer them in a cup of water for five minutes. Cover, leave for 10 minutes, strain and drink warm.

### A NATIVE AMERICAN CUSTOM

Native Americans used wintergreen oil as a treatment for rheumatism. A similar oil, now obtained from birch and sometimes called sweet birch oil, can bring relief when rubbed into affected parts.

Some herbalists recommend adding extract of birch leaves to a hot bath to relieve arthritic and rheumatic pains and stiff joints.

*Lavender
'Twickle Purple'*

*Lavender
'Munstead'*

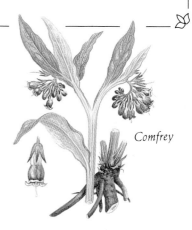

*Comfrey*

# CUTS & BRUISES, BITES & STINGS

Minor accidents that might occur in the home, garden or playground, and result in cuts and abrasions, bruises and burns, bites and stings, can respond to self-help medicine. More severe injuries of any kind call for urgent medical help. Where children are concerned the combination of a gentle remedy and a sympathetic touch works wonders.

## Cuts and grazes

*The first requirement when the skin is broken is to clean it thoroughly. One way to do this is to stir 2.5 ml (½ teaspoon) tincture of calendula in 300 ml (½ pt) boiled water and bathe the wound.*

### Culpeper says . . .

*Nicholas Culpeper, whose seventeenth-century* Complete Herbal *set out to identify the medicinal properties of plants and define their uses, had something to say on the treatment of wounds and cuts, and of certain bites. He described feverfew as "one of the most singular wound herbs". And of mint he wrote that, "applied with salt, it helps the bites of mad dogs . . . and is good to wash the heads of young children with, against all manner of breakings out, sores and scabs . . ."*

Sterilized gauze wrung out in a fresh batch of the solution held in place with a bandage has good healing properties. Smaller areas can be treated with one or two drops of the tincture of calendula on the sticking plaster gauze.

GARLIC AS A POULTICE
As a healing plant, garlic has a long and far-reaching history. The Chinese applied slices of raw garlic to heal wounds, and garlic dressings were used to treat battle wounds in World War I.

You can put its reputation as a protection against infection to the test, and make a poultice of thinly sliced garlic wrapped in sterilized gauze. As an alternative you can harness the twin properties of garlic and another known antiseptic substance, organic honey. The garlic elixir recommended on page

185 for bronchial complaints may be spread thickly on cuts and grazes and held in place with sterilized lint and a bandage. If you find the smell of raw garlic unacceptable, spread "neat" honey on the open wound.

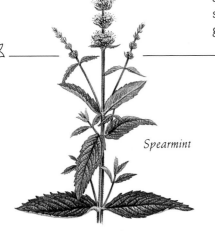

*Spearmint*

*Feverfew*

*Chamomile*

# Bruises

*Comfrey is a herb with a variety of medicinal properties, and recent research supports its folkloric use as a treatment for bruises.*

Bathing the affected area in hot comfrey tea, or applying a tisane as a compress should help alleviate the pain and reduce the discoloration. Comfrey ointment, obtainable from herbalists, harnesses the plant's properties in another form.

Some of the plant's old country names, "knitbone" and "knitback" among them, and its botanical name, *Symphytum*, which comes from the Greek word for union, refer to its ability to help torn flesh heal up cleanly.

The early settlers in New England learned some of their herbal medicine from the Native Americans, who had long used extract of witch-hazel to treat severe bruising. Keep a bottle in the medicine cupboard and use it, soaked on cotton wool, to reduce the discomfort level.

# Burns

*Severe burns and scalds are a matter for urgent medical attention, but the immediate concern is to cool the affected area.*

Further tissue damage can be halted by immersing the burn in cold water or pouring water over the affected part.

Solutions of cold water with a few drops of tincture of calendula or hypericum can be applied to minor burns and scalds. Apply one as a compress with sterilized lint, or dab it on with cotton wool. If you do not have any of the tinctures to hand, cold chamomile tea or comfrey tea can both be used in a similar way.

In cases where the skin is broken, a paste made of organic honey and either of the herbal tisanes is both soothing and healing.

# Bites and stings

*Bee and wasp stings should be pulled out at once. The most effective on-the-spot treatment is bathing with an alkaline solution of water and baking soda (bicarbonate of soda).*

## Quick tips

• Ant bites also respond quickly to a water and baking soda (sodium bicarbonate) solution.

• Dab bites and stings with witch-hazel, the colder the better. It pays to keep a bottle in the refrigerator.

• Perhaps the most widely-known antidote to stinging nettle stings is the immediate application of a dock leaf, a wayside poultice in its simplest form.

• Oil of eucalyptus or essence of lavender dabbed on an insect bite or sting with a clean finger, both take away the heat.

• Country folk reached for an onion to soothe painful bites and stings. A thick slice of onion can be used as a poultice, held in place with sticking plaster or a bandage. Alternatively make a compress with grated or sliced onion in sterilized gauze.

• Feverfew tea, made by infusing 30 ml (2 tbsp) of the flowerheads in a cup of boiling water, is an old country remedy to soothe bites and stings. Dab it generously on to the affected areas and allow it to dry.

• The same infusion was used by country folk as an insect repellant. The plant contains camphor which bees and other insects do not like.

# DIGESTIVE DISORDERS

Many digestive disorders can be attributed to an injudicious diet or even to the
manner of eating. Foods that are high in saturated fats and refined carbohydrates and, most of all,
low in dietary fibre; drinks that have a high caffeine, tannin or alcohol content; and a rapid,
hurried fast-eating routine can all contribute to indigestion, heartburn, flatulence and colic,
acidity of the stomach and disorders of the bowel and colon.

It cannot be emphasized too
strongly that when a severe
condition is suspected, medical
advice should be sought at once.
Home remedies can bring
considerable relief in cases of minor
disorders, but should never be used
to mask symptoms of a more
serious condition.

Tisanes and decoctions might
have been invented to ease the
discomfort of indigestion and
related problems. Opposite is a
check-list of the top ten that can
be helpful.

### DANDELIONS
Dandelion is a versatile plant with
good medicinal credentials. The
root, which can be used to make a
decoction, is helpful in cases of
dyspepsia, and as a mild but bitter
laxative. Due principally to its
taraxin content, dandelion
stimulates the liver and gall bladder
and significantly increases the flow
of bile to aid digestion.

The leaves have a reputation as
an efficient diuretic, a function

attested by the plant's old country
names of piss-a-bed, or, in French,
*pis en lit*. They may be lightly
cooked and served, as spinach,
sprinkled with lemon juice and
pepper, or included in mixed green
salads. The light, bright green
young leaves, gathered in the
spring, are especially good tossed
with watercress. (Watercress is also
a diuretic. It helps to relieve fluid
retention, ridding the body of toxic
wastes from the tissues and blood,
and stimulates the digestion.)

### LICORICE ROOT
Country children used to be given a
stick of licorice root to chew "to
keep their stomachs in order" and
the plant has long been used as a
remedy for indigestion. Its ability
to lower the level of acid in the
stomach makes it effective against
heartburn. It can also ease spasms
of the large intestine and contribute
to the healing of stomach ulcers. A
decoction can be made from
powdered licorice root available
from herbalists.

NOTE Licorice should not be taken
by those who suffer from high
blood pressure.

*Dandelion*

*Watercress*

*Dill*

# Top ten tisanes

## PEPPERMINT

*The terms peppermint and indigestion are inextricably linked, and a packet of strong peppermints is part of many a sufferer's self-help kit. The herb contains flavonoids which stimulate the liver and gall bladder, increasing the flow of bile. It can be an effective remedy for colic and flatulence, and has an antispasmodic effect on the smooth muscles of the digestive tract.*

## PARSLEY

*The herb is a strong diuretic which is useful for treating urinary infections and stones, as well as fluid retention. It is a rich source of vitamin C and iron and aids digestion.*

## SAGE

*The volatile oil has both a carminative and stimulating effect on the digestion. Sage tea, which does so much to ease respiratory disorders, is helpful in relieving discomfort.*

## SWEET MARJORAM

*The wide use of the herb in cooking, as a flavouring for egg and meat dishes, probably derives from its properties as an aid to digestion. Marjoram tea is all the more fragrant if you include a spoonful of the tiny purple flowers.*

## THYME

*One of the many benefits of an infusion of thyme is its ability to soothe the digestive system and ease flatulence. This is due to the antispasmodic effect on smooth muscle of the plant's volatile oil.*

## ROSEMARY

*A cup or two of rosemary tea can ease flatulence and stimulate the digestion, liver and gall bladder by increasing the flow of bile. This is brought about by the action of rosmanicine which, as it breaks down in the body, stimulates the smooth muscle of the gall bladder and digestive tract.*

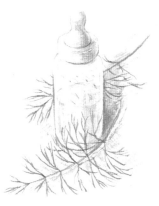

## DILL

*The name comes from dilla, an Icelandic word meaning "lull", and dill water made from the herb has been used for generations to promote good digestion and improve the appetite. The herb is still a constituent of gripe water and other children's medicines, valued for its ability to ease colic and flatulence. The tisane is made by infusing one teaspoon lightly crushed seeds in a cup of boiling water.*

## FENNEL

*Both the seeds and the root of this umbelliferous plant can aid digestion and soothe discomfort, though the fennel tea made by infusing the lightly crushed seeds is more usual. You can buy powdered fennel root, from which to make a decoction, from herbalists. The tisane is good for easing colic in babies, and heartburn and indigestion in adults.*

## LEMON BALM

*The valuable volatile oils in the leaves may be lost during the drying process, and so it is best to use the herb fresh, or frozen. A cup of hot lemon-balm tea sipped slowly after meals is an excellent aid to digestion, and it can relieve colic and flatulence. This is due to the antispasmodic effects of the essential oils, notably eugenol.*

## ANGELICA

*An infusion of lightly crushed angelica seeds, with their pungent, bitter taste, stimulates the digestion and can ease gripe, colic and flatulence. It also has diuretic properties which can be beneficial in the treatment of urinary infections.*

# EYE, EAR & MOUTH PROBLEMS

The unrelated problems of puffy eyes and aching ears can be relieved with the use of a single plant, according to Nicholas Culpeper. In his definitive herbal, he noted of parsley that "the leaves laid to the eyes inflamed with heat or swollen, helps them . . . the juice dropped into the ears with a little wine, eases the pain". He had a remedy for sore mouths, too. In such cases he recommended mint, with the words, "The decoction gargled in the mouth, cures the mouth and gums that are sore, and amends an ill-favoured breath."

## Eye problems

*Sore, inflamed and itching eyes may be caused by lack of sleep, stress and strain or exposure to cigarette smoke. The traditional remedy is a cold compress placed on each eye and rest in a cool, dark room.*

Ice-cold water used to soak cotton wool discs is helpful, but cold herbal teas are better. Fennel tea, made by infusing the seeds, is an old country remedy. More up-to-date is to use cold fennel or chamomile teabags.

SOOTHING EYEBATHS
Sore and red eyes may be treated at home with one of a number of soothing eyebaths. Conjunctivitis and other eye infections call for medical attention. Scrupulous attention must be paid to cleanliness and hygiene. First sterilize an eyebath in boiling water or steam from a kettle. Then use any of these infusions or blends to bathe the eyes. Cool the solution before use, keep it in a stoppered

bottle in the refrigerator for up to 24 hours, and discard the used solution after each application.
*Chamomile tea* made with the flowers.
*Elder-flower tea.*
*Fennel tea* made with the seeds.
*Calendula eyebath solution* Mix two drops of tincture of calendula with 15 ml (1 tbsp) distilled water for each bath, for each eye.
*Marigold petal compress* This is soothing to tired eyes and can be helpful in dispersing styes, as can torn parsley leaves wrapped in hot, sterilized gauze.

### Eye brightness

*Culpeper credited* Euphrasia officinalis *with remarkable powers: "If the herb were as much used as neglected, it would spoil half the spectacle-makers' trade."*

*To make an eyebright solution, mix five drops tincture of eyebright with one tablespoonful rosewater, for each bath. Use a new solution for each eye and each application.*

*An infusion of the leaves may be taken as a tisane, or cooled and used as an eyebath or compress. As a mouthwash or gargle, the infusion is also helpful for sore mouths and sore throats.*

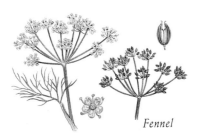

*Pot marigold*

*Fennel*

*Myrrh/Sweet cicely*

# Ear problems

*Earache can be an after-effect of a cold or it can be a symptom of an infection. It is important not to take any chances, and to consult medical opinion at once.*

Minor cases of earache can be relieved by the use of a warm herbal oil. You can make one with 20 drops tincture of myrrh or tincture of eucalyptus and one tablespoon almond oil. Keep the mixture in a stoppered bottle. To use it, pour a little into a teaspoon pre-heated in boiling water. Apply the oil carefully with a piece of cotton wool used as an ear plug.

Garlic oil is another simple remedy. It can be bought in capsule form. Use it as described above, piercing one capsule and emptying the oil into a heated spoon.

Lavender oil diluted with almond oil or olive oil can be massaged around the outer ear to reduce the risk of infection.

# Mouth problems

*Toothache and sore or infected gums are symptoms that should be checked by your dentist.*

Herbal mouthwashes can help to relieve soreness and act as bactericides, and vitamin supplements, especially vitamin C, and the B vitamins are also helpful.

### HERBAL MOUTHWASHES

Tisanes made in the usual way can be used as soothing mouthwashes in cases of sore gums or toothache. Swish the infusion around in your mouth and retain it there for as long as possible. The following solutions should be helpful.
*Rosemary tea* Use fresh or dried leaves.
*Sage tea* Use fresh or dried leaves.
*Thyme tea* Use fresh or dried leaves and, if possible, a few flowers.
*Lavender tea* Use flowers.
*Tincture of myrrh* Dilute the tincture in warm, boiled water. Use in the proportion of eight drops to 150 ml (¼ pt) water.
*Oil of cloves* This is used as a local anaesthetic to ease nagging toothache. Pour a few drops on to a cotton wool bud and massage it on the gums around the affected tooth. Repeat every two to three hours as required.

### BREATH SWEETENER

Any of the tisanes or solutions mentioned above will also help when bad breath is a problem; although the underlying cause will need to be determined. Other ways to freshen the breath are to chew a few caraway, cumin or fennel seeds, or parsley or mint leaves.

*Chamomile*

# AROMATHERAPY

The use of essential plant oils as a means of promoting emotional and physical well-being, the practice of aromatherapy, was widely appreciated by ancient cultures around the world. It formed a significant part of medical practice in both China and Egypt, where the therapeutic powers of the oils were well recognized.

Aromatherapy harnesses the therapeutic properties of essential oils to heal and cure both physical and psychological ailments and to enhance well-being. Oils can be administered by way of the skin, with massage; the airways, in inhalations; and the digestive tract, in tisanes.

Combined with all these are the olfactory pathways along which aromas reach the brain. Neurons – nerve cells – in the lining membranes of the nasal passages enable information to be relayed rapidly to different parts of the brain. Kyphi, the blend of oils developed by the ancient Greeks, had well-documented mood-altering properties.

The use of oils in body massage is one of the most widely known aspects of aromatherapy. The skin, our largest organ, absorbs the volatile oils, which are taken up selectively by different tissues in the body. They also reinforce the body's own natural healing processes. There is an added benefit, since massage is soothing.

Just as the oils themselves are complex, so their action is complex and cannot be fully understood without extensive study. It is, for example, possible to take essential oils internally, but because they are so highly concentrated and have such diverse properties, this is not recommended unless under the supervision of a qualified practitioner.

One of the most intriguing aspects of aromatherapy is the blending of more than one essential oil to make what are known as synergistic compounds, each one

*Purple sage*

*Apothecary's rose*

*Coriander*

formulated to have unique properties and actions. This, too, is an area on which it is advisable to take expert guidance.

### USING ESSENTIAL OILS

Essential oils should never be used neat – they are far too highly concentrated – but diluted in the proportion of a maximum of five drops of essential oil to 5 ml (1 tsp) of a base or carrier oil. This may be a single oil or a mixture of two or more, chosen from, among others, grapeseed, peanut, hazelnut, walnut, soya and almond oils. Usually one teaspoonful of oil is enough for a whole body massage.

Inhalation is another way of harnessing the benefits of essential oils. One drop of, for example, lavender oil on a handkerchief can produce enough aroma to be both calming and relaxing, whilst two or three drops of an essential oil in a large bowl of hot water produces a strong vapour. To maximize the effects of this aromatic steam, hold your face about 25 cm (10 in) from the bowl, cover your head with a towel, close your eyes and breathe deeply through your nose for one minute. The act of deep breathing also contributes to the benefit of this age-old remedial procedure.

WARNING Essential oils must not be used during pregnancy. Many are slightly toxic, or could induce a miscarriage.

*Lavender 'Twickle Purple'*

---

# Choosing an essential oil

*These are some of the oils which can be used for massage, as inhalants or added, three or four drops at a time, to a bath.*

### SANDALWOOD
*The sandalwood tree, native to the Indian province of Mysore, has to be 30 years old before its essential oil is fully developed. The luxurious oil is used to combat anxiety and reduce nervous tension.*

### JASMINE
*It takes eight million hand-picked jasmine blooms to make 1 kg (2¼ lb) of the "absolute" from which the oil is made. It is used to aid relaxation and sleep, and to soothe anxiety.*

### YLANG YLANG
*This intensely sweet oil, extracted from the blossoms of "perfume trees" grown in Madagascar, is both a sedative and an anti-depressant. Its aroma can be somewhat cloying and it should be used sparingly.*

### FRANKINCENSE
*Extracted from the gum resin from the tree Boswellia thurifera, this oil has a calming effect. It is particularly effective when used in a vaporizer as a relaxing environmental perfume.*

### NEROLI
*This relaxing yet stimulating oil, which comes from the bitter orange tree, can ease nervous tension and anxiety and encourage sleep.*

### GERANIUM
*Sometimes sold as geranium Bourbon-la-Reunion oil, for the island where the plant originated, the essential oil is soothing and relaxing.*

### LAVENDER
*This oil is used for its steadying influence on the nerves and as a relaxant. It is effective both as a massage oil and, used two or three drops at a time, as an inhalant.*

### BERGAMOT
*The oil is used to lift depression and encourage a more positive outlook.*

### CHAMOMILE
*This golden oil is used to calm anxiety and dispel anger. It is also effective, used two or three drops at a time, as an inhalant.*

### MELISSA
*Distilled from lemon balm leaves, the oil is used to lift depression and induce a sense of well-being.*

### ROSEMARY
*The essential oil can lift exhaustion and stimulate the senses and can be used to aid concentration.*

### GRAPEFRUIT
*This is the oil to use when a confidence booster is needed. It is warming and soothing.*

### CORIANDER
*To produce this oil, coriander is harvested when the fruit is fully ripe. Its stimulating effect can help to combat tiredness and lethargy.*

### ROSE
*Distilled from centifolia, damascena and gallica roses, rose oil, or attar of roses, is used to ease tension and soothe anxiety, and is especially helpful in post-natal depression. It takes about 5 tons (5 tonnes) of roses to produce 1 kg (2¼ lb) of the oil.*

# CRAFTS

Herbs were once the mainstay of many home crafts, used in dyeing and for decoration. Many decorative uses have their origins in symbolic or religious beliefs – St. John's wort tied in bunches at the window to ward off evil spirits, for example, or mistletoe hung to bring good fortune and fertility. Today, many of these symbolic meanings are preserved in Victorian "language of flowers" listings, even though our seasonal decorations are more usually regarded as pure ornament. The traditional herb dyes have not been forgotten, however. Many craft weavers and spinners still prefer the subtle and variable shades they give compared with standardized chemical products.

*Tansy flowers dry well and are attractive in arrangements.*

*Wreaths look good all year, not only at festive times.*

## Herbs for dried flower arrangements and wreaths

*The colours in dried flower arrangements can be richer and more varied than the familiar shades of muted brown and green. The list below shows herbs that work particularly well in arrangements, retaining colour when dried. It also includes some that make interesting shapes. When choosing herbs to dry, pick them just after they open – their colours when dried will be richer if they have not begun to fade at the time you harvest them.*

| Herb | Parts used | Colours when dried |
| --- | --- | --- |
| Bay | leaves and stems | deep green |
| Bee balm | flowering stems | scarlet |
| Caraway | seedheads | tan and brown |
| Chamomile | flowers | yellow-grey |
| Chervil | seedheads | green and brown |
| Dill | seedheads | green and brown |
| Eucalyptus | leaves | silvery grey |
| Fennel | seedheads | light grey-brown, umbrella-shaped seedheads |
| Lady's mantle | flowering stems | yellow-green |
| Lavender | flowering stems | shades of purple and dark blue |
| Pennyroyal | flowering stems and leaves | purple |
| Rosemary | stems and leaves | deep green |
| Sorrel | seedheads | shades of green |
| Southernwood | stems and leaves | green |
| Tansy | flowering stems | bright yellow |
| Yarrow | flowering stems | pink, white, deep yellow |

# The language of herbs

The chart shows the symbolic meanings of a number of herbs. These could be taken into account if you are making an arrangement for a special occasion.

| Herb | Symbolic meaning |
| --- | --- |
| Bay | honour, loyalty and unchanging affections, faithfulness |
| Basil | best wishes, warm friendship |
| Borage | courage |
| Chamomile | patience, meekness, resignation |
| Chervil | sincerity, warm feelings |
| Coriander | hidden worth, concealed feelings |
| Elderflower | compassion, sympathy |
| Evening primrose | inconstancy, uncertainty |
| Fennel | strength, flattery |
| Geranium | comfort, consolation |
| Lavender | silence, the acceptance and recognition of love |
| Marjoram | happiness, joy |
| Mint | wisdom |
| Myrtle | love, a first declaration of love |
| Nasturium | conquest |
| Parsley | celebrations, festivity |
| Red rose | true love |
| Rose | silence |
| Rosemary | remembrance |
| Rue | repentance |
| Saffron | marriage |
| Sage | esteem, friendship |
| Southernwood | constancy |
| Thyme | activity |

# Herbs for dyeing

Herbs can be used to produce a wide range of natural dyes with colours that are softer and more subtle than the synthetic dyes used commercially. Mordants both fix the dye in the fabric and affect the final colour: those suggested below are for dyeing wool. If you want to try dyeing at home, start with a small amount of fabric in a natural cotton or wool – a wool scarf would be suitable. Mordants can be purchased at a craft shop; consult directions on the packaging and use exactly as directed. You should only think about dyeing with herbs that you have in plentiful supply – because the colour is gentler than that in commercial dyes, you will need quite a large quantity of the herb to achieve a deep enough colour. The following herbs give a good result; the mordants suggested are for wool.

| Herb | Part used | Colour | Mordant |
| --- | --- | --- | --- |
| Elder | leaves | green | alum |
| | berries | blue/lilac | alum/salt |
| | berries | violet | alum |
| | bark | black | iron |
| Marigold | petals | pale yellow | alum |
| Parsley | leaves and stems | cream | alum |
| St. John's wort | flowers | red | tin/acetic acid |
| Tansy | flowering tops | dark yellow | alum |
| Woad | leaves | blue/lilac | ammonia |

*Garlands of fresh herbs can be used to soften hard lines, creating a more natural effect.*

# WREATHS & GARLANDS

It was the practice in years gone by to create wreaths and garlands on a core of grass, bryony and other supple stems and bind them, like with like, with more of their own kind. To this day the *stefani* rings hung on doorways in Greece in celebration of May Day are made, often by children, by binding posies of fragrant flowers on to a circular hoop of grasses.

More substantial wreath forms can be made – or bought in florists' shops – of supple clematis, vine, willow or other twigs twisted and interwoven to form the base for further decoration. These circular forms, as well as long, thick raffia or vine plaits, provide sprays and posies of herbs with support but not a moisture source. They are suitable for short-term festival decorations, and for use with evergreen herbs such as bay, rosemary and sage and all those flowers which will dry naturally in warm air. Bergamot, caraway, chamomile, chive, feverfew, lady's mantle, lavender, tansy and wild marjoram are floral examples; the seedheads of herbs such as chervil, dill, fennel and sorrel have similar properties. A ring or garland of any one of these herbs, or a fragrant medley of many, will dry attractively day by day until it forms a long-lasting decoration that will have lost little of its original glory, or its fragrance.

Wreath bases and garland cores made of natural materials may form not just the structure of the design but a visual element of the decoration. A ring of dried grass stems underpinning over-lapping bunches of marjoram flowers can provide an acceptable and attractive texture contrast.

Wire, rope, string, cord, plastic and other core materials can be masked by covering them with dry sphagnum moss or hay. This should be bound on with green twine concealed beneath the mass of natural stems. The design for a long-lasting herbal wreath uses this technique.

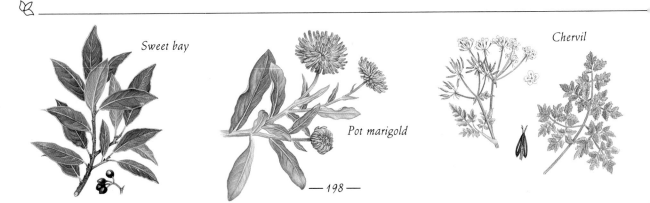

*Sweet bay*

*Pot marigold*

*Chervil*

# Fresh herbal wreath

*Delight the senses with a wreath of fresh herbs that gives off a sweet fragrance as it dries.*

*selection of herb leaves such as bay, cotton lavender, lavender, rosemary and sage*
*selection of herb flowers such as chamomile, chive, feverfew, lady's mantle, lavender and wild marjoram*
*green twine*
*dry hay*
*double copper-wire ring frame, 25 cm (10 in) in diameter*
*silver roll wire*
*medium-gauge stub wires, cut in halves*

Tie one end of the twine to the ring frame. Press handfuls of hay against the frame and bind it around with twine. Gather the herb leaves and flowers into small posies, either of separate or mixed plant materials. Cut the stems to equal length and bind them with silver roll wire. Keep the posies in water until you are ready to complete the decoration. Bend the stub wires to make U-shaped

staples. Hold one of the posies flat against the covered frame and secure the stems in place with the staple. Position successive posies so that the heads of each one cover the stems of the one before. Continue around the ring in this way. You may, if you wish, leave a section of the hay uncovered.

Hang the herbal wreath in a dry room away from direct sunlight. The herbs will dry *in situ*.

# Table garland

*Decorate a summer party or wedding-cake table with a short-lived garland of fresh herb leaves and flowers.*

*long sprays of, for example, variegated mint and golden marjoram leaves*
*flowers such as damask roses or marigolds*
*thick cord or coiled paper ribbon in colours to tone with the flowers*
*silver roll wire*
*hot-glue gun or clear, quick-setting glue*

Plan to make the decoration as close as possible to the opening of the festivities, and keep the plant materials in water until you are ready to start.

Measure around the edge of the

table, or across the front, allowing for loops in the garland if you wish. Cut the cord or other core material to length. Bind the herb stems to the core with silver wire, taking two, three or more together, depending on the thickness you want the garland to be, and the density of the foliage. Cut off the flower stems and stick the flowerheads over the foliage stems. Spray the design with cool water to keep it fresh.

*Variegated apple mint*

# POSIES & NOSEGAYS

Nosegays, posies, herbal bouquets, tussie-mussies, call them what you will, have their roots in both country lore and the learned professions. In Elizabethan England people carried these sweet-smelling or pungent posies to sweeten the air around them, and as a protection against the plague and other diseases; the disinfectant herbs such as lavender, rosemary and rue were favoured for this purpose.

In Victorian times would-be lovers exchanged small floral posies made-up of plants chosen to convey a secret message. In accordance with the traditional language of flowers, there might be sprays of rosemary which, Ophelia tells us, in Shakespeare's *Hamlet*, is "for remembrance"; sweet basil to signify best wishes; coriander for hidden worth (on whose part, it might not be clear); elder flowers as a sign of compassion; fennel as a symbol of strength; and parsley for festivity. A red rose would be almost mandatory in a love posy, as an expression of true love.

Herbal posies can be composed with informality, or created more precisely in the Victorian manner, with concentric rings of aromatic leaves and flowers arranged around a central bloom, traditionally a small rosebud. A simple posy could be given as a token at each place around a dinner table.

### FESTIVE BOUQUETS

A herbal posy arranged in the hand makes a delightful bouquet to be carried by a bride or her attendants at a country wedding. Buttonholes and corsages can follow a similar theme, the stems of short-lived plants given a moisture source by being inserted in an orchid phial.

Matching posies can become part of the setting for a festive occasion. Attach small herbal posies, made up and then kept in water until the last minute, to a leafy garland edging a table, wind them around tent poles or drape across the frontfall of a tablecloth. For an equally charming effect, you can pin small posies to the tablecloth front, arranging them in rows or at random.

## A nosegay

*Make a herbal nosegay as prettily informal as you please, as artless as a bunch of flowers gathered by a young child.*

*selection of herbs and flowers such as feverfew, clove pinks, pink cornflowers, purple sage and variegated mint*

Compose the nosegay in your hand or on a flat surface, with the longest stems—they may be the mint or the sage—at the back and the flowering herbs in graduated heights below them. In that way, when the nosegay is put into a small vase, each herb will be seen to its full advantage. Loosely tie the stems with raffia or twine so that the planned shape—which should look entirely without guile—is not disarranged.

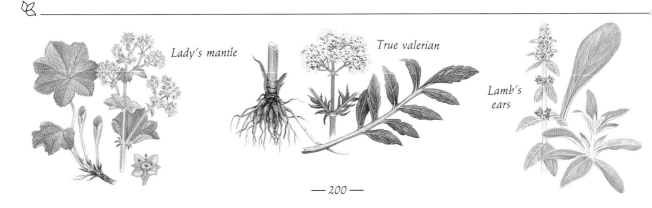

Lady's mantle

True valerian

Lamb's ears

# Decorating candles

*Candles made in plain cylindrical, square or cone-shaped moulds can be decorated with pressed leaves or petals. Pressed rose petals arranged to form flower shapes would be appropriate around rose-scented candles. Establish a colour link by decorating a yellow candle with orange pressed marigold petals or nasturtium flowers. Citrus-scented candles could be accented with small sprays of a lemon-scented herb, and candles perfumed with lavender could be decorated with pressed purple sage leaves and flowers. Use a thin, clear papercraft glue to stick the herbs in place, or lightly brush over them and the surrounding surface of the candle with clear melted wax.*

*You can also buy flexible candle moulds in shapes that suggest the aroma. Orange- and lemon-shaped candles could be scented with the appropriate essential oils. Perfume cone-shaped candles with sandalwood oil to evoke the aroma of incense.*

# A Victorian posy

*It takes a measure of patience to compose a Victorian-style posy of flowers and foliage arranged in concentric rings. For the neatest effect, grade the flowers and leaves according to size.*

*selection of flowering herbs such as rosebuds, feverfew, chamomile, cotton lavender, marjoram*
*fine twine or silver roll wire*
*toning ribbons*

Cut away any thorns from the rose stems. Hold a rosebud in one hand. Surround it with a ring of well-matched flowers, feverfew for example, with the heads at a slightly lower level than the rosebud, and then with sprays of foliage, their tips slightly below those of the previous ring.

Adjust and readjust each stem until the rings are even and concentric, then bind the stems with twine or silver wire. Continue making rings around this central core, binding the stems at intervals.

Finish the posy in the traditional way, with a ring of large protective leaves such as those of lady's mantle. Tie the ribbon around the stems and neaten the ends. Spray the posy with cool water and stand it in water.

*Cotton lavender*

*Feverfew*

*Sweet marjoram*

# HOUSEHOLD PREPARATIONS

In the days before conveniently packaged polishes and detergents, herbs were an important tool for the housewife, used for all sorts of homemade cleaners and disinfectants. One important use was the daily spreading of scented plants on floors to absorb dirt and smells in a far less hygienic world than our own. Plants like lady's bedstraw, meadowsweet, and sweet clover were often used to give houses a rather more attractive fragrance. Pot pourris have their origins in the Middle Ages, too, while the rich would carry pomanders – not only to have something pleasant to smell, but in the belief that they would ward off pestilence and plague.

*Water basil regularly if your windowsill is very sunny.*

*Lavender has many household uses, from candles to insect repellent.*

| APPLICATIONS | HERB | PART USED | HOW TO USE |
|---|---|---|---|
| Candles | Bergamot | flowers | Add crushed to melted wax |
| | Costmary | leaves | Add crushed to melted wax |
| | Lavender | oil | Add to melted wax as scent |
| | | flowers | Add crushed to melted wax |
| | Mint | leaves | Add crushed to melted wax |
| | Neroli/ Orange | oil | Add to melted wax as scent |
| | Rose | oil | Add to melted wax as scent |
| | Rosemary | oil | Add to melted wax as scent |
| | | leaves | Add crushed to melted wax |
| | Sandalwood | oil | Add to melted wax as scent |
| Fabric rinses | Costmary | leaves | Use strained infusion as final rinse for bedlinen, etc. |
| | Eau de cologne mint | leaves | Use strained infusion as final rinse for bedlinen, etc. |
| | Lavender | flowers | Use strained infusion as final rinse for bedlinen, etc. |
| | Lemon verbena | leaves | Use strained infusion as final rinse for bedlinen, etc. |
| | Rosemary | leaves | Use strained infusion as final rinse for bedlinen, etc. |
| Household cleaners | Cedar | oil | Add to beeswax and turpentine polishes and creams |
| | Lavender | flowers | Add to beeswax and turpentine in furniture creams |
| | Lemon balm | leaves | Traditionally added to furniture polish; infuse in linseed oil and turpentine |
| | Soapwort | leaves | Use infusion for washing fabrics and upholstery |
| | | root | Use decoction for washing fabrics and upholstery |
| Insect repellents | Basil | whole plant | Grow on a windowsill |
| | Lavender cotton | leaves | Deters moths if hung in closets or combine with southernwood and other moth deterrents in muslin bags |
| | Lavender | flowers & stems | Deters moths if hung in closets |

| Applications | Herb | Part used | How to use |
|---|---|---|---|
| Insect repellents cont. | Pennyroyal | whole plant | Grow around flowerbeds, to deter ants |
| | Rosemary | leaves | Combine with southernwood and other moth deterrents in muslin bags |
| | Rue | leaves/stems | Deters flies and wasps from a room or picnic table |
| | Southernwood | leaves | Deters moths if hung in closets |
| | Tansy | leaves/stems | Deters flies and wasps from a room or picnic table |
| Mice repellents | Mint | leaves | Strew in affected area |
| | Pepper | ground seed | Sprinkle in affected areas |
| Pillow stuffers | Chamomile | flowers | Use to help sleep |
| | Hops | strobiles | Use to help sleep |
| | Lavender | flowers | Use or for scenting linen and lingerie drawers |
| | Rose | petals | Use for scenting linen and lingerie drawers |
| Pomanders | Cloves | flower bud | Stick into dried orange |
| | Rose | buds | Use to decorate dried oranges |
| | | powdered petals | Use to scent beeswax pomander beads |
| | | oil | Use to scent beeswax pomander beads |
| Room fragrances | Bay | leaves | Use in incense cones |
| | Bergamot | flowers | Use in pot pourri and sachets |
| | Borage | flowers | Use in pot pourri |
| | Cardamom | seeds | Use in incense powder |
| | Coriander | ground seeds | Pot pourri; use in incense cones and powder |
| | Fennel | seeds | Use in pot pourri |
| | Lavender | prunings | Burn on an open fire |
| | | flowers | Pot pourri or store in a stationery box to scent stationery; use in incense cones |
| | | stems | Use for lavender "bottles" to scent drawers, etc. |
| | | oil | Use in incense cones |
| | Lemongrass | leaves | Use in pot pourri and sachets |
| | Lovage | seeds | Use in pot pourri |
| | Marigold | petals | Use in pot pourri and sachets |
| | Marjoram | flowers | Use in pot pourri and sachets |
| | Myrrh | resin | Use in incense powder |
| | Orris | root | Fixative for pot pourri |
| | Rose | petals | Use in pot pourri and sachets |
| | Rosemary | leaves | Pot pourri |
| | | flowers | Use in pot pourri and sachets |
| | | pruned clippings | Burn on open fires |
| | Sandalwood | powder | Use in incense cones & powder |
| | | oil | Use in incense cones |

*Victorian ladies used to carry pomanders. Now, they are used to delicately scent rooms and cupboards.*

*Herbs can be used not only to scent candles but also to decorate them.*

# HOUSEKEEPING PREPARATIONS

Herbs and other aromatic plants can be utilized to keep homes fresh and clean, sweet-smelling and welcoming. Making and using herbal polishes and household soaps offer both a sense of satisfaction and continuity with the past that manufactured products cannot match.

## Lavender furniture cream

*Apply this sweet-smelling cream sparingly, and polish with a soft, dry cloth.*

*50 g (2 oz) beeswax*
*300 ml (½ pt) pure turpentine*
*50 g (2 oz) pure soap flakes*
*200 ml (6 fl oz) lavender infusion*

Put the beeswax and turpentine into the top of a double boiler, or a bowl over a pan of simmering water and stir until the ingredients are well blended. Remove from the heat and cool slightly.

Put the soap flakes and lavender infusion into a small pan and heat gently. Whisk the mixture until it is frothy, then remove from the heat and cool slightly.

Stir the lavender mixture into the beeswax to make a thick, creamy consistency. Pour into an airtight tin or lidded jar, cover and label.

*To make about 600 ml (1 pt)*

## Household shampoo

*This mild soapwort shampoo has been entrusted with the delicate task of cleaning old tapestries and precious carpets.*

*25 g (1 oz) dried soapwort root, soaked overnight, or 3 handfuls of fresh soapwort stems*
*1 litre (1¾ pt) water*

Drain the soaked root, cut it into small pieces and crush it with a rolling pin or a hammer. Cut fresh stems into short lengths. Put the soapwort into a pan, pour on the water and bring to the boil. Cover and simmer for 30 minutes, stirring occasionally. Set aside until it is cool. Strain off the liquid, discarding the herb. Pour it into bottles, cover and label.

*To make 1 litre (1¾ pt)*

*Soapwort*

# Insect repellents

Herbals and country lore abound with ways of ridding yourself of unwelcome pests. Lavender clippings were burned on open fires to deter insects and to scent the room, and in the Middle Ages sprays of mint were strewn on the floor to keep rooms fresh and deter not insects but mice, which were said not to like the smell. Other effective strewing herbs were rue, southernwood and tansy. Tansy leaves were also rubbed over meat and fish to impregnate the food, before covering them with fresh sprays of the herb.

Basil, which has been grown in the Mediterranean region since ancient times, is cultivated in windowsill pots more to repel flies than to flavour tomatoes. By growing pots of herbs such as eau de Cologne mint, peppermint, basil and thyme on the windowsills, hanging bunches of herbs to dry in a warm airy room, and arranging jugs of chamomile and pennyroyal, cotton lavender and southernwood around the home you can discourage an insect invasion.

### Keeping moths at bay

Southernwood, cotton lavender, lavender and rosemary protect woollens from moths. If you wish to try herbal moth repellents, wrap the herb sprays in muslin or cheesecloth, or place them between layers of tissue paper to avoid having to remove silky leaves and tiny seeds later.

### Moth-repellent bags

To make sweet-smelling moth-repellent bags, mix together 6 tablespoonsful of dried southernwood leaves with 2 tablespoonsful each of dried chamomile flowers and dried, crumbled rosemary leaves, 1 tablespoonful of crumbled dried bay leaves, 2 crushed cinnamon sticks, 1 teaspoonful each of ground cloves and orris root powder and 1 tablespoonful of salt. Store in an airtight container for two weeks, shaking every day or two. Use the matured mixture to fill satchets for cupboards and drawers.

# Household soap

*Create a pleasant ambience around the home as you use this soap for household cleaning. It is especially useful for brightening paintwork.*

225 g (8 oz) pure soap flakes
2 tbsp corn oil, plus extra for brushing
5 tbsp clear honey
1 tsp oil of cloves

Put the soap flakes, corn oil and honey into the top of a double boiler, or a bowl over a pan of simmering water and stir occasionally until the ingredients have blended. Stir in the oil of cloves, and continue stirring until the mixture thickens and resists the movement of the spoon.

Turn the mixture into oiled moulds such as dariole moulds or individual dessert cases and put in a warm, dry place to set. This may take two weeks or more, depending on the volume of each bar. Unmould the soap, and polish with a soft cloth.

*To make 325 g (11 oz)*

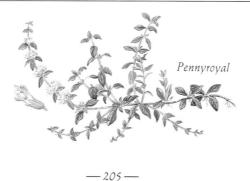

Pennyroyal

Rosemary

# SWEET-SCENTED LAVENDER

Probably more than any other garden herb, lavender has long been associated with serenity and calm, with fresh, clean smells and an aura of luxury. Whoever said that cleanliness is next to godliness must have had a favourite aunt who made use of the herb to scent every room in her home.

For many people lavender evokes bygone days, of Victorian drawing rooms scented with lavender bags tucked between cushions or hung from chairbacks beneath antimacassars. Sachets were even popped inside writing boxes to scent stationery. These and other fragrant notions have as much relevance today, and can greatly enhance our personal environment. If the sweet scent of lavender alone does not create the ambience you seek, spice it up with, say, crushed coriander seeds, a crumbled cinnamon stick, a few allspice berries and dried tansy flowers.

## *Fragrant fillers*

*You can use herbs and other aromatic plants to transform everyday household objects into fragrant decorations.*

### TEAPOT STANDS
*Cut strong cotton fabric into circles, squares or rectangles, or fancy shapes like strawberries or pumpkins. Sew two matching shapes together and fill the "bag" with a sweet or spicy mixture. Every time you put a hot dish on the stand you will release the scent.*

### SWEET BAGS
*You can use the sleep-pillow mixture given right, or a similar one of your choice, to fill sachets. These can be used to scent drawers and cupboards, hang on a door handle or use as a*
*pull for a light or window-blind.*

*Small spherical bags, tightly packed with the flower mixture, can be used as "comforters" to handle in times of stress. Tossing them from hand to hand or squeezing them releases the soothing aroma.*

### PINCUSHIONS
*Make a pincushion in any shape you choose, an apple or pear, heart or hat, and trim it with ribbon or braid, beads or sequins. Pack it with the sweet-bag mixture or with a single herbal fragrance such as dried coriander leaves and lightly-crushed*
*coriander seeds. Each time you insert or withdraw a pin or needle the pincushion will release the aroma.*

### SCENTED PAPER
*Tuck a sweet bag into a box of stationery or face tissues or, for a more long-lasting effect, sew some flower mixture between pieces of muslin. Place these muslin bags between sheets of paper, wrap the paper in foil or put it in an airtight box. Leave it for two or three weeks, by which time the paper should be well impregnated with your favourite herbal fragrance.*

# Lavender bottles

*Sometimes known as lavender rattles for their resemblance to babies'
rattles, lavender bottles have a practical design concept.*

*22 long supple stalks of lavender
in full flower
60 cm (24 in) approximately of satin
ribbon, 6 mm (¼ in) wide*

The lavender flowers are held in a
"cage" of interwoven stalks and
ribbons, so will not spill out. These
decorations were originally used to
separate linen stacked in chests into
dozens and half-dozens, scenting it
at the same time.

Gather the lavender stems
together, with the flowerheads
level. Tie them together with one
end of the ribbon just below the
flowers. Turn the bunch upside-
down and bend the stalks
downwards, from just below the
ribbon, so that they cover the
flowerheads. Space out the stems
in pairs and weave the free end of

the ribbon over and under alternate
pairs of stems so that it encloses
the flowers. Pull the ribbon more
tightly at the top and bottom of the
design, so that the "bottle" has
more fullness in the centre. Tie the
ribbon in a bow, neaten the ends
and trim the stalks.

Tuck a lavender bottle into a
drawer with underwear or
woollens, hang one on a coat-
hanger or arrange three or more in a
dish in a bedroom or bathroom.

*To make one bottle*

# Sleep pillow

*Make a small pillow in the prettiest fabric you can find, fill it with
this relaxing herbal mixture, and rest assured, at home or on an
aeroplane, that it will soothe you to sleep.*

*50 g (2 oz) dried lavender flowers
25 g (1 oz) dried chamomile flowers
25 g (1 oz) dried fragrant rose petals
2 tbsp coriander seeds, lightly crushed
1 small cinnamon stick, crumbled
2 tbsp dried orris root powder*

Mix all the ingredients together and
store them in a lidded jar for two
weeks, stirring or shaking the
contents every day. Pack the dried-
flower mixture into a small pillow
made of closely-woven fabric.

If you decide to vary the mixture,
be sure to include the orris root
powder which acts as a fixative.

Lavender
stoechas

Chamomile

# ROOM FRAGRANCES

Use herbs from your garden or windowbox to contribute to the mood of the moment. Pot pourri, a fragrant blend of dried flowers and petals, leaves and seeds, is a delightful way of enjoying the scents of summer long after the flowers have faded. You can turn back the clock and create both light and fragrance by burning aromatic oils in a traditional burner, or you can perfume candles with fragrant oils to create a romantic mood or an air of luxury.

The most creative element of the craft is in the blending. You can blend the dried plant materials by fragrance – rose petals with rose-scented pelargonium leaves is a perfect example; by colour, creating a sunshine mixture of golden thyme and golden marjoram leaves with pot marigold petals and those from lemon-yellow roses; or simply by season. Few pot pourri mixtures could be more evocative or romantic than one composed of myriad flowers and leaves gathered all on a summer's day.

The origins of pot pourri as an air freshener go back to the Middle Ages when even the heaviest fragrances could scarcely mask the unwelcome odours of daily life! The craft is enjoying a revival of popularity today, when the blend of sweet or pungent aromas, the variety of textures and the limitless colour permutations make pot pourri one of the most delightful accessories for the home.

Although the concept began as a blend of the most fragrant flowers in the herb garden, damask rose petals and lavender flowers, it is possible to include some plant materials which have little or no fragrance, and compensate by adding another pinch or two of a ground spice and a couple of drops of an essential oil.

There are two types of pot pourri. The first, made by what is known as the "moist" method, has the longer pedigree and was made in the still-rooms of the great estates. The second type, made by the dry method is simpler and more versatile.

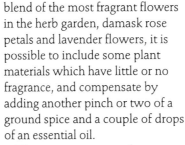

### THE DRY METHOD

To make pot pourri by the dry method it is necessary to have all the materials completely dry; so dry that they rustle like tissue paper. Mix them together with the spices and other fragrances, and store them in a lidded jar for three or four days, stirring daily. Add the fixative and essential oil, cover and leave for six weeks, stirring daily if possible. The pot pourri will then be ready for use.

### THE MOIST METHOD

To make pot pourri by the moist method, partially dry the leaves

*Rosemary*

## Rose garden pot pourri

*Make the pot pourri as described for the dry method.*

2 cups dried damask rose petals
1 cup dried rosemary flowers
and leaves
1 cup dried chamomile flowers
1 cup dried lemon verbena leaves

1 tbsp ground allspice
1 tbsp ground cinnamon
1 tbsp ground orris root powder
4–5 drops rose oil

## Rainbow pot pourri

*Make the pot pourri using the moist method, as described below.*

1 cup partly dried marigold petals
1 cup partly dried bergamot flowers
1 cup partly dried marjoram
flowers, stripped from the stalk
1 cup partly dried lemon grass
leaves, finely chopped
1 cup partly dried lemon verbena
leaves

1 cup partly dried borage flowers
3 cups fine-textured salt
1 tbsp aniseed seeds
1 tbsp fennel seeds
1 tbsp ground coriander
1 tbsp dried orris root powder
5–6 drops essential oil, such as
bergamot

and petals and layer them with salt in a lidded container. Leave them without stirring for two weeks. During this time the salt will have acted as a desiccant, and drawn out the remaining moisture from the plant materials. Break up the block which will have formed, add the spices, the fixative (ground orris root powder) and a few drops of essential oil. Stir well, cover and leave for six weeks, stirring every day if possible. Choose a wide-necked container and mix the developing pot pourri with your fingers; it is remarkably relaxing.

### USING POT POURRI

Pot pourri can be displayed in an open bowl, placed where people can stir it with their fingers as they pass, or in traditional "pomander" bowls with perforated lids. As a more sophisticated alternative to simply filling a glass container with pot pourri, you can embed a nosegay of dried herbs in a block of florists' foam and conceal the block with pot pourri. To conserve the colour and fragrance store it in a lidded jar and lift the lid on the aroma only when the room – a guest bedroom, perhaps – is in use.

The mixture can also be stuffed into sachets and draw-string bags, sleep pillows and other decorative items; there are more details of these notions on pages 206 and 207. A pot pourri blend can be used to create three-dimensional decorations by sticking it evenly over the surface of polystyrene foam balls, piled high in a shallow dish to make a pretty display. A dry foam ring or a heart shape can also be covered in this way. A final flourish of a dried-flower posy tied with ribbon completes a romantic design.

### REVIVING POT POURRI

When your pot pourri loses a little of its original colour and fragrance, it is time for revival tactics. Discard any especially faded petals and leaves, replacing them with more colourful (and fully dried) materials. Put the mixture into a lidded container, shake on a little more spice and essential oil, stir well and cover the jar. Set it aside for about two weeks, stirring it each day.

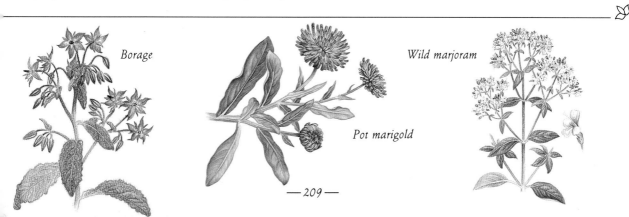

Borage

Pot marigold

Wild marjoram

# Rosebud pomander

*Hang this pretty decoration over a dressing table, on a bed post, a door handle, wherever it will give you most pleasure.*

foam ball, about 7.5 cm (3 in) diameter
2 tbsp cloves
36 small dried rosebuds, approximately
a handful of pot pourri
half a medium-gauge stub wire
narrow ribbon to hang

Stud the foam ball over with cloves. This will give the decoration the pungency of the traditional "clove oranges", or dried-fruit pomanders. Cut the stems of the rosebuds to a length of about 8 mm (3/8 in) and press them into the foam, making neat rows or rings. Continue all around the ball until it is covered. Wrap the pomander in pot pourri in several layers of tissue, or a paper (not plastic) bag. Leave it in a dry, warm place for several weeks. Remove from its wrappings, pierce the top with a U-shaped staple and attach a ribbon by which to hang.

*To make one pomander*

# Scented candles

*A few drops of the essential oil you use in home remedies and cosmetic preparations or home-made fragrant oils are all you need to scent candles of all shapes and sizes.*

9 tbsp paraffin wax
1 tbsp stearin (stearic acid)
candle dye (from craft shops)
3–4 drops essential oil such as rose,
orange, or lavender, or 1 tsp fragrant oil
1 wick
1 wick rod, or pencil or cocktail stick
150 ml (1/4 pt) candle mould, or
yoghurt pot

Melt the wax in the top of a double boiler, or a bowl over a pan of simmering water. Stir in the stearin, which strengthens the wax and slows down the rate of burning, and the dye. Stir in the fragrant oil and stir until well blended. Remove from the heat and cool slightly.

Cut a piece of wick 7.5 cm (3 in) longer than the depth of the mould. Dip the wick in the melted wax and tie it, close to one end, around the centre of the wick rod. Lay the rod across the top of the mould and thread the other end of the wick through a hole in the centre of the mould base. Stand the mould base upright. If it is an uneven shape it may be necessary to support it in a jar or box.

Pour in as much wax as the mould will take, taking care to keep the wick vertical. Tap the mould to release any trapped air and leave the wax to set slightly. As it does so, a depression will form in the top. Gently reheat the remaining wax and pour it into the mould to level the surface. Leave the candle to cool completely.

Remove the wick rod. Peel off flexible moulds, or tap rigid ones to release the candle. Trim the wick and polish the candle with a soft, dry cloth.

*To make one candle*

Lavender
'Hidcote'

Coriander

Myrrh/
Sweet Cice

# Incense powder

*If you have an open fire or are lighting a barbecue, sprinkle a little of this aromatic powder on to the glowing charcoal, but make sure that the room is well ventilated if you are using it indoors.*

*25 g (1 oz) sandalwood powder*
*15 g (½ oz) coriander seeds, lightly crushed*
*15 g (½ oz) cardamom seeds, lightly crushed*
*1 tsp myrrh crystals*
*25 g (1 oz) dried lavender flowers, ground to a powder*
*25 g (1 oz) gum benzoin powder*
*2–3 drops essential oil*

Mix together the sandalwood, coriander and cardamom seeds, myrrh crystals and lavender flowers. Stir in the gum benzoin, which acts as a fixative and "holds" the fragrances, and then the essential oil. Store the mixture in an airtight container. Sprinkle a few large pinches over a fire.

*To make about 100 g (4 oz)*

# Incense cones

*Incense cones bring a hint of the Orient to a living room or hall, and may be used to freshen the air after a party.*

*5 tbsp gum arabic crystals*
*150 g (6 oz) charcoal, crushed*
*25 g (1 oz) gum benzoin powder*
*1 tsp sandalwood powder*
*1 tsp ground coriander*
*25 g (1 oz) dried bay leaves, finely crumbled*
*25 g (1 oz) dried lavender flowers, ground to a powder*
*4–5 drops essential oil such as sandalwood or lavender*

Put the gum arabic into a small bowl and mix it to a stiff paste with water. Mix together the charcoal, gum benzoin powder, sandalwood and ground coriander and stir in the gum arabic paste. Stir in the crumbled bay leaves and lavender flowers and add the essential oil. Stir until the ingredients are thoroughly blended. Form cones about 5 cm (2 in) high and leave them in a warm place such as an airing cupboard for two days. When dry, wrap the cones in foil to keep in their aroma. Unwrap and light the tip to burn.

*To make about 20 cones*

## *Fragrant smoke*

*This simple form of incense captures the fragrance of home-grown herbs in a wisp of smoke. Select the herbs to suit the mood of the occasion. Rub or grind them to a powder, put them in a small fireproof dish, and set light to them.*

FOR A ROMANTIC MOOD
*Lavender flowers or rose petals.*

FOR A REFRESHING AROMA
*Lemon balm, lemon grass, lemon mint, peppermint, rosemary, sage or thyme leaves, dill or fennel seeds.*

FOR AN EXOTIC AROMA
*Bay leaves, coriander seeds or cumin seeds.*

*Sweet bay*

*Apothecary's rose*

# HERB USES

| Herb | Aromatic | Cosmetic | Craft | Culinary | Household | Medicinal |
|------|----------|----------|-------|----------|-----------|-----------|
| Agrimony (*Agrimonia eupatoria*) | | skin care | | | roots: yellow dye | diuretic |
| Angelica (*Angelica archangelica*) | mildly aromatic | | | fruit, cheese dishes, candied stems | | appetite stimulant, digestive |
| Anise (*Pimpinella anisum*) | licorice-like, pungent | | | seeds: curries | infusion of seeds: insecticide | seeds: breath freshener; tisane: digestive, for cough |
| Basil, sweet (*Ocimum basilicum*) | like cloves | | | tomatoes, cheese, salads | insect repellant | tisane: flatulence, nausea |
| Bay, sweet (*Laurus nobilis*) | sweet, woody | | wreaths | meat dishes, sauces, soups | pot pourri | mild sedative, stomach upset, antiseptic |
| Bergamot (*Monarda didyma*) | sweet, light fragrance | oil: perfumery | flowers: floral decoration | salads; flowers: garnish | oil: scented candles | tisane: relaxant; inhalant: chest troubles |
| Birch (*Betula*) | | hair care | | | | oil: rheumatic pain |
| Blackberry (*Rubux fruticosus*) | | skin care | | | | |
| Caraway (*Carum carvi*) | pungent aroma of seeds | | seedheads: wreaths | salads; seeds: cakes, bread, cheese | | tisane: flatulence |
| Catmint (*Nepeta cataria*) | pungent | skin care, hair care | | | | tisane: insomnia, colds |
| Chamomile (*Anthemis nobilis*) | apple scented | skin care, hair care | dried flowers: floral wreaths | | orange or green dye; flowers: pot pourri | tisane: insomnia, digestive; mouthwash; poultice |
| Chervil (*Anthriscus cerefolium*) | anise-like | skin care | seedheads: wreaths | *fines herbes*, bouquet garni, salads, meat, fish | | poultice |
| Chicory (*Cichorium intybus*) | | | | salad, braised vegetable; dried root: drink | | |
| Chive (*Allium schoenoprasum*) | onion scented | | | *fines herbes*, salads, egg dishes | | mild antiseptic |
| Clary (*Salvia sclarea*) | balsam scent | | | soups, sauces, wine making | | eye lotion, gargle, antiseptic |
| Clove (*Eugenia aromatica*) | strong spicy | oil: footcare | | meat dishes, curries, fruit dishes | pot pourri, pomanders | oil: toothache |

| HERB | AROMATIC | COSMETIC | CRAFT | CULINARY | HOUSEHOLD | MEDICINAL |
|---|---|---|---|---|---|---|
| Comfrey (*Symphytum officinale*) | | skin care, hair care | | vegetable | yellow dye | poultice: abscesses, burns, bruises |
| Coriander (*Coriandrum sativum*) | | | | seeds, leaves: Mexican, oriental dishes, salads | ground seeds: incense | tisane: digestive; oil: aromatherapy |
| Costmary (*Chrysanthemum balsamita*) | strongly aromatic | skin care, hair care | | salads, soups, sauces | insect repellant, pot pourri | tisane: digestive |
| Cotton lavender (*Santolina chamaecyparissus*) | strongly aromatic | oil: perfumery | | flowers: garnish | insect repellant | |
| Cumin (*Cuminum cyminum*) | strong, pungent | | | seeds: curries, bread, cakes | | seeds: breath freshener |
| Dandelion (*Taraxacum officinale*) | | skin care | | salads, soups; flowers: wine; dried root: beverage | roots: magenta, brown or orange dye | appetite stimulant, laxative, diuretic |
| Dill (*Anethum graveolens*) | caraway | | seedheads: wreaths | fish, sauces, garnish; seeds: pickles, vinegars, oils | | decoction of seeds: sedative, digestive |
| Elder (*Sambucus*) | flowers honey scented | skin care, hair care | | flowers: fruit preserves, drinks, wine, cordials | | tisane: fever, rheumatism |
| Eucalyptus (*Eucalyptus*) | pungent | skin care | preserved leaves: wreaths | | room purifier | antibiotic; chest troubles |
| Evening primrose (*Oenothera biennis*) | | | | | | oil: skin ailments, menstrual problems |
| Eyebright (*Euphrasia officinalis*) | | | | | | eyebath; gargle for sore throat, catarrh |
| Fennel (*Foeniculum vulgare*) | anise | skin care, hair care | seedheads: wreaths | fish dishes, salad dressings; seeds: bread | | infusion: digestive, diuretic; eyebath |
| Fenugreek (*Tribonella foenum-graecum*) | bitter aroma | | | roasted seeds: curries; sprouted seeds: salads | seeds: yellow dye | seeds: digestive, breath freshener |
| Feverfew (*Chrysanthemum parthenium*) | bitter | skin care | | | moth repellant | headache; tisane: tonic |
| Florence fennel (*Foeniculum vulgare dulce*) | | | | bulb: salads, vegetable | | |
| Garlic (*Allium sativum*) | strong flavour | hair care | | savoury dishes, oils, vinegars | | antiseptic, diuretic |

| Herb | Aromatic | Cosmetic | Craft | Culinary | Household | Medicinal |
|---|---|---|---|---|---|---|
| Ginseng (*Panax quinquefolius*) | | | | | | mild stimulant and relaxant |
| Good King Henry (*Chenopodium bonus-henricus*) | | | | salads, vegetable | | |
| Hops (*Humulus lupulus*) | | | wreaths | | brewing beer, kavening bread | antibiotic, astringent; infusion: sore throat |
| Horehound, white (*Marrybium vulgare*) | bitter | | | | | tisane: chest troubles, digestive |
| Horseradish (*Cochlearia armoracia*) | pungent when bruised | skin care | | root: sauces, fish, meat, fish dishes | | fresh root: chest troubles |
| Horsetail (*Equisetum arvense*) | | skin care, hair care, nail strengthener | | green stems: vegetable | metal polish; grey dye | poultice: wounds; diuretic |
| Hyssop (*Hysoppus officinalis*) | musky | | | salads, meat dishes | insect, moth repellant | tisane: chest trouble, gargle, bruises |
| Lady's mantle (*Alchemilla vulgaris*) | | skin care | posies, wreaths | | | tisane: menstrual troubles |
| Lamb's ears (*Stachys byzantina*) | | | posies, wreaths | | | |
| Lavender (*Lavendula*) | strongly and sweetly scented | skin care, hair care | wreaths | scented oils, sugars; herbes de Provence | pot pourri; laundry rinse; furniture cream; insect repellant; oil: scented candles | tisane: headache, nervousness; oil: aromatherapy |
| Lemon balm (*Melissa officinalis*) | lemon scented | eau de Cologne | | vegetable dishes, milk puddings | laundry rinse; pot pourri; furniture polish | tisane: headache, insomnia; insect bites; oil: aromatherapy |
| Lemon grass (*Cymbopogon citratus*) | | | | Oriental cuisine | pot pourri | |
| Lemon verbena (*Aloysia triphylla*) | lemon scented | skin care, hair care | | meat and poultry stuffing; flavouring syrups | pot pourri; sachets for linens | infusion: digestive, mild sedative |
| Licorice (*Glycyrrhiza glabra*) | sweet, anise | | | confectionery | | digestive, laxative |
| Lovage (*Levisticum officinale*) | celery aroma | skin care, deodorant | | soups, salads, casseroles, Indian cookery | | diuretic; infusion: digestive |

| Herb | Aromatic | Cosmetic | Craft | Culinary | Household | Medicinal |
|------|----------|----------|-------|----------|-----------|-----------|
| Marigold, pot (*Calendula officinalis*) | petals spicy | skin care, hair care | garlands | petals: rice, cheese, meat dishes, salads | petals: pale yellow dye | tisane: digestive; poultice: styes |
| Marjoram, sweet (*Origanum majorana*) | honey scented | hair care, soap | wreaths, garlands | bouquet garni, meats, stuffings, salads, oils, vinegars | insect repellant; pot pourri | tisane: digestive, asthma |
| Marshmallow (*Althaea officinalis*) | | skin care, hair care | | salads | | decoction of dried root: sore throat; bruises, strains |
| Meadow-sweet (*Filipendula ulmaria*) | honey scented flowers | | wreaths, posies | | | tisane: digestive; antiseptic, diuretic |
| Mints (*Mentha*) | | skin care, soap | garlands | bouquet garni, meat sauces, cheese, jellies, syrups, oils, vinegars | insect repellant, scented candles, laundry rinse | tisane: digestive, sedative, appetite stimulant; infusion: antiseptic |
| Mugwort (*Artemisia vulgaris*) | | | | | | digestive; regulates menstruation |
| Myrrh (*Commiphora myrrha*) | musty, spicy | | | | crystals: incense | antiseptic, antifungal; infusion: sore throats, gargle |
| Nasturtium (*Tropaeolum majus*) | spicy | hair care | | salads; seeds: as capers; flowers: salads, garnish | | tisane: chest troubles; urinary tract infections |
| Nettle, stinging (*Urtica dioica*) | | skin care, hair care | | vegetable | | tisane: skin problems |
| Onion, Egyptian tree (*Allium cepa proliferum*) | onion-like | | | as onions | | |
| Onion, Welsh (*Allium fistulosum*) | onion-like | | | bulbs as onions; tops: garnish | | |
| Oregano (*Origanum vulgare*) | | | | meat, vegetable dishes, salads, oils, vinegars | | |
| Orris root (*Iris germanica* var. 'Florentina') | violet scented | dried root: hair care | | | fixative for pot pourri; herb pillows | |
| Parsley (*Petroseleum crispum*) | | skin care, hair care | | *fines herbes*, sauces, salads, egg dishes, soups, garnish | green or cream dye | |
| Pelargonium, scented-leaved (*Pelargonium*) | lemon, nutmeg, orange, clove scented | skin care | | sugar, sorbet, cakes, desserts, decoration | pot pourri, insect repellant | |

| Herb | Aromatic | Cosmetic | Craft | Culinary | Household | Medicinal |
|---|---|---|---|---|---|---|
| Pennyroyal (*Mentha pulegium*) | | skin care | | | insect repellant | plants in flower: colds, nausea; insect stings and bites |
| Peppermint (*Mentha × piperita*) | menthol scent | skin care, hair care | | beverages | insect repellant | tisane: digestive, antiseptic |
| Purslane (*Portulaca oleracea*) | | | | vegetable, salad | | |
| Rose (*Rosa*) | sweet, intensely floral | skin care, soaps, powder | garlands | jam, jellies, decoration, rosehip syrup | pot pourri, scented candles, scenting linen | rose vinegar: headache; rose honey: sore throat |
| Rosemary (*Rosemarinus officinalis*) | pungent | skin care, hair care, soap | posies, wreaths | bouquet garni, roast meats, fish, potatoes, vinegars | pot pourri | tisane: digestive, nervousness; diuretic |
| Rue (*Ruta graveolens*) | bitter | | | | insect repellant | eye disorders; gargle |
| Salad burnet (*Poterium sanguisorba*) | | | | salads, sauces, beverages | | |
| Sage (*Salvia officinalis*) | pungent | hair care, tooth cleanser | | bouquet garni, meats, fish stuffings | insect repellant | tisane: coughs, digestive; mouthwash; oil: aromatherapy |
| Sage, pineapple (*Salvia elegans*) | pineapple scented | | | stuffings | | |
| Sandalwood (*Santalum album*) | musty | | | | incense | oil: aromatherapy |
| Selfheal (*Prunella vulgaris*) | | | | | | infusion: mouthwash |
| Soapwort (*Saponaria officinalis*) | | skin care; dried root: hair care, soap | | | soaps, polish | skin conditions |
| Sorrel (*Rumex acetosa*) | lemon scented | | seedheads: wreaths | soup, vegetable, salads | yellow and green dye | diuretic |
| Sorrel, buckler leaf (*Rumex scutatus*) | | | seedheads: decorations | vegetable | | |
| Southern-wood (*Artemisia abrotanum*) | sweet, refreshing | hair care | | stuffing for meat, poultry | pot pourri, insect and moth repellant; stems: yellow dye | stimulant, antiseptic |
| Summer savory (*Satureia hortensis*) | spicy | | | stuffing for meats; bean dishes | | tisane: digestive, antiseptic, diuretic; insect stings |

| Herb | Aromatic | Cosmetic | Craft | Culinary | Household | Medicinal |
|------|----------|----------|-------|----------|-----------|-----------|
| Sweet Cicely (*Myrrhis odorata*) | sweet, anise | | posies, wreaths | fruit salads, tarts; seeds: beverages | seeds: furniture polish | |
| Sweet violet (*Viola odoratum*) | highly floral scent | skin care | | flavour honey; crystallized flowers | | chest troubles |
| Sweet woodruff (*Galium odoratum*) | like newly mown hay | | | beverage | scenting linen | |
| Tansy (*Tanacetum vulgare*) | pungent | | wreaths | flavour meat, cheese, milk dishes, cakes; salads | orange dye; insect repellant | tisane: digestive |
| Tarragon (*Artemisia dracunculus*) | sweet scent | | | *fines herbes*, salads, tomatoes, poultry, oils, vinegars | | |
| Thyme (*Thymus*) | strongly fragrant | skin care, hair care | | bouquet garni, stuffings, marinades, roast meats, oils, vinegars | pot pourri, insect repellant, scented candles, scenting linens | tisane: colds; digestive, treat cuts, bruises |
| Valerian, true (*Valeriana officinalis*) | repelling aroma | | | | | decoction: mild sedative, headaches |
| Vervain (*Verbena officinalis*) | | | | | | tisane: mild sedative, headaches, gallstones |
| Wall germander (*Teucrinum chamaedrys*) | | | | | | diuretic |
| Watercress (*Nasturtium officinale*) | | | | soups, salads, butters, cheeses, omelettes | | chest troubles, digestive |
| Winter savory (*Satureja montana*) | peppery | | | game, rich meats, soups, bean dishes | strewing herb | infusion of flowers: digestive, antiseptic, diuretic; insect bites, stings |
| Witch hazel (*Hamamelis mollis*) | | skin care | | | antiseptic | bruises, varicose veins; infusion: eyebath, mouthwash |
| Woad (*Isatis tinctoria*) | | | | | blue dye | |
| Wormwood (*Artemisia absinthium*) | | | | | | tisane: digestive |
| Yarrow (*Achillea millefolium*) | strongly aromatic | skin care | wreaths | salads | insect repellant | tisane: digestive, colds, minor wounds |

# ALTERNATIVE NAMES

| DIRECTORY LISTING | ALTERNATIVE BOTANICAL NAME | COMMON NAMES |
| --- | --- | --- |
| *Alchemilla vulgaris* | *Alchemilla xanthochora* | Lady's mantle |
| *Allium cepa proliferum* | | Egyptian tree onion, Egyptian top onion |
| *Allium fistulosum* | | Welsh onion, Japanese bunching onion |
| *Allium schoenoprasum* | | Common chive, onion chive |
| *Allium tuberosum* | | Garlic chive, Chinese chive |
| *Aloysia triphylla* | *Lippia citriodora* | Lemon verbena |
| *Anthemis nobilis* | *Chamaemelum nobile* | Chamomile, English chamomile perennial chamomile |
| *Artemisia abrotanum* | | Lad's love, southernwood, maid's ruin, garde-robe |
| *Chenopodium bonus-henricus* | | Good King Henry, goosefoot |
| *Chrysanthemum balsamita* | *Balsamita major* | Costmary, alecost, bible leaf |
| *Chrysanthemum parthenium* | *Tanacetum parthenium* *Matricaria eximia* | |
| *Cochlearia armoracia* | *Armoracia rusticana* | Horseradish |
| *Coriandrum sativum* | | Coriander, cilantro, Chinese parsley |
| *Glycyrrhiza glabra* | | Licorice, liquorice |
| *Iris germanica* 'Florentina' | *Iris florentina* | Orris root |
| *Isatis tinctoria* | | Woad, dyer's weed |
| *Monarda didyma* | | Bee balm, bergamot, Oswego tea |
| *Myrrhis odorata* | | Sweet Cicely, myrrh, garden myrrh |
| *Nepeta cataria* | | Catnip, catmint |
| *Oenothera biennis* | | Evening primrose, night willow herb |
| *Origanum vulgare* | | Oregano, wild marjoram |
| *Petroselinum crispum* | | Parsley, curled parsley |
| *Salvia officinalis* | | Common sage, garden sage |
| *Santolina chamaecyparissus* | | Cotton lavender, lavender |
| *Stachys byzantina* | *Stachys lanata* *Stachys olympia* | Lamb's ears |
| *Taraxacum officinale* | | Dandelion, piss-the-bed, pis en lis |

# PLANT CLASSIFICATION

**Family** A category in plant classification which gathers together a group of related genera.

**Genus (pl. genera)** The category in ranking between a family and a species. Species with closely similar characteristics are grouped within a genus.

**Species** The category ranking below genus, linking very similar plants with specific characteristics.

**Subspecies** A division within a species.

**Cultivar/Variety** The term "cultivar" is abbreviated from "cultivated variety". It denotes a plant cultivated for specific distinguishing characteristics. In plant identification, cultivars are labelled "cv" and their names are contained within single quotation marks. The term "variety" denotes a variant within a species which occurs naturally, rather than being deliberately cultivated. It is labelled "var."

**Hybrid** A plant created by cross-breeding different types. Hybrids can occur between varieties, cultivars and species.

## HOW PLANT CLASSIFICATION WORKS

When herbs are labelled for sale in a shop or garden centre, the labels will define the plant for the purchaser. The labels below show three typical definitions, and what they mean.

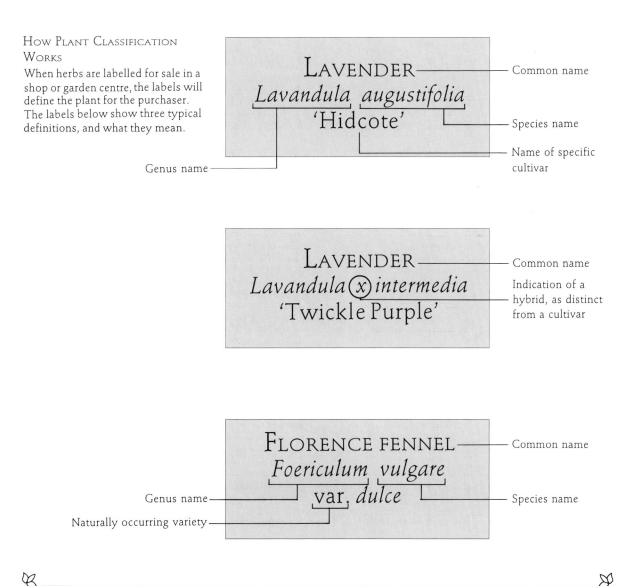

LAVENDER —— Common name
*Lavandula augustifolia* —— Species name
'Hidcote'
—— Name of specific cultivar
Genus name

LAVENDER —— Common name
*Lavandula (x) intermedia* —— Indication of a hybrid, as distinct from a cultivar
'Twickle Purple'

FLORENCE FENNEL —— Common name
*Foericulum vulgare* —— Species name
var. *dulce*
Genus name
Naturally occurring variety

# INDEX

# PHOTOGRAPHIC CREDITS

Key: *a* above, *b* below, *l* left, *r* right

Ace 130*a* (Brian Green), 131 (Anand Razdan), 141 (Mauritius), 173 (Bo Cederwall); A-Z Botanical Collection 7*r*, 17 (Francois Merl), 33, 44, 57, 70, 73, 95, 109, 110, 179; J. Allan Cash 6*b*, 114, 182; et archive 8*a* & *b*, 9*l* & *r*, 10*b*, 11*a*; Greg Evans 180; Derek Fell 1, 65, 80, 121*b*, 122, 123*r*, 124/5, 127; Peter McHoy 16, 19, 20, 22, 28, 31, 32, 34, 35, 36, 37, 39, 41, 42, 45, 46, 47, 48, 49, 50, 52, 53, 55, 56, 58, 59*l* & *r*, 61, 62, 63, 67, 71, 76, 78, 79, 81, 82, 85, 86, 87, 89, 90, 91, 92, 93, 96, 97, 98, 99, 102, 103, 105*a* & *b*, 106*a* & *b*, 111, 117, 123*l*, 128, 135, 137, 186; Maggie Oster 115; Photo/Nats 43; Pictor 133, 188, 206; John Searle 11*r*; Holly H. Shimizu 118; Harry Smith Collection 23, 25, 26, 29, 30, 68, 74, 101, 104, 107, 119, 120, 121*b*, 129, 160*b*, 202*a*.

All additional photography by Paul Forrester, Nelson Hargreaves and Chas Wilder.